BEING A MAN

The women's movement has brought profound change to the lives of men – to their marriages, their working lives, their perception of their lovers, their children, and to themselves and their expectations of women. Yet what has there been by way of a serious male response to the feminist challenge? In *Being A Man* David Cohen provides a thoughtful, sometimes amusing, discussion of the changing position of men in society.

Cohen combines his personal history and reactions to feminism with a review of existing ideas. In so doing he outlines a way forward to overcome the entrenched positions within the feminist debate. At the same time he emphasizes the excessive role that work plays in men's lives, and the many vicissitudes that relationships can bring in post-feminist times.

Cohen draws together these strands to give a critical view of the pleasures and pains of being a man today. He has successfully combined the personal with the psychological in a book that will ring true among both male and female readers, as well as making a relevant contribution to the study of psychology, sociology, and women's studies.

The author
David Cohen is a film maker and journalist. His books include *Psychologists on Psychology*, *J.B. Watson – The Founder of Behaviourism*, *Broadmoor*, *The Development of Play*, and *Soviet Psychiatry*. He has made many documentaries including a banned series on sex, Untying the Knot (on divorce), and many on mental health. He founded and co-edits *Psychology News*.

BEING A MAN

DAVID COHEN

ROUTLEDGE

First published 1990
by Routledge
11 New Fetter Lane, London EC4P 4EE

Phototypeset in 10pt Baskerville by
Mews Photosetting, Beckenham, Kent
Printed and bound in Great Britain by
Mackays of Chatham PLC, Chatham, Kent

British Library Cataloguing in Publication Data
Cohen, David, *1946–*
Being a man.
1. Man. Sex differences. Social aspects
I. Title
305.3

ISBN 0-415-02815-9
0-415-05580-6 (pbk)

CONTENTS

To Aileen with love and sadness

ACKNOWLEDGEMENTS

The author and publisher would like to thank the following for permission to reproduce copyright material: Faber and Faber for Herbert Read, 'To a Conscript of 1940', *Collected Poems* (1953), on pp. 28–9; and Grafton Books for e.e. cummings, 'may i feel', *Complete Poems*, vol. 1 (1913–35), on pp. 124–5. Every effort has been made to obtain permission to reproduce copyright material throughout this book. If any proper acknowledgement has not been made the copyright holder should contact the publisher.

Chapter One

WHAT IS A MAN?

When I was a little boy I was often told to be a man. When my marriage was breaking up my mother told me 'to be a man'. By this, she seemed to mean that I shouldn't go back to my wife. Being unforgiving and hard was the proper posture for a proper man. Her curious harshness made me remember times when, as a boy, I was told to be a man. Sometimes, I was crying. I cried quite often since my parents bickered, shouted, and fought most of the little time they spent together. Sometimes, being a man (as far as my mother was concerned) meant standing up to my father. This was necessary, she said, since he was forever being unfaithful, stingy or acting as a barbarian. He couldn't help it, she conceded when she was in a conciliatory mood, though she never clarified whether this was because he was a man, or an Arab, or due to some darker unmentionable flaw.

In theory, boys are supposed to take their fathers and grandfathers as role models. Father teaches son how to be a man. The behaviourist John B. Watson, for example, was determined to teach his sons masculine skills. He spent hours teaching them how to do woodwork, how to box, and even how to build roofs. Watson's son, James, who became an industrial psychologist, told me his father was never emotional. He never hugged him. Parents and children ought just to shake hands. Watson wanted to prevent children getting sexually fixated on their parents. James, his son, thinks his father had a chronic fear of homosexuality. The result of this scientific regime was that the young Watson felt emotionally starved. Learning how to do carpentry was no substitute for affection. It wasn't, James Watson stressed, that his father didn't care. He didn't know how to care and it showed. The eldest son, Billy, became a psychoanalyst, much to his father's sorrow, and later committed suicide.

My role models were few – and odd. I knew neither of my grandfathers. Both men were, apparently, in the business of breaking their
wives' hearts. My mother's father was a Romanian businessman who
had endless mistresses, scorned synagogue, and, final decadence, had
a gold telephone in his bathroom. He used it to make assignations
so that my grandmother couldn't even have a bath without worrying
about his unfaithfulness.

My father's father was not much better. He was an itinerant pepper
merchant who returned home every four or five years to make his wife
pregnant and, eventually, to die. He was the only human being my
father was romantic about; he would often describe how much he had
learned from his father and how sad and proud he was that his father
had chosen to die in his arms.

Since both of these ancients died before I was one, I only had my
father to model myself on in my immediate family. He had an eccentric
view of being a man. It meant doing well at school. Real men got
O levels, A levels, and scholarships. They could quote French authors
like Boileau (who wrote *L'Art Poétique*), Ernest Renan (who wrote a
Life of Jesus), or Pierre Loti (who wrote about Icelandic fishermen and
lived on top of a hill in Istanbul!). My father wasn't interested in money
or in pushing me into a respectable profession. He wanted a perpetual
succession of scholarships. There didn't seem to be any end purpose
to this frenetic education, and I sometimes suspect he would have been
quite happy if I had acquired a never-ending string of degrees and
done nothing else in my life.

The only other proof of virility required was standing up to anti-
Semites. While we lived in Europe, he was always ready to scrap in
the name of Yahveh.

In the mid-1950s, I was playing in a park in Geneva when another
small boy asked if he could play with my gun. I refused. The boy ran
to his father who confronted me severely. It was selfish not to share
guns. Then, he asked what my name was.

'David Cohen,' I said.

'Filthy Jew', he said, 'get out of here.'

I ran home in tears. My father did not like to see me crying. He
demanded to know what was wrong. I explained. He put on his hat
and announced he would give this Swiss anti-Semite a 'good hiding'.
(My father had worked for the British during the war and picked up
nuggets of slang.) If he didn't give him a good hiding, at least he would
read him 'the riot act'. My mother, whom he denounced as a craven

Romanian, begged him not to go. She called him a berserk barbarian. If the Swiss police found him giving a good hiding or reading the riot act to a native Swiss, they would probably throw us out of Switzerland without time to pack our bags.

The boy, my father replied, had to learn to stand up for himself.

There was no arguing with him in this mood so we hurried through the park looking for the anti-Semites. We never did find them. I rather admired this violent streak in my father, which he lost when we came to Britain. He believed, like many a colonial, that the Brits were gentlemen and couldn't, therefore, be dishonourable, anti-Semitic, or less than perfect. It took him some time to realize that the English are only human. Apart from this one trigger point, my father only became violent when I got bad marks or when oil shares fell.

His work determined where we lived. My mother was expected to help in his work. She complained that she too had a lawyer's degree and had no intention of using her qualifications to clean his office. She had not used her qualifications to do any other work, however, but I suspect that if she had ambitions of her own, my father would have done his best to undermine them. After all, if 'business opportunities' – he was always looking for them – took him abroad, my mother was expected to follow if he wanted her to. She did not want to go to India, for example, because she was convinced we would all die of cholera, but she went nevertheless. For six months, we lived in a hotel in Pondicherry which was, effectively, for whites only. We ate largely out of Libby and Hero tins, which my mother imported. She hated the mosquitoes. She only left India, though, when she convinced herself he was being unfaithful and, worse, with an Indian secretary. Secretaries ought to be relabelled 'sex-retaries'. After this crisis of lust in the tropics, she stormed back to Israel.

Their marriage was not a happy one, but it was unhappy in a very traditional way. Till I was 13, though my father was often not there, I led a normal existence. When my father was around, for example, we usually waited for him to return to have dinner. He would complain about, or compliment my mother on, her cooking, her housekeeping, and, even her make-up. As their marriage became more bitter, he would often accuse her of ruining her eyesight by wearing too much mascara. She was not defenceless against these onslaughts and accused him often of various barbarisms. He never did any housework.

My father might be powerful but he had no interest in many conventional masculine activities. He did not drive. I do not believe he has ever handled a screwdriver. He refused to do any manual work. He thought sport was a waste of time and I had to fight to be allowed to play cricket and football, until I discovered that there was an Alf Gover Academy of Cricket. That made it academic, perhaps! Anyhow, my father was perfectly happy to pay for cricket lessons. My mother was much more interested in sport and was a fitness fanatic long before Jane Fonda. She encouraged me to box, play tennis, and be fit. My father mocked all these efforts at gymnastics, hinting they were rather decadent. Like most things Romanian.

It hadn't occurred to me to analyse these roots and my assumptions about masculinity and its origins till I was forced into it when I was married. Aileen became very involved in the women's movement. It changed her life radically and, in the undertow, it changed mine. In not thinking what being a man involved, I was typical of most men of my generation. Though many writers have analysed the human condition, there is very little writing by men of the problem of men. If anyone had a problem it was women.

During the 1970s, some men described themselves as feminist men. Many feminists were very suspicious of that self-labelling and, in one way, at the very least, their suspicions were just. The few men who have come to consider these issues have not usually done so willingly for themselves. We reacted to feminism or, as in my case, initially to a feminist woman. That doesn't invalidate what might be discovered, but it seems important for men to acknowledge that we didn't start to think about sex roles on our own initiative. Feminist writers in the late 1960s and early 1970s were frequently vitriolic about the macho left who might have been expected to confront such issues. Instead, radical women were meant to admire their policies and penises.

Greer (1970) denounced the demands men made on women as did Shulamith Firestone. In her book *Free and Female*, Seaman (1972) said that 'Today many Women [her caps] recognise that they were forced to become what Men wanted them to be. They are understandably angry'. Seaman argued that all women should 'feel greatly indebted to these militant feminists'. That mood is not dead. In a recent book, *Reflecting Men*, Cline and Spender (1987) interviewed a number of women who felt that they had been destroyed by men's demands. For example Jackie, who was 18, just married, and felt forced to have acrobatic orgasms. 'As far as I'm concerned having orgasms the way they like it is important to keep them sunny side up', she told Cline and Spender. Listening to her and her friends with similar tales made the authors conclude that:

> It is a sad reflection of our society that orgasms, like smiles, should be yet another way women feel forced to pleasure and flatter men. Orgasm in a free society should express ultimate sexual excitement, the exquisite feeling of senses pinpointed to meet flesh, the physical truth of love or passion. But in our social world, male-dominated and ideologically heterosexual, female orgasms are too often physical gestures that lie. They are gestures of a manipulated heart pressed into male supportive service.
>
> (Cline and Spender 1987: 101)

Books of the 1970s show no sign of men considering their position. Women put sexual politics on the agenda. The women's movement has had its own developments and disappointments. In the last twenty years, we have moved from pre-feminism through feminism to post-feminism. The games of intellectual dissection we have come to play make it easy to forget the impact that feminism could have on individual couples as it 'swept through the suburbs'. I know the phrase sounds defensive, but if you were a man, you did often feel defensive or that you had to justify yourself. Life was changed, not through one's own will. I remember suddenly having to cope with the fact that Aileen was heavily involved with women's meetings, with consciousness-raising groups, with an extraordinary intensity about her women friends and, then, women lovers. Every gathering threatened a row. I found myself reading books by Greer, Rowbotham, and Adrienne Rich, which I never would have read otherwise. I found myself minding the children of the Blackheath Women's Group when they went gambolling to the Isle of Sheppey. I found myself arguing and listening to long lectures on why lesbian sex was superior. None of my role models had prepared me for this.

It's hard, and painful, to remember the emotional impact all this had. In some of this book I describe feeling flattened, depressed, ashamed by it. After all, you couldn't be much of a man if your woman did this to you. But, as well as feeling depressed by it, I was also at times excited. A good child of the sixties, I did believe that people had to explore themselves. The Gestalt guru, Fritz Perls, had proclaimed, after all, that if I did my thing and you did your thing that was OK (Perls *et al.* 1972). Should our things coincide, bliss was OK too. It sounds naïve to say I believed in what sounds like a hippy

Mills and Boon plot, but I did think that you couldn't achieve happiness by fencing people in. Boundaries were bad. For all the confusion, I still think there is value in the idea that we don't have the right to limit those we love. It may hurt, but it isn't completely foolish. I had a sneaking admiration for Aileen and her relentless exploration. And there was self-interest too. Eventually, I did some of my own exploring.

The few men I met who were going through similar problems and were willing to discuss them seemed to suffer a vast burden of guilt. Gatherings of so-called 'new men' often wallowed in guilt. I went to one men's group where one man described how he had felt utterly broken-hearted but, to make amends for aeons of oppression, he had brought breakfast in bed to his wife and her lover. In 1975, the Islington Men's Group noted that they had come together because 'guilt forced us to do something about it . . . to be part of an anti sexist struggle'. Alas, the group didn't use its guilt to change enough, and two gay men made them feel even guiltier when they accused 'the conference of male chauvinism, of which there were many examples, and compared it to an Employer's Federation'. Most men were being so nice 'they had forgotten that sexual oppression was a material force; it was on the streets, not in our heads'. This criticism made the Islington group feel yet more guilty.

It is worth quoting the Islington group's response in full because it was typical, I think, of some of the feelings evoked. They noted:

> in short, a lot of nonsense that seemed indicative – to us at least, after some thought – that men in men's groups, ourselves included, hadn't sat down seriously to a dose of real self criticism in the attempt to work out what it really means to fulfil this society's definition of male. We hadn't attempted a serious analysis of its power, its privileges, its oppressiveness, and with that its self destructiveness. Sure, we've acknowledged it in the abstract but perhaps the naîveté – or arrogance – of some men at the last conference shows how much we must realise that oppression by men has a material power that we share in whatever our consciousness. Criticism by ourselves and by others may help us to a better understanding of sexism for ourselves; maybe we can chisel away at it inside our heads. But, until it's equal out there on the streets, discussions about a people's movement, men's oppression, the ancillary status of men's groups and all the other essentially

political topics will remain what they are – an attempt, however unconscious, to recuperate the real criticisms that women and gay men have to make of us. We thought many men went away from the conference feeling quite sick.

There is nothing that the 'hetero sexist' male can do right. Some feminists encouraged this guilt or, at least, thought it was historically necessary. Adrienne Rich in her memorable poem 'From an Old House in America' (1974) surveyed how 'other lives were lived here'. In the house, women had long suffered. They had been alone and abused, 'hanged as witches, sold as breeding wenches'. She acknowledged that the men of the house had also suffered and that she still had

> A dream of tenderness
> wrestles with all I know of history
> I cannot now lie down
> with a man who fears my power
> or reaches for me as for death.

The sonorous evocation of life in this old house moved forward to a climax. Given all the misery, all the reasons for women to be furious with men, Rich wrote:

> *But can't you see me as a human being*
> he said
> *What is a human being*
> she said
> *I try to understand*
> he said
> *what will you undertake*
> she said
> *will you punish me for history*
> he said
> *what will you undertake*
> she said
> *do you believe in collective guilt*
> he said.

Rich's chilling final line excluded men totally, for she concluded:

> Any woman's death diminishes me.

Men had earned that exclusion, she seemed to be saying. No wonder we felt guilty.

I want to suggest that this guilt was not, and is not, helpful. Individual men have reasons to feel guilty about the way they treated individual women. Analysing the way one responds to women in one's life, admitting where you have power and how you use it is important, but I neither can, nor should, carry the burden of the past. I am not guilty for what my fathers or grandfathers did towards the women of their time. I don't believe that I will respond more sensitively to today's problems by agreeing to feel guilty for actions I didn't commit. Hug all the guilt you can, revel in male masochism. The trend had its attractions for much of the late seventies and eighties. Both liberal men and feminist women need to abandon such all-encompassing guilt. It may also be that because such guilt was demanded that there was so little useful response from men.

WHY DID MEN NOT RESPOND TO THE FEMINISM OF THE SEVENTIES AND EIGHTIES?

It has been suggested that many men were just too threatened to frame any coherent reply. We had much to lose and were too afraid. So, we took refuge either in saying nothing or in making fun of feminists. The media lampooned bra-burning 'militants' who were probably dykes out to castrate all men. There were, of course, extremists like SCUM, the Society for Cutting Up Men, that played into the hands of the great majority of men who wanted to portray feminists initially as 'loony', a tactic used against the suffragettes.

Nevertheless, small groups of men did, almost from the first, try to make some response, however timid. The trouble was that they were few and, often, divided. From 1972 onwards, there was an annual conference on 'male liberation' in America. It tended to be captured by those in the Encounter movement who saw 'personal growth' as the road to liberation. The 1975 Conference newsletter caught this mood perfectly with a 'poem' that urged men to 'play/feel/love/joy/grow'. Psychobabble ruled. Men who were interested in exploring 'male liberation' had to 'grow'. Most other men made fun of them as wimps while feminists tended to be suspicious, hostile or, at best, rather uninterested. Women had their own agenda, after all. Did men have to dominate them so much that they triend to muscle in on 'liberation'?

As a result of these factors, there was little writing and analysis of the position of heterosexual men till the 1980s. There were earlier gay writings as the Campaign for Homosexual Equality became more confident both in Britain and America.

Since then, things have changed,though not radically. Dillons, London's leading bookshop, has hundreds of books about women in the sexual politics section but no more than ten on men. Most of those deal with fatherhood. Nevertheless, it's possible to discern three different approaches to the 'problem of man' which have begun to emerge. Crudely put, these are:

1 gay studies;
2 empirical studies/personal growth;
3 Marxist theory.

Gay studies

These approaches have very different emphases. Personal growth and therapy clearly aim to change men. Give us insight, teach us to feel and we shall be more perfect creatures. Gay studies were initially evangelical, or perhaps seemed especially so to non gays. If you were gay, be proud of it. And if you weren't sure whether you were gay or not, explore. The Campaign for Homosexual Equality (CHE) produced in 1979, for instance, a teacher's handbook which urged young people who were uncertain of their sexual orientation to contact it, leading Peter Simple in the *Daily Telegraph* to snipe:

Young people who are uncertain whether they are heterosexual, bisexual or homosexual are advised in a new Teacher's Guide produced by the Campaign for Homosexual Equality to contact any number of organisations including CHE, the Samaritans, Gay News.

This is far too casual and unsystematic. There is a failure here to affirm strongly the importance of making young people think about their 'sexuality' most if not all of the time. The 'media' are doing a lot to bring this about, but teachers can and must help.

The 'Guide' also fails to take into account the large number of young people who must wonder whether they are potential foot fetishists, mac fans, paedophiles or gerontophiles or drawn to another of thousands of other choices described by the pioneer Krafft-Ebing and his successors.

Once these young people have made their choice or choices (mere bisexuality is surely laughably inadequate in our omnisexual times), they should be able to register with a central agency called the 'Sexual Agency Opportunities Board' which would help them make the most of the roles they have chosen by arranging introductions, organising social clubs and supplying literature and other aids.

Peter Simple recommended therapy for the 'few maladjusted people who react to the booming sexuality industry by losing interest in sex altogether'.

Peter Simple's satire reveals both that sex is an uneasy subject and, of course, his blatant hostility to homosexuals. If people have to be gay, let them at least be decently ashamed of it. Gay theorists reacted, naturally enough, to such hostility by being defiant. They said they were proud to be gay and pointed to the contribution that gay men had made to the wider culture. Where would the British theatre have been without Oscar Wilde and Noel Coward? Gays argued that, like women, they were persecuted by male society.

The full force of that feeling only became clear to me when I collaborated on the making of a series called 'Sex in Our Time', which was banned. We were especially proud of our film on homosexuality because we felt it went beyond the liberal view that homosexuality ought to be tolerated because the poor men couldn't help it. We showed a wide variety of ways in which men were homosexual. At the 'conventional' end of the spectrum, we filmed a cloyingly happy couple who lived together and held hands while listening to Brahms. Their kitchen would have done the Women's Institute proud and they revelled in that irony. Kitsch country scenes lined the walls. At the other end of the spectrum, we looked at the work of Gay Sweatshop and one of its founders, Drew Griffiths, who was later murdered. In their plays Gay Sweatshop highlighted the emotional and social pain of being gay. All of them had had a tough time finding out that they didn't conform to the norm. Griffiths was defiant. He, like Joe Orton, trumpeted the fact that he liked having as many fucks as possible. The more fucks the more of a man you were. Being gay opened up possibilities and fantasies that heterosexuals couldn't have in their dirtiest dreams. For Griffiths, a one-night stand was too long and too involving. A lesbian co-worker of his from Gay Sweatshop complained that it was just this unfeeling, mechanical attitude that she hated most about men. Sex was about feeling, not scoring. Griffiths did not argue, as has now become fashionable, that there are no such creatures as homosexual men or women but only homosexual acts. He didn't, I suspect, because gay pride demanded that you were proud of being gay. It was a total identity. The Aids crisis and the mix of real and hysterical fears it has led to have altered the mood. It is easy to forget how chic gay chic seemed. Gay fervour made heterosexual men often defensive. Feminists were urging separatism; gay men, the delights of other men. In a generally unpleasant piece on gay men today, Roy Kerridge in the *Spectator* in 1987 remembers an Islington conversation where a woman said, 'The trouble with Adrian is that he doesn't realize he's one of a dying breed – the heterosexuals.'

I want to suggest that, for straight men, a gay analysis of maleness can only be of limited value. Society conditions and oppresses straight men but not in the same ways that it oppresses women or gay men. We collude far more in the oppression and appear to gain out of it. To summon up the rage and hurt of persecution that these 'out' groups have wouldn't be real. Moreover, for most heterosexual men, a key area of life is how to define and work out their relationships either with women or with the one woman who is their sexual partner. To attempt to identify the problems of gay men as the problems of all men would be false though, in many areas to do with work and success, all men face identical problems. Empirical studies in psychology, psychiatry, and sociology offer a different kind of response.

Empirical studies and/or personal growth

Tellingly, it was a woman psychologist, Sandra Bem (1974), who pioneered innovations in the study of sex roles. She devised the concept of psychological androgyny. The perfect person, Bem claimed, wasn't exclusively masculine or feminine but had a variety of gender traits! She could fix a fuse and rustle up a soufflé; he could mind the baby and be decisive. Bem frankly said that she wanted men to change. Her empirical surveys of attitudes and feelings about certain tasks had a political purpose. Many of the other social scientists and commentators like Janet Spence, Gloria Emerson, and, in Britain, Mary Ingham who studied men also hoped for some change. It took longer for men to publish in this field. Slowly, now there is evidence of change in men – both in terms of attitudes and of behaviour in areas like child care. Some of the books that have examined some of these differences are *Men* (Ingham 1984), Emerson's *Some American Men* (1985), and Astrachan's *How Men Feel* which is honestly subtitled 'their response to women's demands'. There have also been a set of recent papers on patriarchy and the proceedings of a conference called 'Men in Feminism' (Jardine and Smith 1987). All these pieces of evidence suggest that men may not have been quite as rigidly 'male' as has been imagined and that we are changing. The change may be slow and subtle but it is there to be discerned.

Some of the men most committed to change have also been committed to the personal growth movement. Not all are convinced of its value. Astrachan argues that the connection is a mixed blessing indeed. Personal growth means, in the USA, *personal* growth. It has nothing to do with social changes. The movement is apolitical, Astrachan argues, except for access to children and custody. Separated and divorced fathers have become vocal. Yet many other crucial issues are political, involving questions of power, economics and status. All the insight in the world won't resolve them. But, given American history and fear of socialism, it has proved hard for American men to see the economic and power issues in sexual politics. They prefer to focus on therapy. Ironically, personal growth is being used to foster corporate growth. Relax, meditate, grow and you'll soon be a super executive.

Britain's tiny male liberation movement has been more political. Anti-sexist men tend to be left wing. They have often tried to establish links with anti-racist and anti-nuclear groups. It is nice that British men have been more willing to accept the importance of economic and employment issues, but it has proved of little practical impact. Britain has not kept a consistent male liberation movement in being. There is no recognized body, no publication like *Spare Rib*, nothing but sporadic conferences.

The American love of therapy has influenced research – most of which has been carried out in the States. Studies have focused on individuals. What leads men to see they need to change? What kinds of programmes do it best and quickest? Will liberation help your career? And you can manage to achieve all this in your little ego-shell. Few American psychologists recognize that this is a limited, very American view.

The Marxist view

Marxist theoreticians highlight the political and economic injustices –

both in the First and Third Worlds. They argue that this contributes to the alienation of men, but, in general, Marxist writers remain theoretical and impersonal. Few of their texts or analyses have the passion of feminist writing. Partly this is because, in their emphasis on economics, it's hard for them to focus on what men lose personally. Partly, too, it reflects the ambivalence to feminism of the 'working class'. Many unions were hostile, for example, to giving women the sole right to be paid child benefit because men wanted to keep the economic privilege of handling the money. Trade unions throughout the seventies and eighties remained essentially white, male and pretty proud of it, as many women trade unionists have complained. There was little eagerness to fight on issues like paternity leave and job sharing.

Such attitudes discouraged Marxist writers from examining issues raised by feminism too personally. But in so far as there is expertise in this field, it comes partly from experience. Living through the dilemmas makes you think and might eventually make you act. It is easy to be too academic, too detached, too political. The impersonal approach protects you from contemplating having to change your own life.

Ironically, before men have been able to frame a proper response to these questions, the ideological climate has changed and there is now danger of a backlash.

THE BACKLASH

These three approaches came from men who either sympathized with the women's movement or saw there was a problem. Many men just mocked feminists. The more serious New Right denounced feminism and all its works. We needed a return to faith, family, and fidelity. Let old oppressions thrive. Even some feminist writers have become oddly defensive. The failure of the movement to change the world has left its mark, and its disillusion. Segal (1987) has recently produced a sympathetic analysis of the troubles of feminism in post-feminist times. The revolution didn't come and is now not expected. There have been also signs of a backlash in, for example, the Tory government's attack on the defunct ILEA's policy of introducing books that countered sexual stereotypes. I intend to argue that men have nothing to gain – and a great deal to fear – from this backlash.

For me, none of these positions felt true. I knew that I both liked and desired women. I also knew that I was willing to change but, after much pain, that I didn't want to go under. There seemed little point in exchanging male oppression for female oppression in which, after centuries of bad treatment, the other side got their own back. It took me some years, and some misery, to realize that, but I eventually did.

The second point is that we are now in a situation where there is a historical opportunity to look at the role of men – in their relationship to women, to one another and to society. Partly that is the result of feminism. Partly, I intend to argue, it's the product of larger social and economic changes in the developed world. In Britain, one in three marriages ends in divorce. The average age at which men retire today is 62 and, by the year 2000, it is expected to be under 55. Most men will have twenty years of fairly active life after retirement.

The latest analysis of trends suggests that by the year 2010 men will be divided into two groups. The majority of men will find their hours of work reduced to about 25 hours a week. A small group of managers and 'high-level' workers will find they work at least 60 hours a week – more if you add travelling time and time away from home. This second group will see work as central to their identity, the focus of their lives. The group of '25-hourers' will see work as something they have to do to make money, and the problem for them will be how to spend the rest of their time. Research suggests too that many men have become insecure and reluctant about work. More women are working than ever before in peacetime – and women expect far more out of their work. These are all profound changes.

Psychology has helped fashion another change. We are more self-conscious than ever before. We analyse our lives and our crises. We no longer just live, but we pick over our living to see if it is the best we can do. The personal growth movement has, according to Lasch (1980) created not just narcissists but self-conscious narcissists, who dwell on how interesting and profound their thoughts about themselves make them. I intend to argue that Lasch has been too judgemental. Self-consciousness has its uses. As the French writer, Serge Moscovici (1976) has argued, psychoanalysis did make us self-conscious but, in doing that, it offers us a chance to discuss ways in which we can change. Psychoanalysis may not be true; it may not solve anything. But it has created a vocabulary in which we can discuss where our lives are and our options. It has affected the way in which we think of ourselves and how we can imagine changing ourselves. For men, it makes it possible to think about the kinds of men we want to be. In the rich West, we need to remember how lucky we are and that, if you are hungry, there is no point in discussing your complexes and repressions. But for the full-bellied the possibilities of conscious change do exist.

This book attempts to contemplate such a change and risks a personal view of how we need to change. I hardly claim to be that heroic new creature, the 'new man' or offer myself as an example. The method of this book owes much to feminist writers. It tries to weave together personal history and social science. It has been a painful book to write. It uses some notes I made ten years ago. I've retained some of these in all their rawness because they reflect the anger and confusion I felt then. Feminism was very frightening to men of my generation, and, if you don't admit that, you are not likely to get very far.

Chapter 2 looks at the role of the hero in developing men's ideas of what it is like to be a man. We have such a welter of heroes these days, making contradictory self-images, that it adds to confusion. Chapter 3 is very personal, examining what happened to me and my marriage when Aileen became a radical feminist. Chapter 4 is more academic, and looks at the literature and evidence for the stereotype that men are emotionally illiterate and obsessed by success. I have frequently been called a workaholic and have been said to take refuge from personal problems in work so perhaps I'm in a good position to examine the role of work. In Chapter 5, I argue that men pay a heavy psychological and physical price for this obsession with work. I also ask just where this idea that work is everything stems from since there is an honourable tradition in political thought (written, yes, mainly by men) which condemns work as dehumanizing. Chapter 6 looks, somewhat personally, at the area of sexuality and relationships. I acknowledge that men often are oppressive and clumsy but claim there is no reason to abandon heterosexuality. We can improve it. Chapter 7 looks at the twin fears – of loneliness and commitment. It argues that it is no longer true that men are more frightened of commitment than women. It suggests that the demands we now place on relationships in the self-conscious, post-Freudian world make everyone both eager to connect and fearful of being conned by a connection (or relationship) that isn't as good as it might be. Men, and women, risk becoming victims of a quest for the perfect relationship, the 'real' real 'Real Thing'. Chapter 8 looks at fatherhood. It suggests that much research indicates that men's attitudes to fathering have changed. For me, becoming a father was a crucial, wonderful event.

15

In all these chapters, I argue that while it is true that the personal is the political, the last fifteen years have shown that the 'personal' isn't enough. It's obvious that men and women need to share far more the care of the children, domestic drudgery and the chance of good careers. But individuals, and couples, have often found that the changes they agreed to try, changes that were the result of much arguing after much pain, fell apart. It wasn't that one party didn't try hard enough but that changing one-to-one relationships often depended on other social and political changes. To get anywhere, couples had to make extreme sacrifices giving up careers. For me, the clearest evidence of that was when in 1974, Aileen and I took off for Greece with our 4-year-old son, Nicholas. We spent a lovely three months. But our money began to run out, we had to get Nicholas back to school and there was a limit to the stories either of us could write for English magazines from the middle of the Peloponnese. So we came back – sure we had mended our marriage. A year later, when I was back at work in TV, all the problems we had originally had were destroying our relationship again.

We could have an equal, equally satisfying relationship, as long as we were cocooned from the pressures of making a living in a competitive society where both of us were ambitious to succeed. But holidays can't last for ever. I didn't draw the conclusion quickly, but, slowly, it became clear to me that the kind of issues I deal with in this book aren't just personal ones. They are political and require rather more mundane, dogged political reform than most feminist theorists contemplate. They involve patching patriarchal society to help create a context in which we can change. Feminist writers tended to ignore conventional politics. They either mapped a grand alliance of feminism and Marxism or just wrote off ordinary politics as patriarchal irrelevance. In the last chapter, I try to argue for some structural changes which will make it possible for men and women to negotiate better, happier relationships. I'm sure that I will be accused of 'Utopianism', a very old species of mud to sling, but the last fifteen years haven't left me defeated or pessimistic. They've left me convinced that there is a lot of work to do, a lot of pain to go through and a lot of pleasure to be had.

For both men and women.

Chapter Two

THE HOBBLED HERO

Heroes were constructed.
Deconstruct the hero.

Hero
H/ero
He/ro
Her/o

It is a cliché that the late twentieth century is a time of rapid social changes. In one of his Wessex poems, 'In the Time of the Breaking of Nations', Hardy (1960) writes of a boy and girl courting while politicians threaten, armies clash, fortunes are made and lost. Human life carried on, for Hardy, as it had always done. Lad lusted for lass despite great political changes. Contemporary changes bypass ordinary lives less. They affect the way we live and think of ourselves, and what we might do with our lives. Most psychologists accept that the women's movement has changed the self-perception even of women who don't identify themselves as feminist. Their ambitions and their sense of what they might do with their lives have been influenced by feminism. Fewer Western women think of themselves only as wives and mothers with a successful family as the ultimate accolade. Feminism convinced women that they ought to try to succeed (and enjoy themselves) in lots of different ways: at work, in marriage, in relationships with other women, with their children, in their sense of growth.

Modern men haven't had an equivalent of the women's movement and their conflicts and confusions have hardly been expressed. In this chapter, I want to examine the fate of the hero. The hero, like the boys and men who are supposed to identify with him, is in something of a state of crisis. Moreover, I want to suggest that many feminists ought to recognize the shape of that crisis.

Today, it's hard to admire a hero without ambivalence. Heroes almost parody themselves. Even films which appear to glorify the macho hero of old tend to undermine him. James Bond cuts a slightly ludicrous figure. Rambo, wild man of the techno-West, has a name that sounds uncomfortably like Dumbo (the elephant) or Sambo. Can that be entirely accidental?

We can no longer be simple or easy in our attitudes to heroes and heroics. I don't think that is particularly the product of feminism but it does have implications for men's view of themselves. In this chapter, I want to argue both that we find heroes harder to accept and that men now have a bewildering variety of heroes and role models to identify with and imitate. Too many heroes confuse the ego.

The psychoanalyst Otto Rank, who was a pupil of Freud, published *The Myth of the Birth of the Hero* (1922). Freud relied on many of Rank's ideas when he came to write *Moses and Monotheism* (1930), his account of the origins of religion. For Freud, Moses was one of the seminal heroes. Freud claimed there was a pattern to all heroic myths from Babylon on. The hero, Freud argued, has a typical life history. He is the child of very aristocratic parents. His conception is not easy. One or both of the parents have been barren; the gods, or God, have been against their breeding. Our hero is lucky to be born at all and, as soon as he breathes, he is usually doomed to die. Oedipus, for example, was exposed on a rock when his parents heard that he would kill his father and marry his mother. Freud found that often the heroic babes were sent to die on the water. Moses was typical in being sent to float to his death down the Nile. The role of water was significant, for water symbolized the forces of life, Freud argued. Our hero wouldn't be dispatched so easily. Inevitably – for otherwise there would be no stirring legend – the fledgling hero is saved from death. His rescuers are either humble persons or wild animals. From then on, the hero progressed. He could grow up, grow strong and grow famous by avenging himself. Revenge would involve triumphing over his father or his apparent father. Thus Moses defeated the Pharaoh, and became free.

Freud claimed that Sargon of Agade, who founded Babylon round 2800 BC, was the first historical person to have such a myth woven around him. Others who shared this biography were, of course, Moses, Cyrus and Romulus. Rank had also included Oedipus, Karna who featured in the Sanskrit epics, Perseus, Heracles, and Gilgamesh. Universal laws seemed to apply, indicating that the hero was an important figure in our species' psychological growth. Freud (1930) claimed that 'A hero is someone who had had the courage to rebel against the father and triumph'. The hero was thus uniform.

Freud wanted to understand the deepest roots of the hero. For those with simpler ambitions, however, the characteristics of the hero conformed to a set pattern. Robert Graves (1974) defined the hero of Greek myth as strong, brave, wily and favoured of the gods. He didn't squander his qualities on ignoble causes. In Western culture, the Greek hero was the model for all subsequent ones. But it's interesting how little difference there seems to have been between heroes in most cultures.

In both Western and Eastern literature, a stereotype of the hero evolved. He was young, aggressive, sexually powerful, masculine and, when faced with problems, could resolve them. Heroes solved the Oedipal riddle and cut the Gordian knot.

Initially, heroes were, like Oedipus, victims of fate or of the gods. It wasn't Oedipus' fault that he killed his father or married his mother. Wily deities decreed that doomed fate. By the sixteenth century, however, authors created tragic heroes with tragic flaws. Marlowe's Dr Faustus could have had an excellent career if he hadn't been ensnared by the necromantic arts, vanity and vast ambition. Even Hamlet, whom Freud saw as being most like Oedipus, had acquired character defects by 1600. His indecision was his undoing; he couldn't act the hero. Freud was sympathetic. Hamlet had been put in the most Oedipal of all binds. Any action he took had to be psychologically agonizing.

It wasn't just in Western literature that the hero surfaced. Japanese literature sang of samurai who were brave, proud and decisive. For all their individual and cultural differences, heroes belonged to a similar type. Jung (1925), indeed, argued that the hero was one of our psychological archetypes.

It would have been useful to know the extent to which people in the past identified with such heroes. Clues suggest they did. In analysing the impact of plays, Aristotle argued that tragedies were cathartic. They gave audiences the chance to experience pity and terror on behalf of their characters. In *The Poetics* Aristotle called this 'an innocent pleasure'. Ross (1954) has pointed out that 'a whole library has been written on this famous doctrine of catharsis', and there are learned arguments about how 'purgative' watching a tragedy was. It could only purge if the audience identified with the hero. We all are Oedipus, Freud claimed, which is why the tragedy is terrifying and moving.

Later playwrights, like Shakespeare and Racine, clearly wanted audiences not just to understand heroes but to identify with them. Sadly, there were no social scientists in the theatres to ask duly controlled questions about whether people identified with these heroes, but writers like Freud and Jung assumed that as a given.

THE FATHER AS HERO

The heroes of fiction are powerful but, according to psychoanalysts, most children find their original hero in their families. Boys look up to their father and try to be like him. Daddy is the first hero. Children identify with their parents, and boys, in particular, are often taught to be like their father. Freud tended to see this as an inevitable, unconscious process, but it is often very conscious as parents try to school boys to resemble their fathers. This is not a new development at all.

In her account of childhood, Pollock (1984) found that fathers were emotionally involved and that they kept diaries of how they interacted with their children. She found that books on how to rear children often emphasized the need for the father to provide a good model.

Writers often criticized fathers for demanding too much influence and authority over their offspring. The French essayist Montaigne noted, 'I dislike the custom of forbidding children to call us Father and insisting that they use some more distant appellation to show greater respect as if nature had not sufficiently provided us with authority.' Montaigne sniped that we did call God Almighty 'Father', and wondered whether fathers meant to imply that they were as potent (Montaigne 1972).

James Mill, the father of the philosopher John Stuart Mill, was very certain that it was his duty to bring up his child, John Stuart, in his own image. From the age of 2, as J.S. Mill noted in his autobiography, he was taught the classics and given a reading list of improving works. Play was frivolous. Like his father, J.S. Mill was very bad at using his hands for practical tasks. It is telling that Mill, who was a sceptical, libertarian philosopher, came to question many assumptions about human knowledge and society, but he never questioned his relationship with his father. Papa was revered. Like most Victorian fathers, the elder Mill believed his position entitled him to automatic respect.

Patriarchal power could make sons ill or neurotic. William and Henry James shared a domineering father who attempted to impose on them a particular kind of occultist 'Swedenborgian' philosophy. William James spent years trying to break away from his father – either through illness or travel. He was well into his thirties before he managed to become independent enough to get a job of his own. There were many drawbacks to such unbridled parental power but it also offered a kind of clarity. The father was strong and authoritative. Much of Freud's work assumes that, normally, fathers are so domineering. In fact, the father of the original human horde, as Freud described him in *Totem and Taboo* (1913), had many of the characteristics of the Victorian paterfamilias. He ruled his sons like iron, laid down the law to his wife and children, and was not to be questioned. In *Totem and Taboo* the sons eventually rebelled against this tyrant and killed him since he controlled access to all the women. Victorian children didn't have to go so far. But the father remained a crucially strong figure. He offered a clear model, and a clear model for sons to rebel against.

One of the psychologists to rebel against Victorian values was the behaviourist, John B. Watson. He preached sexual education. He wanted psychology to be used to allow people to control their lives. He rejected the Victorian ideas of soul. His views as a father are well known, however, for two reasons. First, he wrote *The Psychological Care of the Infant and Child* (1928), which was the bible of perfect child care. Second, his son, James Watson, has given a set of interviews in which he reflected on his past. The interviews are interesting because they show that first, for all Watson's progressiveness, he still believed that a father ought to mould and fashion his sons and, second, that it was becoming harder to do so. Watson's children were too well-educated, too analytical not to react against their father. James Watson told me that his father found it very hard to express any emotions. He was aloof and often depressed. Yet, though his son was very critical, he had gone into the same profession. He was a psychologist too and, as his father advocated, used psychology very practically working for a big American corporation.

The role of fathers has changed. It is harder than ever to play god in the living room any more. Much research has highlighted the fact that society today questions all authority more than ever before.

There is evidence from research in family therapy that children question their parents in ways that J.S. Mill would never have dared. This isn't a social history so I can't examine the causes of that, but I want to suggest that the psychological result is that children, especially boys, no longer have such a clear role to model themselves on. Of course, fathers in the past were far from perfect. John Watson's own father was a drunk in a Baptist community, and eventually ran off to live with two American Indian women. But the role that fathers were meant to play was clear – and many fulfilled it. Today, the position is more confused.

However, as fathers change, as many men spend more time with their children, and as family relationships become less authoritarian, it may well contribute to the fragmentation of the hero. The father can no longer be the dominating figure that Freud cast – the source of all authority.

Even popular culture can no longer take heroes seriously. It's quite true that there were braggarts and ridiculous heroes in Roman comedies, but the trouble with these swaggerers was that they were not real heroes. They were poor imitations. They had unflattering flaws like cowardice, big feet, flatulence, and manic greed. Such a catalogue of failure could be compared with the perfect qualities of the true hero. No being was more serious, blessed, or straight than the properly fashioned hero. In the sixteenth century, there were comedies which included ridiculous heroes like the Knight of the Burning Pestle, but Jasper, the so-called knight, was, as the title suggests, no true knight. Shakespeare had real heroes like Henry V, tortured heroes (Hamlet), and braggarts like Falstaff, but none of his proper heroes was absurd. The subversive notion that the real hero could have an undermining touch of the absurd came later – and, initially, it surfaced in social comedies. Authors like Fielding, Jane Austen, and Thackeray made fun of the young men who acted as if they were brave soldiers in the comfort of eighteenth-century drawing rooms. Fielding's Tom Jones is an early anti-hero, splendidly short on morals, but his only conquests are in bed. When sentenced to be hanged, he has to be rescued. Poor show for a hero!

The hero survived best in the cinema and popular fiction. In its first fifty years, Hollywood produced a succession of uncomplicated heroes who were strong, manly, and good. Douglas Fairbanks, Errol Flynn, and John Wayne were ranged against the weak, evil, and sly. Of later, the cinema has not been able to sustain these heroes. As I've suggested, even box-office hits like Rambo and the James Bond movies show a slightly absurd hero. Our ambivalence towards the image of the straight hero comes out nicely in films like Woody Allen's *The Rose of Cairo* or *Something Hot*, both hits of 1987. In *The Rose of Cairo*, Mia Farrow is a cinema fan who falls in love with the character of an archaeologist in a film. Suddenly, the character crosses the divide between fact and fiction. He walks out of the screen and into real life. But, making the film in the 1980s, Allen has to subvert this hero who gets totally confused when a night club won't accept his prop money, and in the end he dumps Mia Farrow for the sake of his screen career. Allen's hero has to be compromised, a shade ridiculous. The hero of *Something Hot* is more realistic. He allows a girl he picks up to take him along thieving, to her reunion ball, and, in many ways, she sets the pace and style of their relationship. Yet the casting (Jeff Daniels as the 'hero') is exactly of the kind of physical type who would have been the classic hero.

The theatre has seen interesting developments too. Brecht suggested that modern audiences cannot accept traditional heroes. There has also been the angry kitchen-sink hero (Jimmy Porter) or the nihilistic hero (Vladimir in *Waiting for Godot* or all the characters in Sartre's *Huis Clos*). Samuel Beckett's characters are not heroic and they all inhabit a bleak, totally isolated landscape. Maybe the point of Beckett – if one can vandalize Beckett to suggest he has a point – is that the only way to cling to unity and integrity is to live with as little contact with the world as possible. Most people reject that choice.

The demise of the simple hero in fiction corresponds with the rise in sociology and psychology of role theory, which suggests that any human being has a multiple number of identities. Role theory was originally developed by a sociologist, J.L. Moreno, who went on to create psychodrama. Moreno (1946) argued that through acting different roles, we would come to understand how we behaved and how others behaved towards us. If I have to play my father as he relates to me, I may see not just that I am frightened of him but that he has his own terrors.

THE HOBBLED HERO AND ROLE THEORY

Moreno's work has led to a number of sociological and psychological theories which claim that there are in us competing minds or selves. Authors like Robert Ornstein in his *Multimind* (1987) and Jan Elster

23

in *The Multiple Self* (1986) tend to trace the origins of this idea to Freud's division of the mind into the id, ego, and superego. But Freud did not just divide: he saw an integrating force in the ego. It was in some sense superior because it mastered both the wild lusts of the id and the hysterical defences of the superego. It negotiated between our desire and our disgust. It used the energy of the id and the conscience of the superego to achieve a balance.

Later theories place less emphasis on integration. The sociologist Erving Goffman (1969) argued that we play an endless variety of social roles. When I go to the doctor, I play the patient; when I take my son to the football match, I play parent. I am different in all these situations. Arguments rage about whether there is a core which is more 'me', an authentic, unifying self. Ornstein (1987) argues that we have many different minds. Some are intellectual, some are practical, some emotional. They don't connect very much, and it is naïve to think that the stream of consciousness binds them together. Ornstein doesn't explain how, given such fragmentation, I still wake up each morning knowing I'm David Cohen whose history is X, Y, and Z. How do I achieve that sense of identity? But though he posits that view in too simple and extreme a fashion, Ornstein has a point. Certainly any attempt at a grand theory of the human condition today – something of which psychologists tend to be wary as being too cosmic – has to recognize our ability to fragment, to be different selves at different times. We are very self-conscious about it. Yet it's a fragmentation that's constantly reinforced. The media tell us each day that we are taxpayers, consumers, motorists, voters, drinkers. As a drinker, I may want to be less on booze but, as a motorist, I know that may mean more road tax while, as a parent, I believe in more taxation since that will mean more money for schools.

Perhaps because of this feeling that we are so split, we also have a terrible desire for intimacy and authenticity. Lonely hearts ads (which now even exist in magazines for social workers) advertise how desperate people can get for the true relationship in which you can be your true, whole self wholeheartedly. Yet, you can't advertise yourself as a simple soul. A glance at most lonely hearts columns shows that, paradoxically, one of the ways in which we preen ourselves for mating is to draw attention to our very complexity. The more complex, the more seductive we are. Today, the stream of consciousness is made up of many different rivers – and they don't all flow the same way.

Goffman's work was influential, and it coincided with work on the split brain which proved that the left and right hemispheres lead rather independent existences. The right sees things to which the more logical left is blind, and vice versa. Such very different patterns of research have made us accustomed to the idea that our consciousness is split, not united. The mind is not a unity but, as Robert Ornstein has called it, 'the multimind', with different departments which often feud.

Feminists used the concepts of different levels of consciousness and competing roles to analyse the various expectations that women are expected to fulfil. Too many roles create too much strain especially since, in many of these roles, women were expected to nurture and 'be' for others.

With men, the process is not identical but it has similarities. The variety of roles causes confusion. Moreover, precisely because men had power and because of the taboo on analysing the personal, men did not examine their situation in a personal way. Marxist theory focused on alienation at work and the oppression of, in effect, 'not doing one's own thing'. Isolated romantics like D.H. Lawrence argued for greater freedom but Lawrence was curiously hostile to Freud, as is shown in his polemic *Fantasia of the Unconscious* (1971). Men did not have a nineteenth-century tradition of analysing their personal histories to rediscover and apply to the different situation of the late twentieth century.

Yet the lack of a clear hero, of a role model that tells men what they ought to be, if only to rebel against, is a problem. It means we each have to invent our own futures, structure our own lives, set our own goals, make individual choices. Our forefathers had a more set and settled agenda. Consistent, stable heroes made useful sign-posts. The fragmented hero is a novelty, a challenge, and a trauma. Today, there are far more competing, contradictory figures for us to identify with. These contradictions between different kinds of hero leave men with no clear sense of what 'role model' to fit in with. Different men will deal with this situation differently. Many will not think about it at all or deny it exists. Many will absorb some of these points without dwelling too self-consciously on them. Some will think about, even brood, about them. But since many of these contradictions turn up in popular culture – on television, in advertising, in newspapers and magazines – it's hard for most men to cut themselves off from such confusions.

In this chapter, I want to outline some of the competing role models men can choose from. I'm not claiming that the list is exhaustive. I may well miss out some models, but such omissions are less crucial than the fact that there are a host of potential heroes, each with its own lobby, its own fan club. For the fans, that vision of being a man is the true one. Often, these visions of the perfect or proper man happen to conflict with each other. I have had fun devising the following menu of heroes and, if I have left out your favourite one, I apologize. The point is that there are now so many of them.

THE CLASSIC HERO

In Greek times, heroes were military men, skilled at fighting, javelin throwing, and other athletic skills. Plato in *The Republic* suggested that this hero had to be improved upon and given philosophical qualities. He should be both gentle and aggressive. Plato wanted to ban certain Greek myths and stories, like that of Zeus becoming a swan to seduce Leda, and of the wailing when men went into the underworld. Zeus made deceit seem acceptable, and proper heroes didn't quail at death. Plato said that children needed nobler stories to inspire them. Traditionally, the hero was strong, firm, and just, but he was not a psychopath. To be his enemy was unwise. The hero did not tolerate insults or equals. Usually, each tale could only have one hero, which could pose problems.

The Greek hero evolved into the hero of medieval tales and legends. But the 'verray parfit gentil knight' praised by Chaucer was different in some significant ways from his Greek predecessor. The Grecian hero was not usually interested in women. It seemed less than glorious to Plato that the Trojan War should be started over a woman. *The Republic* praised orderly love between boys and lamented the frenzy of sex. 'Corinthian girlfriends' (who were presumably specially sensuous) were condemned, as were over-spiced Sicilian food and over-elaborate music. The hero and Plato's philosopher king had higher aims than good relationships with women.

By the Middle Ages, the hero had acquired the Christian faith, the chivalrous rose, and an obsession with romance. The perfect knight was often hopelessly in love. He rescued damsels in distress and sometimes didn't even require adultery afterwards. Medieval tales are often full of fantasy but, then, the hero is himself a creature of fantasy. From then on, most heroes were brave, romantic, and willing to defend their, and their beloved's, honour. The image was, and still is, powerful. It helped fashion some of the greatest figures in Western literature, from Lancelot to the hero in the film *Mona Lisa* where Bob Hoskins risks all to save the tart/damsel in trouble.

It is surprising how little the stereotype of the strong hero changes from the Middle Ages to the end of the nineteenth century. In his play, *Arms and the Man*, first performed in 1900, George Bernard Shaw poked affectionate fun at mock heroes in a clever but traditional way. The play opens with Raina, a young Bulgarian lady and her mother drooling over the exploits of Sergius, her betrothed, who led the cavalry charge that swept the Bulgarians to victory. Her mother trills:

> He was . . . the first man to sweep through their guns. Can't you see it Raina, our gallant splendid Bulgarians with their swords and eyes flashing thundering down like an avalanche and scattering the wretched Serbs and their dandified Austrian officers like chaff. And you, you kept Sergius waiting a year before you'd be betrothed to him. Oh, if you have a drop of Bulgarian blood in your veins, you'll worship him when he comes back.

Raina feels wretched that she doubted him and doubted whether he was a real hero. How could she be sarcastic and carp that Sergius was just a man who'd read too much Byron and Pushkin? Slowly, it emerges that the cavalry charge was a mistake, that Sergius has been unfaithful with the maid and that the real hero of the battle is a Swiss mercenary (who owns a chain of hotels) and who is skilled at providing fodder for the horses and food for the infantry. He is called the chocolate cream soldier.

Yet, like many, Shaw was ready to glorify proper heroes who were worthy of GBS. He also wrote *The Man of Destiny*, a play about Napoleon. Napoleon, unlike the chocolate cream soldier, was a real hero who, after a discourse on how fear keeps armies together, tells the lady who is hiding a vital letter from him that 'Pooh there's no such thing as a real hero'. What could be more heroic? Shaw might be a socialist inclined to pacifism but he too was susceptible to the lure of a real hero as opposed to a fake one.

The world wars did not change this human love for heroes. But, more than before, writers praised the heroic characteristics of ordinary men. Take a poem by Herbert Read (1953) to a conscript:

TO A CONSCRIPT OF 1940

Qui n'a pas une fois désespéré de l'honneur, ne sera jamais un héros.

Georges Bernanos

A soldier passed me in the freshly-fallen snow,
   His footsteps muffled, his face unearthly grey;
And my heart gave a sudden leap
   As I gazed on a ghost of five-and-twenty years ago.

I shouted Halt! and my voice had the old accustomed
      ring
   And he obeyed it as it was obeyed
In the shrouded days when I too was one
   Of an army of young men marching

Into the unknown. He turned towards me and I said:
   'I am one of those who went before you
Five-and-twenty years ago: one of the many who never
      returned,
   Of the many who returned and yet were dead.

We went where you are going, into the rain and the
      mud;
   We fought as you will fight
With death and darkness and despair;
   We gave what you will give – our brains and our
      blood.

We think we gave in vain. The world was not renewed.
   There was hope in the homestead and anger in the
      streets
But the old world was restored and we returned
   To the dreary field and workshop, and the
      immemorial feud

Of rich and poor. Our victory was our defeat.
   Power was retained where power had been misused
And youth was left to sweep away
   The ashes that the fires had strewn beneath our feet.

But one thing we learned: there is no glory in the deed
   Until the soldier wears a badge of tarnished braid;
There are heroes who have heard the rally and have
     seen
   The glitter of a garland round their head.

28

Theirs is the hollow victory. They are deceived.
    But you, my brother and my ghost, if you can go
Knowing that there is no reward, no certain use
    In all your sacrifice, then honour is reprieved.

To fight without hope is to fight with grace,
    The self reconstructed, the false heart repaired.'
Then I turned with a smile, and he answered my salute
    As he stood against the fretted hedge, which was
        like white lace.

Like Kipling's Tommy Atkins, the ordinary soldier had the qualities of the old heroes, and more: a certain modest ordinariness.

The classic hero survived the 1939–45 war. One of the best analyses of the post-war hero is to be found in Tom Wolfe's *The Right Stuff* (1970). The book examines the US Navy and Air Force programme that initially led to breaking the sound barrier and, then, to the Gemini and Apollo missions. At the start of the book, Tom Wolfe tries to sketch the way in which the young men joining were made to feel that certain subjects like death were taboo. Plato would have approved. No moaning about the risks or the River of Death. It's worth quoting Wolfe at some length:

A young man might go into military flight training believing that he was entering some sort of technical school in which he was simply going to acquire a certain set of skills. Instead, he found himself all at once enclosed in a fraternity. And, in this fraternity, even though it was military, men were not rated by their outward rank as ensigns, lieutenants, commanders or whatever. No, herein the world was divided into those who had it and those who did not. This quality, this *it*, was never named however, nor was it talked about in any way.

As to just what this ineffable quality was . . . well it obviously involved bravery. But it was not bravery in the simple sense of being willing to risk your life. The idea seemed to be that any fool could do that if that was all that was required, just as any fool could throw his life away in the process. No, the idea here . . . seemed to be that a man should have the ability to go up in a hurtling piece of machinery and put his hide on the line and then have the moxie, the reflexes, the experience, the coolness to pull it back in the last yawning moment – and then to go up again the next day, and the next day, and every next day, even if the series should prove infinite – and ultimately, in its best expression, to do so in a cause that means something to thousands, to a people, to a nation, to God. Nor was there *a test* to show whether or not a pilot had this righteous quality. There was instead a seemingly infinite series of tests. A career in flying was like climbing one of those ancient Babylonian pyramids made up of a dizzy progression of steps and ledges, a ziggurat, a pyramid extraordinarily high and steep; and the idea was to prove yourself at every foot of the way up that pyramid that you were one of the elected and anointed ones who had *the right stuff* and could move higher and higher and even – ultimately, God willing, one day – that you might be able to join that special few at the very top, that elite that had the capacity to bring tears to men's eyes, the very Brotherhood of the Right Stuff itself.

(Wolfe 1970: 18, 19)

The test pilots of the high-altitude planes that preceded the Gemini programme and the Apollo astronauts became such heroes. They risked all for America, and a grateful nation duly swooned at their feet.

For Britain, the Falklands War saw very similar attitudes. A few commanders became heroes, especially Major H Jones who died during the taking of Goose Green. But, for the most part, the laurels went to the ordinary men, Tommy Atkins again, who 'yomped' across the islands with stealth and speed. The British press noted that the Argentinians couldn't match this –probably because they had too many Corinthian girlfriends (see Plato's *Republic*). In the Argentine, the war created its own heroes – mainly the pilots who wove and bombed their way among the big British ships. The reporting in both countries highlighted how there is still a desire to find the classic hero.

Some biologists and psychologists believe that our passion for heroes doesn't just reflect the Freudian melodrama of *Totem and Taboo* but also our biological inheritance. The ethologist Konrad Lorenz devoted his book *On Aggression* (1972) to the subject. In his observations of animals, Lorenz found that there was a link between aggression and 'love'. Mating rituals often started with mock fighting. In species that moved in herds, there was a lot of play fighting between the males to establish what the pecking order was. These 'battles' create bonds as well as establish rank. The difference between animals and men, Lorenz pointed out, is that animals draw the line at killing their own species. With us, aggression has no limits. But given our fighting biology, it wasn't surprising we could often be moved to tears (a paradox, when you consider the unmanliness of tears) by the aggressive hero. He recalled the leader of the ancient human pack.

In *The Naked Ape* (1965), Desmond Morris, following Lorenz, argued that human beings had to learn to make do with less aggression. But Morris pointed out that the neurological facts were not very promising. Aggression seems to be 'wired into' the limbic system, an area of the mid-brain which is the oldest part of the cortex. The limbic system controls some basic functions: eating, fear, and flight. A number of training programmes have tried to reform the over-aggressive, but none of these has been successful. Penal reformers sometimes think they have struck the solution – a new form of counselling or token economy programmes which reward inmates for restraining their natural desire to punch. Very often, follow-up research reveals that those who took part did not change fundamentally but just grasped the rules of the game they were asked to play. In prison or a secure hospital, they knew they would lose privileges if they showed their aggression. There was no mileage in it so they suppressed it. In the real world, where they might not get caught, they let their hostilities out.

The classic hero was a model of good aggression often used for a noble cause. He did not have to function in a society where there was a growing critique of aggression. Despite the message of Christ, there was virtually no 'peace' movement in Christendom until the Quakers who, for much of their history, were regarded as eccentric. Today, the underlying assumptions are different. Lorenz, like Morris, noted the quirk in human evolution. We needed aggression to survive and to evolve, but what was useful on the savannas is counter-productive today. Men do not need to go hunting in the supermarket. The kind of aggression that made a samurai a hero in sixteenth-century Japan would make him a psychopath today in Tokyo. Moreover, in the 1960s, a different hero began to star. Pop philosophers like Bob Dylan and John Lennon preached love, not war. They were heroes who appeared to be against heroics. The butch hero was a macho dinosaur, fit only to be parodied. And the culture of the time reflected that with movies, like the early Bond films, making their mark as stylish parodies. Bond was never quite serious, after all.

The lure of the classic hero still exists. He surfaces in advertising campaigns like Cadbury's Milk Tray and in the Lucozade ads starring Olympic champion, Daley Thompson. An interesting example of how we have come to parody heroes comes from a look at the history of comics. In the 1930s, comics created supermen. At first, they were serious heroes. Then these relatively sober super-antics have exploded now so that we have a whole galaxy of weird, wonderful, and improbable super-heroes. Who can take seriously the heroics of creatures like Captain Atom, Booster Gold, Rocket Red, Green Lantern, the Martian Man Hunter, and the deliciously named 'Thing from the Swamp'? The final parody is perhaps a new ad for Domestos, the lavatory cleaner, which is 'Big Bad Dom'. Big Bad Dom is macho and attacks lavatory germs. When the hero is represented as a lavatory cleaner, ancient values might seem to be in a state of flux or flush!

THE ANTI-HERO

The anti-hero is a more complicated figure. His 'anti-ness' can consist either of thinking and not acting, or of acting deliberately anti-heroically. John Lennon, for example, was an active anti-hero. He preached against violence. He defied authority by taking drugs, leading protests, and poking fun at orthodoxies. Eventually, when he and Yoko Ono took to their bed and sang 'Give Peace a Chance', it was stirring stuff. The more conventional anti-hero preferred, like Hamlet, to agonize. Inaction was all. Hamlet would have solved most of his problems if he had had the courage to organize a rebellion against Claudius. Instead, he soliloquized. The Romantics made such self-analysis fashionable and, eventually, a link with drugs developed. Junkies like De Quincey and Burroughs saw themselves as exploring the lower depths. It was consciousness rather than continents they explored. Astronauts might step on the moon but the anti-hero knew that the moon really was inside your head.

The anti-hero was tortured about aggression, was artistic and was more concerned about integrity than valour. He believed in being true to himself, which meant defying established values. Some anti-heroes achieved this through being more tortured than anyone else, like the Danish philosopher, Soren Kierkegaard. Others did it with literary swagger, like Nietzsche.

Nietzsche's great book, *Thus Spake Zarathustra* (1890), is a hymn to the anti-hero who takes on all forms of established authority. Usually, Zarathustra prefers to stay in his cave up the mountain. When he ventures down to the Motley Cow (which is a town, not a pub), he rails against all orthodoxies. 'I see many soldiers', he rails in 'On War and Warriors' (p. 159), 'would that I saw many warriors. ''Uniform'' one calls what they wear; would that what it conceals were not uniform.' Zarathustra fulminates against hypocrisy, noting that 'war and courage have accomplished more than love of the neighbour'. So much for the Christians. In a splendidly vitriolic chapter called 'On the Rabble', he preaches against those who 'have poisoned the holy water with their lustfulness' (p. 208) and 'when they called their dirty dream "pleasure", they poisoned the language too.' Priests, governments, and the bourgeois were also the butt of his invective. Nietzsche was the first writer to perfect nihilism. Nothing could please him. He thundered,

> Not my hatred but my nausea gnawed hungrily at my life. Alas, I often grew weary of the spirit when I found that even the rabble had esprit. And I turned my back on those who rule when I saw what they now call ruling, higgling and haggling for power – with the rabble. I have lived with closed ears among people with foreign tongues: would that the tongue of their higgling and haggling for power might remain foreign to me. And, holding my nose, I walked disgruntled through all of yesterday and today.
>
> (Nietzsche 1890: 209)

The vision is bleak but is told with relish.

Many twentieth-century writers built on this foundation, creating cynical, nihilistic heroes who believed in nothing much, not even themselves. But not to believe was proof of a higher truth. Until the 1950s, the anti-hero was reserved for the elite. You had to be an intellectual, to read Sartre, Kierkegaard, or Nietzsche in order to appreciate their antics and anti-heroics. But, with the rise of *film noire* round 1946, Hollywood adopted this not so heroic hero, of whom Bogart was perhaps the finest exponent. Films like *Casablanca* made the nihilistic, rebellious hero fashionable.

Advertising campaigns that reflect this hero today include that for Canadian Club which show the drinker hiding inside a grand piano and a recent ad for the Bristol and West Building Society which features an incompetent Soviet security man who urges a girl to '*defekt to the West*'.

THE BREADWINNER

In Greek myths, the hero often became a father and handed on his values to his children. For Freud, the father was the principal hero and he enshrined him as such in the psychoanalytic literature from 1900. Two of the most crucial heroes Freud wrote about – the father of the human horde and Moses – were actually breadwinners. They didn't so much win wars as feed, and sustain, their families and flock. The father of the human horde organized the hunting; Moses organized the manna. Both provided.

This 'hero' has rather fewer dashing qualities but he is dependable, present, a figure of authority. He is the father who controls the family. The old Greek hero was usually a young man without a sense of family, though there were exceptions. It's interesting though, that the provision of food is central to this version.

Many images in advertising present this hero as the model of the ideal man. He takes his sons fishing or to football matches. He waits for his wife, who is a good woman, to present him with dinner on the table. He is married and solid, and yet that solidity is glamorous.

Advertising campaigns for products such as Oxo and those of Birds-Eye reflect this image of the solid fatherly man. Curiously, a number of recent campaigns subvert this paragon. One campaign for cereal had a father playing games with his children. Father was unfair. He would only let his son bowl underarm and then hooted with triumph when he hit a six. When his son hit a boundary, he was cheating (father said) and was disqualified. The campaign painted a picture of a petty father who couldn't lose gracefully. The punch-line was when the wife and mother said the cereal was 'for children of all ages' – who very obviously included the father.

CASANOVA – OR THE HERO AS LOVER

When Zeus descended from Mount Olympus to seduce all and sundry, this was not considered a heroic trait by Plato, who wanted all references to these less than divine antics deleted from Homer. Zeus' compulsive bed-hopping was an all too human sign. I have not been able to find a book that traces the history of seduction but, certainly, when Giacomo Casanova penned his erotic memoirs (which Zeus would have loved) he was the first writer to ask to be admired for the number of women he had slept with. Casanova happened to write entertainingly about eighteenth-century manners, travel, and the cult of the occult but, essentially, he was engaged in number fucking. The more women he had, the better man he was. It mattered, of course, that most of them should be women of honour because there was no conquest in seducing dishonourable tarts.

Casanova preferred to pursue nuns (a special favourite) and the virtuous wives of other men, and, if possible, to make love to two women at the same time or, at least, in the same evening. Seduction was a chase and a challenge. There was no delight in buying virtue.

Despite the bawdy nature of Restoration plays like (Ethelridge 1964) *The Man of Mode* and of Samuel Pepys' *Diary* there were no sexual boasters in print before Casanova. Casanova claimed thousands of conquests and, according to the American computer which records interests in Ph.Ds, there are two projects which involve counting up just how many people he did sleep with.

Casanova's uncensored memoirs were published posthumously in 1822 and immediately had rivals for the position of prince of the cocks like Byron, but, by 1837, social fashions had changed. Morality was à la mode. Casanova became a shameful figure. There was nothing to boast about in sexual conquests. But the seducer hero began to surface again in the naughty nineties. Undoubtedly, there were men who enjoyed pursuing women, but, outside a small artistic circle, it was considered something to be ashamed of. The sexual conqueror as hero did not re-emerge till the 1950s, though he was always a figure that some feminists warned against. In *The Second Sex* (1949), Simone de Beauvoir took great pleasure in putting down this phallic narcissist. She argued that many women suffered because men were rough and brutal. They were only interested in their selfish pleasures and, having made love insensitively, would then often be violent. For men, the sheer act of conquest, of 'having' seemed to be much of the pleasure. Women wanted not just more tenderness but more erotic attention. Men, obsessed with penetration and as much penetration as possible, were unable to give them what they wanted.

By a curious historical coincidence, de Beauvoir published *The Second Sex* the year after Kinsey published his first researches on sex. His 1948 Kinsey Report dealt with men, and it seems likely that it boosted the idea that it was manly to sleep with a number of women. Kinsey provoked outrage by claiming that for men between the ages of 15 and 25, the median number of ejaculations a week was between two and three. The majority of young men masturbated frequently. But there was also a considerable amount of pre-marital sex. The more educated men were, the more likely they were to have pre-marital sex. Kinsey also found that adultery was more frequent than might have been expected. Kinsey's work contributed valuable scientific and social information. It also helped create a new climate in which sex was less of a taboo. His quantification also focused attention on how much sex one might be expected to have. Men did not want to lag behind, to be below the norm for orgasms.

Feminists now argue that the sexual revolution of the sixties was a sham and another instance of male oppression. Not to fuck was to be unfashionable. The revolution also created its own pressures for men. You had to perform well. To be good in bed meant acquiring experience. If you couldn't persuade a number of women to sleep with you, you were a failure. Books on sex usually didn't quite preach the necessity of promiscuity, but how could you satisfy a lover or a wife if you hadn't been around? Worse, what happened if someone sat up and said, 'Fred was far better'. It was a far cry from the outrage that Casanova and Byron had provoked as masters of immorality.

Many advertising campaigns glamorize the sexy instant lover as hero: the Smirnoff ads, countless ads for after-shave, and, recently, the ad for the Montego where passion flares in a petrol station. She only has to see him at the wheel of his smart car to drool with desire. But here too some ads now subvert the seducer. Take the Red Mountain coffee romance. A young man brings his date home for the first time. He dabs on after-shave while making the coffee. He dims the lights. She tells him she loves the coffee but says it is 'a pity about the after-shave'.

He will not get very far.

THE GAY HERO

Gay men were the most willing to learn from the women's movement. They saw their own situation as parallel to that of women – and in some ways worse. Homosexual acts between consenting adults were illegal till 1969. Even afterwards, there was much discrimination. In 1976, I saw *Gay Sweatshop*, the theatre group. In an angry play, the company screamed against the pain, confusion, and discrimination of being gay. They accused famous homosexuals like Somerset Maugham and Noel Coward of betraying the cause. Neither had ever 'come out'. The pain (to a non-gay man) seemed to turn all too quickly into arrogance that suggested that the only way to be male at this particular point in history was to be gay. It made things possible that straight men only dreamed of – like constant anonymous fucking. Joe Orton in his letters and notebooks, for example, praised the ability of gay men to score, to engage in 'impersonal' sex in atmospheric cottages. He logged many encounters, as W.H. Auden had once kept a list of 'Boys had'.

Advertising has made little use of the gay hero in the United Kingdom so far – though it has become more fashionable to use beautiful men's bodies not just in ads but in photos in fashion magazines.

THE NEW SENSITIVE MAN

The 'new' man isn't entirely new. It is possible to see some traces of him in the 'Romantic' man of the early nineteenth century. Poets like Wordsworth made much of the glories of feeling, though, as feminists pointed out, that didn't stop them exploiting their women. Wordsworth relied heavily on his sister Dorothy; the more flamboyant Shelley, while protesting the rights of women, let his wife Mary have the drudgery of running their nomadic household. Still, it would be a mistake to suppose that we are the first generation of men to see the possibilities of feeling.

The modern version of this hero is the sensitive, androgynous man for whom the 'right stuff' includes being able to feed the baby, doing his share of the shopping, and being able to listen to his partner when times are hard for her. The new man can be masculine and feminine, strong and weak, active and passive. Many feminists are sceptical of this creature, and others complain, rather unfairly, that any new men are really *wimps* – and not worth the bother. Since I talk a good deal in this book about the new man, I won't embellish him here. It is telling, though, that advertising agencies have woken up to his potential. They produce ads showing men looking after children, shopping and cooking as ordinary activities. Such ads are still few and, according to the *Guardian*, advertising agencies are very uncertain just what is the appeal of this new man.

My list doesn't claim to be exclusive. Add your own favourite brand of hero. My point is that there is no longer one classic hero for all men to identify with and be inspired by. Worse, many of the heroes I've outlined conflict with one another. How can you be a classic aggressive hero and a new pacific man? How can you be an anti-hero who despises authority and also the conformist breadwinner? How do you choose which to be?

So many different possibilities create choice and confusion. Some men have reacted to feminism by claiming that 'poor' men now also have too many demands made on them – by their own conditioning, by society, by demanding women. I intend to argue something different: that we have a crisis in masculinity precisely because we are more aware than ever before of these different options and of what we could become. In what appears to be a very psychologically oriented society (as the rich West has become) you ought to know where your life is heading, what 'direction' you are taking, 'what the development plan' is for your career, your personal life, and your soul. Men are facing a problem that parallels one that feminists have identified. Women are being asked to take on a variety of roles. Superwoman has to be mother, mistress, career women, wife, and washer-up. It isn't easy.

It isn't easy for men either, especially as we have even less tradition of framing personal questions about ourselves. Yet we have to do it. Otherwise, you drift. There was a time when the range of choices was limited and there was no necessity to make self-conscious analyses of where one's life was going. That isn't so any longer. It is important, in the wake of these social and political changes, not to feel powerless. This may sound paradoxical since I've claimed that men hate feeling powerless and that we devote vast effort to appearing in control. Yet there is considerable evidence that men feel the world is changing in ways they can't comprehend. For some, it means a drift into drink or depression. Others desperately try to impose control which may explain the growing popularity of some churches like the Mormons which offer a total answer to the confusions of life. I want to suggest remedies that are different from alcohol or religion. Our growing self-consciousness is there. We can make it useful. We can use it to explore the state of our life and of our relationships. We can use it to acknowledge areas where we have power, areas where we are powerless, and areas where we might change. My own experience tells me that it is hard and frightening to change. You may decide, when you look at it, that you don't want to. But my tale of the fragmented heroes suggests that all men feel pulled in different ways. We can feel powerless in the face of those pulls or we can look at them – and use the knowledge. It is an opportunity for change.

In the next chapters I examine some areas that are central to masculine identity: work, feelings of triumph, sexuality, our need for relationships, sex, and fatherhood. But I start with some personal history because if that had not happened, I am sure that I wouldn't be writing this book.

Chapter Three

PERSONAL

One of the important points feminist writers made is that 'the personal is the political'. They argued convincingly that, in their analyses, men were too detached, too academic, too unwilling to examine what they did and what happened to them. In this chapter, I try to analyse what happened during part of my marriage. Like all such narratives, it's bound to be one-sided and I'm sure there are many points that Aileen La Tourette will question, disagree with and have her own very different views on. Nevertheless, it's an attempt to examine honestly what happened between us – and despite us.

I met Aileen in Oxford in 1965 outside Blackwell's. She was an American from New Jersey on a one-year study visit with eleven other girls from Trinity, a Catholic university in Washington, DC. She had never been to Europe before. She was attractive, clever, and ambitious. She knew she wanted to be a writer. We started to go out together. I relished the idea of picking her up from the convent in the Woodstock Road where she lived. After a few weeks, we became lovers. I assumed that, at the end of the year, she would return to America and that would be that. It would have been warm, lovely, fun, but the last thing I was interested in was marriage. I had seen what marriage had done for, and to, my parents.

Aileen did not see it like that. She was convinced we were meant for each other. I was her first lover: 'pathological, isn't it,' she sometimes smiled. After she went back to America, she wrote fervently. I was much cooler and, eventually, told her that I was having an affair with another student. For Aileen, that wasn't the end of it. As soon as she graduated, she got herself a job in Britain. She arrived back shortly after I left Oxford and my then girlfriend and I split up. We started going out together again. For eighteen months, our relationship was traumatic, passionate, off and on. Like many young men, I didn't want to get 'caught', but it would be wrong to give the impression that she was always the pursuer. Twice, when she tried to break it off, I went back, persuading her that we should give it another try. Once I did this after she moved in with another man.

In May 1970, we eventually got married. The ceremony had its comic, telling moments. When the Registrar asked me to give my full name, I forgot it and had to be prompted by my cousin. When he congratulated the new Mrs Cohen, Aileen turned round to my mother wondering why the Registrar was congratulating her. My father and mother met for the first time in years. He brought her a bunch of flowers 'as a symbol of peace because I am a peaceful man' and she asked him why he had turned up in a top hat looking over-dressed. Aileen's parents lived in America and could not come to the wedding at all. They did, however, give us a honeymoon in Bermuda but forgot to tell us we would be sharing a house with a middle-aged couple who were friends of theirs. Gus and Louisa were not happily married and, at breakfast, Gus would often leer that he bet I'd had a nice night which was more than could be said for him because Louisa 'had the red flag flying'. Louisa lectured us on how cancer didn't exist and had been invented by American doctors for the purpose of fleecing their patients.

I was ambivalent about getting married but we had a good time in Bermuda. The island was abuzz with a political trial. There had been a number of incidents in which a number of 'subversive elements' had attacked the police. Some were charged with using umbrellas as offensive weapons. Since there didn't seem to be any London journalists on the island, I persuaded Aileen that we should cover the trial, so we spent two days of our honeymoon in court. I wasn't then a 'new man', of course.

For all my initial ambivalence, I decided that now I was married I ought to give it my best. My parents' marriage had given me both a jaundiced view of marriage and no clear idea of how a marriage should work. Aileen's parents were still together but far from happy. We needed time to work out how to be married, to have fun together and find our way in being a couple. We never got it because Aileen became pregnant. She was very keen to have a baby and, after all the traumas we had gone through, it seemed a good idea. In some ways, as the ensuing narrative shows, we would have been wiser to wait a while before having a child but I've never regretted it and I don't think she has either.

We lived at first over my father's television shop and then bought a flat in Greenwich. Aileen loved being pregnant even though she had bad morning sickness. Both of us were, in different ways, mesmerized · by her pregnancy. For her: she was finally going to have the child she so much wanted. The boring parts, getting fat, feeling lethargic, being too involved with it to do anything else were minor irritations. She was joyful and enjoying it, too.

For me: it was a shock. I had never thought of myself as a father and, from the age of seventeen on, my reaction had been to flee the possibility. Sensible young men clung to their freedom, and, whenever I was asked to justify that stance, the exciting new permissive morality was there to back me up with progressive chapter and verse. Women wanted the children. Now that we were going to have a child, it just seemed a fact. There was no question or panic about it. It was an exciting event for eight months in the future. Meanwhile I observed it a little bit like an intruder. Every time I placed my hands on Aileen's stomach to see if the baby would kick, I found it hard to grasp that the living thing inside was partly mine, partly caused by me.

I had no idea what babies entailed. I had never held a baby. None of my parents' friends had children under 15. My cousins who had small children lived either in Israel or in America. Even more than to most men, babies were a complete mystery to me.

I didn't question really that women had the responsibility for looking after children. From my knowledge of psychology, I knew the evidence that fathers cannot make an equally strong bond was rather poor and largely based on prejudice. Social rather than biological reasons prevent paternal bonds. Men do not have the chance to make those bonds. Some feminists claim that this is a deliberate male ploy. This, to me, overstates the duplicity of men, and ignores the fact that many men suffer because they have so little to do with the care of their children. To suggest – stridently – that men have taken a conscious and collective decision to dump all child care on women tries to ascribe personal responsibility to a process which is essentially social and political.

Though I could accept in my head feminist arguments when Aileen was pregnant, I did nothing very practical about them. Nothing I knew, had learned, or wanted to learn, suggested that a normal man had much to do with bringing up his child. I did want to be different. But not that much different. I wanted to go to the delivery and carefully read parts of the natural childbirth book Aileen had bought. She meant to give birth 'naturally'. There was a chapter on the role of the father.

Just as Dr Spock back in 1970 devoted only a little space to fathers – who were, after all, amateurs when it came to babies – the natural childbirth book had only a few pages of advice for men. I mugged up on how to help Aileen during the delivery, on massage, and on assisting her rhythm. My only other contribution was to paint a clumsy-looking blue elephant in the corner of the room where we placed the baby's cot.

And while Aileen took care of the baby, I could continue my frenetic chase after money, success, and work. The year 1969 was not the one in which I made it to Hollywood. I got a small medical documentary to direct which has the dubious distinction of being shown to patients before they have their limbs amputated. I was hired to do the sixth rewrite of a film which was very loosely based on Dante's *Inferno*, though much of the action moved from the circles of hell to sauna baths or erotic massage parlours. In December 1969, as Aileen was growing truly large with child, I got another rewrite job in Switzerland. I asked if they would pay for Aileen to come out with me as we didn't feel like being apart, and reduce my fee.

Busy as I was with pushing my own career, I paid much less attention to what Aileen was doing. She was writing a novel, the early part of which described the life of a young, tomboyish Catholic girl. There were almost no boys around in her emotional world which was the convent school, and the emotional bonds between the girls were intense. In one chapter, she described the games she played with another girl when they were both 10 and 11. Many of the games were frankly sexual. They caressed each other; they sat on top of each other; Aileen wrote that she remembered exploring parts of the other girl's body. There was a hot, passionate description of a walk the two girls had taken together which ended with a tumble in the hay. The tumble was more ignorant than innocent.

I was surprised by all this. The rest of Aileen's book was very autobiographical. I asked if all that had really happened.

'Oh yes,' said Aileen.

But I didn't really ask anything else about it. It didn't echo my own childhood. I remembered a period round about 11 when I was very intrigued by the sight of other naked boys. I might have been intrigued, and excited, by any naked body but there was no likelihood of seeing any naked girls. I never took part in any games like Aileen's though there was a curious ritual at my prep school. One boy would guard his crotch with a school cap while another boy, using his cap also, would try to touch his cock. In front of the class they danced around each other like duellists making thrusts with their caps at each other's cocks. Aileen was writing of herself when she was 11, and my psychology degree did tell me that we were all bound to go through a homosexual phase. Aileen's memories seemed uncommonly vivid but she had never said anything else about them. Her lesbian games were part of growing up, I assumed. In her own rather autobiographical novel, *Nuns and Mothers*, she sees them very differently, a side of herself she was taught to repress.

It's always easy not to see a point you're nervous of seeing. I didn't ask too much about these adolescent romps described in the novel and, by the time we were in Switzerland, I had forgotten all about them.

We spent a strange three weeks in Vevey on the banks of Lake Geneva. I had been hired to rewrite a screenplay of *Jane Eyre*, and James Mason, the actor who hired me, put us up in the most expensive hotel in Vevey. All the other guests were either, or had once been, fabulously rich. The hotel had an enormous Christmas tree that was decorated with real candles. They blazed away, the biggest fire risk ever. Bell boys stood around armed with fire hoses. At the prices of the Grand Hotel, they could offer this unique touch. Whenever a branch caught fire, whoosh, some sharp-eyed bell boy would douse it down. In the same hall a very old pianist played erratic excerpts from *The Sound of Music*.

Aileen and I were broke, and loved being broke, in the midst of this rococo splendour. We had a magnificent room overlooking the lake and we lolled on the huge, ornate bed late in the mornings. I wrote for most of the day and dreamed, of course, that the brilliance of my script would soon transport me to Hollywood. On Christmas Day, I went out and bought her one rose. The pound was chronically weak. It was all we could afford. She loved the rose.

In Switzerland, in between writing, we discovered Patrick White. Patrick White has the distinction not only of having won the Nobel Prize but also of having written one of the few books that Aileen and I both fell in love with, *Riders in the Chariot*. Aileen frequently disdains my taste. P.G. Wodehouse is not among the great literati as far as she is concerned, and there have been many books she loves which seem to me intense, self-concious, or just boring. She liked to tease that her taste was better since the books that I failed to love (or read to the end) included *Ulysses*, *Under the Volcano*, and *Ultramarine* (they can't all have started with 'U'). To find a book that hit us both as magical capped our odd experience of Vevey.

And, as Aileen's belly grew and grew and grew, the presence of that baby-to-be got more and more real. It was a lull of extraordinary happiness.

Just before the New Year, we took the couchette back to London and waited, anxiously, for the birth. Aileen began to be bored with being pregnant and she couldn't wait for the time to come. We went to natural childbirth classes. We scraped together the money to buy the things the baby would need. My mother who, like many middle-class foreigners in London, believes that the only two shops are Harrods and Fortnum and Mason, treated us to an immense Harrods pram, which needed a starched Victorian nanny to push it. I, too, had been infected with Harrodsmania and dragged Aileen there to buy nappies. We found some reduced shop-worn nappies and, delighted I had found a bargain, we bought twenty-four of them.

Two weeks before the baby was due, I went with Aileen to a natural childbirth class. One such visit was meant to be as much as fathers required, and I can't claim that I went out of my way to ask for more. We were lectured on the various phases of labour. We were told what role we might play in the great event. Sympathy, massage, and a little help with the rhythm of breathing were the most a man could offer. I was awed, too, as we listened to the baby's heartbeat. It was hard to make out that steady beat amid the gurgle of all the other body noises but the idea seemed extraordinary. Inside Aileen, there was a human being. Each man had two or three minutes straining to listen to that throb of life. Then, the efficient doctor whisked the next couple in. I had not made it my business to seek out any more preparation.

Day by day, Aileen grew more tired and yet more excited. We were into the last week of anticipation and everyone we knew who had had a baby warned that the beasts never arrived on time. Aileen had some contractions one evening. Then, they petered out. The next evening, when I came home, she told me she had been having contractions throughout the afternoon. I panicked with delight. She told me to calm down. I told her, knowingly, of course, that this was the night. We ate, we tried to read. It was rather hard to concentrate. We were waiting. Then, suddenly, as Aileen was sitting on the bed there was this gush and plop. Her waters had broken. As she sat in the puddle, I told her – sagely again – I knew it was coming. I rang for the ambulance and wondered what on earth would have to be done if Aileen suddenly started giving birth there and then. Images of myself as a male midwife (and hero) coursed through my mind. Luckily, the ambulance turned up within five minutes.

The hospital gave Aileen a hard time. They would not believe her when she said she thought that she was very close to giving birth. They insisted on giving her an injection of Pethedine to 'relax you, dear' even though Aileen muttered she didn't want it. I felt too intimidated by the hospital atmosphere, by my confusion at being about to become a father, to help Aileen stand up to the omniscient nurses. They left us alone in a small room.

After an hour, we rang the bell because Aileen was sure she was very close to giving birth. She felt the instinct to push. The midwife asked me if I really wanted to attend the birth and intimated that this was a very peculiar request. Men were not supposed to attend the mystery of birth. I insisted and so I was made to dress up like a surgeon.

In the delivery suite, Aileen was having difficulty in maintaining the natural rhythm her childbirth classes had taught her. The Pethedine injection had played havoc with her reactions. I sat by her side but I had not really understood the intricacies of the breathing rhythms well enough to do more than hold her hand and encourage her. In and out, in and out, I coaxed her like a feeble-minded cox.

For a while, all appeared to be going well. Aileen was not in too much pain. The head was engaged and was starting to come out. I could sense a mounting fever in myself. I began to be sure that our child would be born speaking and carrying a message. God – I happen to be an atheist – would trumpet his message through our child. Nonsense, insane nonsense, I knew perfectly well, and yet the idea rolled on and on. I couldn't get it out of my head. I concentrated on holding Aileen's hand and mopping her brow. Soon, soon, very soon, the baby would be born.

Suddenly, the nurses got a hush of anxiety in their voices. Was the baby breathing all right? Was the cord not tangled? How long was he or she going to be in the birth canal? The baby seemed stuck. Far too relaxed because of the Pethedine, Aileen's muscles slackened and just would not muster the energy for the final shove. Those minutes were the most terrible I have ever experienced. I was in a giddy panic. There could be brain damage if a baby was stuck too long in the birth canal. Never mind atheism, I started to pray to God. My mind couldn't stop flashing on the worst, most disastrous, outcomes. Just as I had been convinced, a few minutes before, that our child would enter the world uttering a profound message, now I was jelly, praying to the God I didn't believe in it would be all right. Behind the surgical mask, I was sweating, fidgeting, and, somehow, not uttering any of my own anxiety.

45

I dared not look at Aileen's vagina because I was sure that, if I presumed to look, I would only see catastrophe.

Eventually, eventually, Aileen managed to rise above the Pethedine and pushed the baby out. He was safe. I could have yelled with relief. Nicholas duly screamed as he hit life. He was washed down and proclaimed male, and was given to Aileen to hold. She burst into tears and just kept repeating that he was beautiful. The nurses told us he weighed 7 lbs 4 ozs. Aileen hugged him, rocked him, cried over him. The nurse announced his length in inches. I was allowed a very brief moment to hold Nicholas. But, naturally, it was considered dangerous for the father to hold on to his baby for too long. Even Aileen was only allowed a very limited hug.

Half an hour after Nicholas had been born, the routine of the hospital had imposed itself. He had been taken off into the nursery.

The birth had been one of the great highs of all my life. I felt elated. Aileen felt elated. But at this precise moment, medical practice dictated that we all had to be well apart. I hugged her and kissed her. Aileen was more excited than exhausted. But, like a good girl, she had to go to sleep now. We didn't want to say goodbye there and then. We wanted to talk, to celebrate, to hold each other, to stare at our child, to cuddle him. But all that was impossible. I gave Aileen another hug, another kiss. The pressure from the nurses was clear: I had to go now, to leave. My time was up.

The delivery had been a sea of emotions – joy, panic, weird thoughts that gushed into my head, delight – but I never got a chance to talk about any of them. I would not be allowed to see Aileen or our wrinkled baby till the next evening. That was a stupid and cruel delay imposed simply for the sake of hospital tradition and routine.

And so, after a final hug, I left Aileen. She was taken off into the maternity ward. I walked through the quiet corridors of the hospital. It was about 4.30 in the morning. The moment I got out of the hospital, I couldn't contain my delight. I ran all the way up the hill to the block of flats where we lived.

Visits to the hospital. Ten minutes before seven; a straggly queue of men forms outside the ward. Inside the ward, one perceives much bustle. Later, Aileen would laugh and say that the sisters would act as if mothers and babies were going on parade. 'For goodness sake, Mrs Jones, you don't want the men to see you looking like that!' Come 7.00 and we males would be admitted into the sanctum. Holding your baby was discouraged because men just did not do that kind of thing, and that only strengthened my own hazy fear that really I was so clumsy I might damage this delicate, embroidered little being.

During the visits, it was almost impossible to speak at all openly. The institutional atmosphere stifled all contact. I would ogle the baby, hold Aileen's hand, and ask her how she was. She was bored and frustrated but she shilly-shallied round that. Looking forward to getting home, she said. I didn't have the sensitivity to guess how irritated and unsure of herself the hospital was making her feel. She found that she was not producing enough milk and the nurses managed to make her feel inadequate. Decent mothers gush with milk. Then, the nurses did nothing to stimulate the flow. By the time eight days were over and it was nearly time for Aileen to leave, she felt sure she had failed Nicholas because of not having enough milk.

On Sunday morning, we took the cab up Greenwich Hill to our flat. I had got in nice food and a bottle of wine to welcome my wife and child back home. It seemed that here, as we placed Nicholas in his cot for the first time, was what we had wanted and battled for – battled against each other as much as anything. She had wanted our child so much and made me, eventually, want that child too. We drooled over our lovely Nicky, freed at last from the hospital's clutches, and we kissed him and kissed each other.

That night, when the blessed baby refused to go to sleep, it was a joke. There had to be problems that first night. Soon, he would settle down – to living.

After three days, I returned to the routine of work. Aileen stayed at home to mind the baby. Neither of us expected anything different. Aileen had been taught to believe that these first weeks of a baby's life would be hard but that they would also be a wondrous high. The delight of having a baby would quite outshine the boring business of nappies, bottles, and burping and rocking the baby to sleep. We had indulged in a lovely old rocking chair just for that. Aileen knew that her mother had adored tending her children when they were tiny babies and so she had every reason for thinking that bliss was at hand.

It turned out less ecstatic. Aileen was entranced when he smiled at her when he was less than two weeks old. He was alert, beautiful, and bright, and Aileen was besotted from the start.

But Nicholas was difficult as well as delightful. Besotted or not, she found the relentless caring and tending got her down. Her life had to change completely overnight. She had to stay at home most of the day. She saw no one, apart from an older woman who had also just had a baby. It was not just a question of isolation. Because Nicholas slept so badly, and because Aileen had by far the greater burden of his care, she got very tired. He had to be rocked often during the day and, at night, it was almost impossible for her to get a long period of sleep. He was restless and had to be comforted. Aileen probably felt under even more pressure to respond to Nicky's every fret because she had not been able to breast-feed, which depressed her and made her feel guilty. Not having the energy to read, let alone to write, also made her feel that part of herself was dying. She was losing herself in becoming a mother.

I make it sound as if I did nothing. Every evening after my chasing after commissions – and even doing some work – I would get home tired. Work was hard to find, and neither magazine editors nor movie moguls were exactly queueing up for my juvenile services. It became clear that neither *Jane Eyre* nor the sixth rewrite of dirty Dante's *Inferno* was going to be filmed.

When I got home, Aileen desperately wanted to talk and to be stimulated. She wanted me to take over Nicholas for a few hours and she wanted me to ease her out of her loneliness and depression.

But I wanted something quite different. Having tried to get work out of a hostile world, I wanted constant love, support, and admiration from my wife.

I wrote a student film script at the time in which there is a young married couple with a child. In one scene, chubby hubby gets home. His wife tells him: 'You've missed *Civilization*', as at that time retailed by Kenneth Clark. Not too dismayed by that shock because he is slightly zombie-looking, hubby pecks his wife and, after a few minutes, is in danger of falling asleep before the television set. When she complains, he says that that is what marriage is about. In the film I tried to play it for irony but, in my life, I wasn't so different from smug husband.

Looking after Nicholas turned out to be largely Aileen's responsibility, even when I was there. Men are encouraged to feel diffident about babies just as women are encouraged to feel diffident about 'male' activities such as mending fuses. Nicky felt so small and fragile. I felt sure that any creature as clumsy as I was would be bound to hurt him if I touched him too much. That wrinkled bag of flesh seemed too vulnerable. Touch it – and it might break. I did learn to change nappies but, for a long time, I had the sly knack of getting Aileen to change the really dirty ones. Shit is for women. I was very proud of my prowess with the sterilizer and I did learn to make up a bottle but, still, Aileen had to check it to make sure it was right. We shared rocking-chair duty to some extent. But my energy was more precious than hers. After all, come to next morning, I would have to issue forth into the world again. I couldn't spend the whole night rocking. She could; she had nothing better to do.

And then it was she who had so desperately wanted a child. I could always fall back on that.

I might nor really feel as responsible for Nicholas' care but I was very proud of him. Back in 1971, few employers granted paternity leave and a man who requested a month off to help with his new baby would have appeared distinctly odd. As it happened, as I worked for myself, I could have given myself a month off and gone on the dole. Aileen would have had less of the total strain. She could have gone out: I could have become more confident in handling Nicholas. But such a radical step occurred neither to me nor to her. After the first three days, my life returned to normal. Hers was completely changed.

It took me a long time to realize how changed Aileen's life was. Day after day at home with a baby sapped her. She became very tired and very quiet. She was depressed, and depressed that I did not recognize her depression. But she didn't herself seem to recognize her depression. Often she shrugged off tears. They were just a sign of tiredness and she was so tired because stubborn, lively Nicholas refused to sleep for more than two or three hours at a time. But that was good. Bright babies were restless and difficult.

Later, Aileen admitted there were times when she wished she could die because, dead, she could get a good night's sleep. It didn't help that she could hardly believe she was unhappy. After all, she finally had everything she had wanted: a baby, a marriage, and me. To be unhappy would be perverse.

It never occurred to me either that she might be unhappy. We struggled and sulked but, after a few days, we always made passionate love. And that, I imagined, was a sign that everything really was OK.

Aileen was a victim of her own expectations and I did not have the wit, or inclination, to notice how badly she felt. My own male prejudices did everything to help Aileen not to see. I had always assumed that women were so keen to marry in order to have children. That she did not want all the responsibility of children – or, at least, that a baby was a problem as well as a joy – never crossed my mind. It took an outsider to point out the obvious.

Three months after Nicholas was born, Aileen's mother announced that she was flying in from New York. Though Aileen's mother was only 45, and adamant that she was not to be called 'granny' or 'grandma', she did want to see the first grandchild. It was through your children, and their children, that you snatched immortality, she often said.

The visit was a rescue dash, but I only learned that later. As soon as her mother landed, she confided that she had come because Aileen's letters were so depressed and distraught. She was convinced there was something wrong between Aileen and me and she had rushed to the help of her daughter. I was surprised. Nothing seemed wrong. We were coping well, I thought. Aileen was tired but managing, and I, heroic male, was making bottles, changing nappies when these were not oozing with slimy shit and sitting up with Nicky for part of the night. How ungrateful of Aileen to be less than happy! I knew that it wasn't ideal for an intelligent woman to be stuck all day at home with the baby, but I had to work. There was no alternative. And since I knew that it wasn't easy for her, I resented her complaining. Wasn't it enough that I was sensitive enough to know there were such problems?

So far, the story in this chapter sounds depressingly familiar, a commonplace of the seventies. In the *Guardian* cartoon strip, 'Mrs Weber's Diary', the women are often moaning about the fact that all the child care is left to them and that it sucks them dry, often sucks out of them most of the love for their children.

But not only did I not realize what all this was doing to Aileen, I didn't realize what I was missing as a father. Half-hearted feeds during the night and changing the cleaner nappies were all signs of the fact that I was only a part-time parent. It wasn't that I was half-hearted about my son. I bubbled with pride when Aileen said he had smiled or started to make clear babbling noises, but I wasn't there. I missed a great deal of that. He was more her son than my son.

The partial nature of my relationship with Nicholas became clear one evening when he was about six months old. He was sitting up by then and I was sitting facing him, for some reason. I had decided to devote a few minutes to being a good daddy and was about to roll a pink plastic ball towards his toes. Improve his co-ordination. Suddenly, this little baby started to laugh at me.

And laugh and laugh and laugh.

I laughed back.

We sat there, fixed by these gurgles of laughter, for minute after minute.

The laughter kept on bursting, flowing, popping. Usually, there is a clear focus to laughter, a joke, a cartoon. But here there was nothing except recognition and love. Sitting in his nappy, ignoring the plastic pink ball I had conscientiously rolled at his toes, Nicholas laughed and laughed at me. And I laughed and laughed at him. Aileen came into the room, saw what was happening and watched. I didn't notice her there for ages because she just watched quietly.

It was wonderful. There isn't a moment, of course, when a child really becomes your child but there are moments that change you, that you remember as changing. In the laughter, we really became related.

I was lucky. I don't know what triggered off this overflow of laughter because once I was in it, I forgot everything except the strange intensity of it. Nothing was strained. Long bursts of laughter often are strained. And I'm so grateful for that outburst. It changed my feelings towards Nicholas and it also had rather more practical effects. I lost my inhibitions about touching him. I could bear to change the shittiest of nappies, and, in the night, I did rather more of the feeding than I had ever done before. The conversion was hardly total. More of the care, far more, still fell to Aileen but, at least, there were some signs of change. But I did feel completely involved with my young son.

That summer, work was scarce. The idea occurred to me to go to Holland where there were a lot of good medical and social science stories. A week there should bring in plenty of articles. While I bummed around Amsterdam, spent the night in Vondelpark and interviewed interesting psychiatrists, Aileen stayed at home. From Amsterdam, I went to Paris to meet Berta Salkind, the wife of Alexander Salkind who was to produce the *Superman* movies. She had written a play. A mutual friend, James Mason, had given them my name and they offered to pay my fare to Paris to discuss rewriting and directing it. I met Berta at her friend's who was a faith-healer. Berta liked me: I quite liked the play which was a comedy about a Jewish film producer (her husband) trying to set up a huge prduction while being plagued by creditors who had lost their patience, and his mystical wife (none other than Berta). Much of the play was funny but towards the end, it veered off into visions in which the producer turned into a Christ-like figure.

'Forget your economic worries,' the producer told me after Berta

51

said she liked my ideas which I had tailored a bit to her mysticism. Eager for the job, I said that I thought the play should end with the producer figure lugging a tripod and camera shaped like a cross up a hill. The Celluloid Christ!

Instead of getting the best fee I could get, I would ask if they would pay for Aileen and Nicholas to stay in Paris with me as we worked on the script. That way, we would have a holiday, Aileen would get out of her isolation and we would enjoy Paris together.

'Of course, of course,' beamed Alex.

After that magic laughter I was beginning to get a sense of what I might be missing. I felt part of a family. The feeling that it was Aileen and Nicholas against, or apart from me, disappeared totally. I got enormous fun out of Nicky, bouncing him up and down, singing him songs out of tune, scampering after him as he learned to crawl and then to walk. I also took more and more pride in my ability to cope with him on my own if Aileen went out for the evening or, occasionally, for the day. It sounds silly perhaps to highlight things like scampering with a ten-month-old but babies and children make it possible for adults to play again. The only adults you can tickle and romp with and cuddle are, after all, your lovers and we are so attuned to performance in sex that we play less than we should. Men, especially, tend to lose that freedom to play, to make complete fools of themselves by being a bellowing elephant on the living-room floor, by pretending to be Cinderella or throwing teddy bears across the bed.

Also, I got a certain awareness of feelings of tenderness. Rocking Nicholas to sleep was exhausting and boring but very tender. Trying to burp him was exasperating but lovely when the burp finally came. Coaxing him and cuddling him when he had colic was agonizing because it was hard to see him tighten and suffer, but I found a strange comfort in trying to comfort him. All these mixtures of warmth and play came, for me, only when I began to take a serious part in looking after Nicholas.

By going out to work, coming home tired, and hardly seeing their babies most men seem to me to lose a chance to grow themselves. Much as I detest the jargon of the growth industry, I did grow in that time and, if I had pushed it more, might have done so more. The economic structure makes it impossible for most men to make that choice without sacrificing both their long-term career and short-term money. I wish now that I'd been more committed to trying something more 'extreme'. I was probably in a better position than most men to take anything like such a step, and I didn't.

So I made my gesture about Paris. Having lost our push-chair, we had to carry Nicholas around everywhere, but it was worth it. He dozed in his carry-cot in many restaurants as Aileen and I ate. After a few days, the three of us and Berta set off for the country where we were to do the bulk of the work on the script. Berta's secretary had found us a remarkable hotel which had once been the haunt of artists. Frequently broke, they had often been unable to pay for their dinners. The indulgent owner let them paint pictures on the dining room wall to settle up and, among his impromptu murals, there were two Toulouse-Lautrecs. Aileen seemed happy. I felt pleased with myself for having done something bold.

We did eventually put on the play but there were dramas in the drama. Twice, Berta sacked members of the cast. Once I was sacked. Once she lambasted an Irish actor because he was so disrespectful to the text. Next, she sacked one of the actresses, who had to be hired back the next day at a quadrupled salary. Alex hired another writer to work on the script – a man I'll call Bandis.

If I hadn't been so desperate, I would have walked out. But it was my big break, my chance to be spotted as a real director. The play was being done in the Roundhouse. Ambitious, believing that somehow I could finesse it so that it would be all right, I went on. I worked incredibly hard. The cast was larger than any I had dealt with. The tensions in the production were a nightmare. Berta kept on changing bits of the script.

From the start, I had wanted Aileen to be involved. I had asked her if she wanted to do the publicity since she had worked on magazines. She said that she did even though she didn't. Later, she told me, she had been so angry because she knew she could write a much better play and, of course, no one was giving her the chance. I was playing big director: she was meant to be the meek wife. As the production became more and more frantic, I leaned on Aileen for more and more support. Who else should I moan to? Who else should I look to for giving me strength to cope with all these impossible people? Doing the play took over my life for something like six to eight months.

But Aileen had Nicholas to care for. As the production of the play became more fraught, as I became more anxious, all those good, fatherly intentions collapsed. I spend much less time looking after Nicholas. That made Aileen angry, and being so close to something creative made her feel so frustrated. I needed more and more support and she was less and less willing to give me that.

Towards the end of the run of the play (which failed, surprise, surprise, to become a hit) there were economic problems. Equity had to use its money in escrow to pay the actors. The bank refused to meet some cheques on the production. All that added to the general stress and strain of the show. Neither Hollywood nor West End theatres called.

The play left me tired and depressed. I had driven myself like a slave. To what end? For months afterwards I would have angry letters from people who claimed they were owed money. I knew, too, in my heart of hearts, that I would have been stronger if I had been less ambitious. I had tried to accommodate Berta with her whims of a mystical millionairess. If I had walked out dramatically, they might well have accommodated me. But I didn't have the confidence then to do that and so I had patched on, compromised on, tried to get the play on.

I was exhausted by the time we finally struck the set so late that I missed the end-of-production party. I didn't miss much, Aileen told me. By the time she got there, all the booze had disappeared and one of the actors was dancing around in a leotard which had so many holes in it, it might have been a colander. Neighbours complained. The police were called. A few people were getting stoned and the party got raided. It was a fitting end. Aileen had had the wit to get out a few moments before the police arrived.

The best thing seemed to have a holiday. Gathering together what money we had, we booked ourselves on a package tour to Spain. On that holiday, some wonderful things happened. Nicholas caught his first sight of the sea and he laughed and laughed at it, laughed as much as he and I had done that lovely time. The beach was slightly frightening. It was still in Franco's time and the sinister Guardia Civil patrolled with machine guns on the sand. (They never put those scenes in the tourist ads.) But it was just what we needed to get relaxed. Nicholas also crawled up his first long flight of stairs by the side of the villa we had rented and, thank God, he had pulled the stove over himself and, miraculously, he was safe. Aileen is still agog at how lucky he, and we, were.

But if Nicholas was lovely, the holiday only opened wounds between us. We went for a walk one evening to a small restaurant at the far end of the beach. Thunder threatened; huge clouds, bulbous like swollen cauliflowers, kept running across a full moon. Moonbeams scattered across the sea. A wind picked up. We picked our way across rocks and holiday litter, taking turns carrying Nicholas. The evening was meant to be a treat. It was the best restaurant in town.

Aileen told me she had nearly fallen in love during the play.

'With whom?' I asked almost before I had had time to be taken aback.

With the writer whom maliciously I had called 'Bandy'.

'Oh,' I said, surprised, because he had seemed a pretentious man to me.

He had, she said, talked to her, seen her as a human being, not treated her through the fog of being wife and mother, that creature made up of those twin roles. 'I wanted to sleep with him when he came to say goodbye. We were at your mother's flat. I'd arranged it so we'd have time alone.'

I felt jealous, hurt, and angry.

'But we didn't.' He had been honourable or diffident or thought better of it. He was married himself. Pure malice to call the man 'Bandy', for it was not his doing that he should happen at a point when Aileen was so ready to fall in love with someone else.

It all tripped so cruelly off her tongue. I tried to justify myself. The play had been a bad patch. I was sorry I had been so absent. She was being unfair, by which, of course, I meant unfair to me who deserved nothing less than total loving.

'I'm just not happy,' she said. She was even more unhappy because I didn't seem to realize how unhappy she was. 'It just isn't what I thought it'd be.'

It was a shock. I stopped on that beach and stared dramatically at the sea. From the start, I had assumed that Aileen wanted me more than I wanted her. My love had been grudging and, when we married, it felt to me like a triumph for her. At least, I remember telling myself, I'll always have her love. If I lost my freedom in marriage, at least I would be more loved than loving. Now, it was suddenly, stunningly, different.

Most of the last year, Aileen said, she had been unhappy. I had opted out of looking after Nicholas. I always demanded and demanded her attention, her support, and she got so little back in return. 'It just seems empty, stupid,' she shrugged.

She was accusing me of having failed her completely. I promised I would change. I promised I would help more with Nicholas. I promised I would *improve*. Inside myself, I felt a shudder as I said that word.

Snug on my shoulder, Nicholas dozed. We had an expensive meal neither of us enjoyed much. It was a restaurant made for lovers. Fishing nets hung about the walls. There were cheap prints of little fishing boats and candles struck in bottles. I looked across the table at Aileen and I was sure that if I took more care, if I was more loving, she would soon be as happy as she had been at the best of times between us. I could make her love me again as much as she had before. And it would be quite easy.

A few days later, back in London, Aileen saw an ad in a newsagents which advertised a women's group. 'I'm going to go,' she said. It felt rather good, a sign of change, that I should be baby-sitting at home while she was out. Nicky was a pest to get to sleep, and when I had finally got him down I succumbed to television. *News at Ten* finished. It was eleven. It was half past eleven. I was beginning to wonder when Aileen was going to be back. Just before midnight, she returned, sat down and with a long hiss of pleasure, said: 'That was the best, best thing I've done for ages. All those women – women, note – actually understand some of what I'm unhappy and miserable about and, oh, I could talk to them.'

That last phrase was aimed at me. If I and our relationship had not been a failure, then she would not have had to scurry to a women's group for understanding. It seemed unfair, but I stopped myself saying it. Here, on the verge of making this great effort to make our marriage work better for her, she sailed off to a women's group. I sulked delicately. (Despite our inability to feel, men are able to sulk; I am proud of a soulful, smouldering sulk provoked by snubs to the ego.)

Aileen became a firm member of the group. It sharpened her own anger. She felt guilty no more about wanting me to look after the baby. The women's movement made her see that her demands were modest – indeed, the result of her own background. If I refused to budge to such an extent, then I could hardly be classed as human. Some specific things really riled her. Why did I never clean the lavatory? Were my male hands too pure to be sullied? Or Nicky's really shitty nappies? If I ever did more than the washing up, she accused, I looked like a martyr. An unpleasant one, too.

Conversations often ended abruptly with her saying: 'Oh my God, it's the oh my God I'm a martyr look.' Then she would leave the room.

The martyr thought, however, that as he was making the money off which we lived, he should be spared these domestic chores. As it happened after our flight to Spain, we had no money and work was hard to find. I had a pink and pliant bank manager who had a bizarre fascination with circumcision. Twice, I managed to get an overdraft extension after long conversations on this unlikely subject.

'This has nothing to do with money, strictly speaking', he once said, patting his sweaty, bald head, 'but I have been told that if you're circumcised it makes it easier to wash the gubbins.' He seemed to expect a response.

I thought it was odd what one did to get a £50 overdraft. I nodded and said I expected so. After these unlikely conversations, I would be allowed to draw another ten pounds. 'You must be more disciplined,' he declared, patting his pink pate.

Eventually, banking patience wore out and we had to borrow money from my mother. Aileen blamed me for not being around more; I blamed her for not doing anything to make money.

'You could write articles.'

'I don't want to do that.'

'There must be something you could do.'

'I'd rather be a waitress and write in the evenings.' She was furious, because she had abandoned her novel after 250 pages.

Aileen's women's group constantly raised the question of money, who made it, who controlled it, and the tight links between capitalism and patriarchy. I saw myself as a generous person who was broke; Aileen saw me as a man who used, as all men, economic power. I might be going through a period of no economic power, but when I had had economic power I had used it against her. When I had it again, I would use it against her again. Unless she fought. I made her feel guilty about spending money and guilty about not having money. Whenever she said that I should give up some of that power, I became defensive.

It's easy to forget the energy of discovery that the women's movement had in the early seventies and the impact it had on men involved with feminist women. I prided myself on not wanting to stop Aileen, on not being frightened, like some of the other husbands, of these issues.

The group did not just raise tensions about money. Some of the men whose women had joined the women's group became apoplectic. One man refused to leave the house when the women were meeting. No coven, randy for liberation, was going to drive him out of his castle on which he paid the mortgage. A diffident man rang me and said he wanted to meet in a pub to discuss his wife's frightening, weird ideas. In the pub, he confessed that he usually did the washing up after dinner. He looked a bit hesitant. Was it tantamount to a sin? Had this 'concession' spurred his wife to experiment with liberation? Now, she wanted him to do half the cleaning, and, given his domestic incompetence, she was proposing to give him lessons in hoovering, running the washing machine, ironing, and mopping the kitchen floor. In return, he could teach her how to mend electric plugs. He told all this anxiously. Was it unnatural? Should he consult a doctor?

The anger and the energy among some of the women – often in Aileen – certainly made me very uneasy. It burst out unexpectedly often.

There was a party which Aileen took me to. Most of the women in her group were there and many had brought their husbands along. It was a sign of suburban ambivalence about the movement that, although men were rigorously excluded from consciousness-raising groups, there was hope that feminism would make us all grow. We would have better parties because of it. If only the prickly, prick-laden men could get off their defences and be alive without being aggressive.

The party went well, though there was some sense of being on your best behaviour in alien territory. Only liberal opinions were safe. We discussed adventure playgroups. Everyone was very positive about adventure playgrounds. We discussed threatened cuts in public spending. Everyone agreed they were evil and presaged the end of civilization. We drank to that. We danced to that. Towards the end of the party, Aileen and I were dancing together.

We got a ride back from Sammy and Jake. Sammy was a small, angular woman. Her jaw was thin and craggy. Husband Jake was all vagueness. He was tall but covered his weak chin with a beard. Being all vague, even his beard had failed to take proper root. It was sparse and the skin underneath a patchy red. He always wore a corduroy jacket. As a couple, they had impeccable left-wing political opinions and were planning to go to the Far East.

Jake put the car in gear and, at once, it stalled. The mellow mood went.

'You watch what you're doing,' snapped Sammy.

'I usually do', Jake whined.

'You haven't had too much to drink,' warned Sammy.

'No.'

'Because if you have, you'll probably kill us. If there's one thing I can't stand it's someone who drinks too much and won't admit it.'

'Take that turn,' Sammy ordered.

'I was going to.'

'Don't lie . . . you're always getting lost.'

Jake said nothing. I was sweating.

'For Chrissake why don't you learn to drive properly,' Sammy yelled suddenly. It wasn't clear to me what Jake's new sin was. 'You don't need to go that way. It's shorter this way. Where do you think you're going *now*?' She leaned forward at the next turn. 'Can't you get anything right? This is the road you take, you fool,' she shouted. I looked at Aileen as you do when you're with someone and a third person is behaving outrageously.

We reached our block of flats. I thanked Jake for the ride and he returned a blank nod. Aileen and Sammy hugged and then she thanked them both for the lift. We watched them disappear and staggered towards each other. There was a moment's peace in our hug.

Then Aileen smiled: 'I suppose you're going to say that she's like that because she's a feminist.'

'She was just vicious.'

'But you really think it's because she's a feminist.'

'No.'

'Of course you won't admit it. But if she is like that, what do you think has done it? Being with him?'

Aileen disentangled herself from my arms and went inside.

Men were neurotic about success, Aileen repeated. There was no hope if I refused to be less driven to succeed. I said that I did have to earn our living and that required energy. Nonsense, she countered, I loved being neurotic about work. She loved to make fun of me when I waited for the postman to arrive. Every morning, come ten to eight, 'you start stealing these little glances through the window'. True. 'And then I can see you hoping, hoping that in his hand there might be letters carrying all sorts of successful goodies.' The ultimate, golden contract.

'All right, some truth.' I did watch the postman enter the building, I did listen for his steps on the stone floor. Then there would be a shuffle outside our door. Anything might pop through the letter box. I admitted it but I didn't see any other way. Much of the post was rejection slips and letters from television companies that did not want my services. Aileen never had to put up with persons such as the silky publisher who commissioned me to write a book on the police. I was to be paid £40 for each chapter as I delivered it. The week after I delivered chapter 6, which described the history of corruption in the police, I expected the cheque. We needed it as relations with my bank manager had taken a turn for the worse since he seemed to have lost interest in circumcision. I rang the publisher. He said, coldly, he wanted to talk to me. In his smart office stuffed with Georgian bric-à-brac and posters from a Matisse exhibition, his silkiness glared at me with his most judgemental mien. The book was dreadful. He was always over generous to young would-be writers.

'But you wrote that you liked it.'

'I was drunk at the time.'

'I did deliver the chapter and, to be honest, it cost me quite a lot of research to put together.'

'Would-be writers always say that.' What did he expect me to do? Argue it was brilliant? Beg? He knew I had a young child and that I had devoted weeks to this chapter to make it good. 'Your wife just brought forth, didn't she? Well, in the circumstances, I'll let you have £20. Not that you deserve it and really I should ask for all my money back.' He wrote out a cheque and, for a moment, it lay there between us. I wanted to spit. I took the cheque and said I was grateful and raced to put it in the bank.

This was my economic power.

The manager let me withdraw £8 after issuing 'Stern warnings in vitriol if I may put it like that, not to be extravagant'.

'I'm not extravagant,' I promised, clutching the eight quid.

Aileen had none of this to complain of. While she went to the women's group, she insisted on our talking more about what was wrong. We 'explored our resentments', shared them, chewed them, failed to resolve them but basked in the glow of having been mature and sensitive enough to discuss them. I did change in some ways. I looked after Nicky more. I became less afraid of being alone with him. I mastered the arts of washing the lavatory and the kitchen floor. It did seem to me that we were learning from our mistakes. Aileen must be starting to love me again, I thought. She was writing every day as well as seeing her friends from the group. Things were getting better, I thought. I never made much of one strange fact.

Every day, as I waited for the post to arrive, I knew there would be a letter for Aileen from the States. She and old friend, Mo, seemed to be having the most intense correspondence. Mo was fat, funny and the last time I had seen her she had been dangling herself seductively in front of a hippy war-lord. The letters were thick and Aileen read them avidly. She would shut herself up in them, read them once, twice over and then set to writing her reply. I envied the intensity of that correspondence and so asked about the letters. But Aileen always fobbed me off. They were her letters, her business, her life. Not man's business.

She fobbed me off until one evening.

There is a scene in a Truffaut film where a 50-year-old businessman falls in love with a stewardess. He is fat, rich, balding. What started as a one-night stand (in a five-star hotel) turns into real passion. His wife suspects nothing. He wants to be honest and kind but, when he comes to tell his wife the truth, he is also gloating. He tells her that he hates himself for what he is doing to her. And that is true. But he also loves doing it and handing her an unexpected shock of pain and distance.

One evening, Aileen sat down opposite me. She leaned forward seriously, waited as if she were deciding something. 'I suppose I should tell you something.'

It did sound like the start of a confession. 'What?'

She wavered between a look of remorse and a very businesslike air as if she were going to refuse to extend my credit. She tossed the remorse aside.

'I'm in love with Mo.'

'Oh,' I said, flummoxed. What did *being in love* mean between two women?

'She's coming over to see me.'

I repeated my *Oh*.

'Is that all you can say?' Aileen hardened.

'I don't know what to say.'

'We've been writing all these thick intense letters you're so curious about because we're in love. I want her badly.'

She had jolted that physical reality down between us. For a definite fact. Let there be no cosy male illusion that being in love for these two women meant something tame, pretty, spiritual rather than sexual. The love spoke its name and spelled out its intentions very clearly. I had no idea what to say. I hurt. I poured myself a drink very slowly and sat down opposite Aileen. I stared at her, hunched myself up for comfort.

'Is that all you're going to say?'

'What can I say? *Why*, I suppose? Why?'

Aileen said she could rattle off a good list of good reasons for having fallen out of love with me and in love with Mo. Should she start the recital?

'I don't see why you're being angry with me,' I snapped.

'Of course. You're my husband. I'm going to be unfaithful. I belong to you. You have every right to be angry. Of course.'

'You don't belong to me like that but I'm still hurt. Isn't that allowed?'

'Yes, I suppose so.'

Still not knowing what to say, I seized on the practical. 'When is she coming?'

'In two weeks. For Christmas.'

'Where's she going to stay?'

'I invited her here,' said Aileen in full defiant splendour. 'It's my flat too.'

Should be cosy, I thought, but lacked the confidence to say. My first reaction was to play for pity. After all, Aileen should feel guilty. 'What do you want me to do?'

'That's up to you.'

As Fritz Perls recommended, she was going to do her thing. What I did about that was up to me.

'I see,' I said.

'I doubt that,' she said, angry again. 'What you do is up to you. What I do is up to me. But Mo is coming here to stay with me.'

'I don't seem to have much choice.'

'No, for once, you don't.'

Writing this, I wonder if Aileen did relish it so much, if she revelled in her harshness. She needed her anger to keep her determined; I wanted her to console me and felt she ought to because she ought to feel guilty. She warded off any accusations by pointing out various crises where I had made one 'big mistake' after another, as if living with her required one to pass a series of emotional and sexual exams. My marks were very low. She had dwindled in the marriage. So had I turned from a romantic rebel into a suburban slob.

My reaction was to deny her experiences. But she told me she was happy. Only last week when we were in the park. Didn't she remember the night when we made such erotic love? She brushed all my good memories away. Every time she had been happy, she said, she was compromising, clutching at straws or thinking of Nicky. She was lazy and she did hope against hope it might work out between us. But it never did. Did I know that during this period when I lapped up her affirmations of happiness she had been having an affair with an old friend of hers? Being clandestine gave her a thrill. When we *explored our feelings* and played therapists, we swore to be honest. But having such a perilous secret was too precious for Aileen to give it up. A friend who worked in the law was her secret lover. He finished his cases and hoped Aileen had got Nicky to sleep on time. I never found out, though a few times he must have left seconds before I arrived, climbed up to the next landing, waited for me to go in, and then ambled safely out. I had no suspicions; and, when I found out, I admired the cool calculation with which Aileen carried it all out. If there were any tell-tale signs – a lingering aroma of after-shave, an unaccountable sock under the bed – I failed to spot them. I hadn't even noticed, she sniped, how unhappy she was. Now, I was trying to make her feel guilty. She didn't want to feel guilty; she didn't feel guilty. She had hardly had a monopoly of cruelty, she bit. When she had wanted me, I had been cold. I knew I had been brutal – I had left her stranded, abandoned her. I had always expected her to fit in with my needs.

'I don't want to be a wife,' she said bitterly.

'Well, you're not behaving like a wife.'

'I can't stand myself when I do. And the trouble is', she smiled almost fondly at me, 'the trouble is that though you always said you didn't want a wife, you do want a wife.'

For the next two weeks, we tried to live normally. I knew that there was no point in pleading with her to tell Mo not to come. And apart from not wanting to abase myself, part of me felt that she had every right to try and be something else. Our evenings were almost jolly, often because Aileen seemed cheered by her confession. I knew. I had no moral grounds on which to complain. I promised that I would try to understand her side of it, why she found being my wife so obliterating. A few evenings before Mo was to arrive, I said I would go away – at least for the first night and the first day. Flight was better than fight, especially when there was no prospect of winning the fight.

The morning of Mo's arrival I hugged Nicky, hugged Aileen who allowed herself to be hugged. She was impatient I should be gone because then she could start being someone else. I spend the day working round the City and, about six, when I knew Mo had arrrived, I went to eat. It was Christmas time and London was decked in lights. Tinsel, trees, shoppers, families rushing. I bolted my food even though I had told myself I would eat slowly, meditatively. I had bought a P.G. Wodehouse book to read over dinner. There was no friend I felt safe to confide in so, I walked, and I went to see Woody Allen's *Play It Again Sam* and sat through it twice, laughing hysterically. But since the film centres on Woody's inability to get anywhere with women, it wasn't the cosiest comedy. I wondered if the real reason was not in anything as vague as the emotions but sex. And in the middle of one gag in *Play It Again Sam* images of *Cat on a Hot Tin Roof* rushed into my mind. The scene where Big Momma tells Elizabeth Taylor that every problem marriage starts going wrong here in the bed. Aileen no longer wanted me. I was not the demon lover.

I left the cinema and walked down the Strand, killing time, looking in incongruous windows like that of the Western Australia office. Should I emigrate? There was a Fleet Street café, Micks, which would be open, full of smoke, full of chatter, a place to feel lost in. I stared at my large mug of tea and nibbled some thick toast. In an alley cross the road, once, Aileen and I had been so hungry for each other that we had just about made love in the shadow of a City church. I glared with envy at the other men in Micks. Their lives weren't in shreds. Their women weren't at home screwing with another woman. I bought the first edition of the *Daily Telegraph* which did nothing to take my mind off my insistent question: how could she prefer Mo to me? Or anyone to me?

By three in the morning, I tottered into my mother's flat. Luckily she was away so I didn't have to explain my appearance. I hated the silence and found smoochy romantic music. Didn't the radio stations realize that the only people who listen at three in the morning are the ones whom love has given up on? I switched off the radio. The silence was nasty. I tried to find a book. As a teenager, I had loved *The Murder of Roger Ackroyd*. Now, after three pages, I tossed it aside because it seemed so awful. I yawned, and prayed to find that I was so drained I would fall asleep. I didn't, of course: I worried. For myself. For Nicky. At least, I was in touch with my anger and, as a result, scored over most men in sensitivity. Painful as it was, it could be used.

Being abandoned felt not only painful but embarrassing. I thought of ringing an old girlfriend and talking to her. But how do you say that your wife has left you for a woman? The burgeoning gay literature of the past few years describes the joys and difficulties of *coming out*. Even though your family and friends may be shocked, and even though they may occasionally cut you dead, a gay man or woman has the consolation of knowing that they are now being themselves. To come out is to recognize and to accept yourself – a major triumph. Being married to someone who is excitingly *coming out* while you wail your solitary hetero woes has none of that triumph. It's a loss. And a brutal one. The best I could do was to repeat to myself that I wasn't stopping Aileen finding herself. It struck me as pathetic that I felt queasy about talking about it. I felt I might be pitied or laughed at and that, somehow, anyone would regard the whole thing as weird. If Aileen did prefer a woman to me, I had to be pathetic and weird.

Rationally, I knew there was her side, her story, but, just then, I couldn't concentrate on it. I wasn't so weird. Ironically, of course, I wanted to talk to her, and what you can't do when your wife/husband has gone off with someone else is talk to them.

Eventually, I fell asleep. I woke up early, fended off images of Aileen and Mo, and went out to buy the papers. Come ten or eleven, I would have to ring Aileen. I knew, theoretically, that I could take a train to Cornwall or disappear in the City or just hole up at my mother's, but that was theory. Come ten, or eleven, or noon, if I held out stoically, I would ring Aileen.

And what then?

What if she told me to stay away?

What if she told me to come back?

I waited, returned to the flat, and just tried not to ring too soon. I tried *The Murder of Roger Ackroyd* again and, this, time, stayed with it until he actually was murdered. It was 11.18 To have lasted past eleven seemed something of an achievement. I started to dial our number. What if nobody answered? What would that mean? That they had skipped off with my son into a lesbian idyll. I sweated. The phone rang. Once, twice, I hate waiting. Three times, four times. They were probably in bed. Five, six rings. If she hadn't answered by ten, they must be out or she wasn't answering. Our flat was small. *Our flat* – who was *our*? Seventh ring. The phone is picked up.

'I thought it would be you.'

'How are you?'

'Fine. And you?'

'Less fine, I guess.'

'Well don't expect me to shed any more tears over you. I've shed enough.'

Long pause. At that time, our phone conversations were usually packed with long pauses that grated on Aileen.

'Don't you have anything to say?' she asked, finally.

'I suppose I'm asking if I can come home.'

'No-one's stopping you.'

'You do sound welcoming.'

'Don't be childish. You know what's going on.'

Any lingering hopes that it hadn't turned into a sexual love disappeared.

'I don't feel like spending another night out here on my own.'

'It's up to you. Only don't make any assumptions.'

Don't make the assumption that I will be with you. She didn't say that but it lay there.

'Nicky'll be glad to see you,' she said finally.

With some trepidation, I went back home. I wasn't expecting to find Mo attractive. She was still plump, but her hair had grown long and wild. She looked on me with double suspicion. I was a man and I was Aileen's husband. She made me nervous and afraid but, still, I liked her.

Mo wanted to go for a walk round London and Aileen said that she wanted to write. So, Mo and I, rivals, took a 53 bus and went sightseeing through London. On top of the bus, we edged towards some revelations.

'I didn't realize that you and Aileen were still so much together,' she said almost apologetically.

'I didn't realize any of that.'

'She isn't very happy.'

'I didn't do a great job of noticing it.'

'Men usually don't.'

We had reached the Elephant and Castle and I told Mo how it had got its name. There was a pub called the Infanta of Castile but no one could pronounce the name properly so the 'infanta' became the 'elephant'.

'I thought it was kind of nice of you not to be there last night.'

'I don't imagine it would have been too much fun for me.'

'Or for me. I still get bad attacks of guilt. It wouldn't have been much fun for Aileen either.'

'I hate scenes anyhow.'

'You a coward?'

'I don't like cowards.'

I grinned sheepishly. Neither of us were too eager to ask what would happen next. We got off the bus and walked around the city. As we stood outside the National Gallery, for some reason, I put my arm around Mo – we were, somehow, in this mess together – and instead of shaking it off, she put her arm around me.

If all this seems bizarre, it was partly a test of all our 'advanced'

66

ideas. I had never believed in fidelity. Why did there have to be possessiveness or hatred? Here was the perfect chance to be progressive. And, then, if I kept my cool maybe we could retrieve something from the mess.

Mo stayed for three weeks, three weeks which veered from fun to pain.

Fun: one evening, we were watching television together. John Wayne and Maureen O'Hara were cast in an Irish epic in which they loved, and lost, each other. True to the sexually confusing situation, we decided to act the film over again but with me playing Maureen O'Hara and John Wayne being played by Mo. A significant part was also played by our half-broken Hoover which acted the broom. In the film, Maureen O'Hara was always brooming bits of her Irish home free of dust. Aileen sat giggling away on the bed. We laughed and we laughed till we all three fell on the bed and started to kiss in a jumble.

Both Mo and Aileen felt they had to make such formal declarations in case I made assumptions which, given my history and male history in general, they assumed I was only too likely to make.

Least fun were the nights when they declared almost formally they wanted to be together. I went out to walk the streets. I would tick time off and go back when they were asleep. Eventually, after all, they would fall asleep. It was bitterly cold. I walked down the hill towards the river at Greenwich. It was slippery from rain and the wind was blowing keen and cold. I stopped, leaned over the railing, and listened to the lapping of the tide mesmerizing me. I huddled on the steps in front of the Naval college. It was too cold to fall asleep and I was crying, which kept me awake. I wondered if they had finished making love now, if it was quiet, if I could go back and not have to confront their obvious passion.

I walked back up the steep hill. When I got to the door, I found I had forgotten the key. Deliberately, says Freud. Probably right, Freud. I knocked. Irritated, Aileen came to the door, demure in a dressing gown.

'Couldn't you just let yourself in quietly?'

'I'm sorry.'

'Goodnight.' She turned on her heels.

'I'm very cold. Can you give me the spare blanket?'

I went to lie down on the sofa. Aileen appeared with the blanket. 'There's the blanket. Now leave us in peace.'

She hurried back. I cloaked the blanket round my shoulders and put on some Bach to drown out whatever sounds they made. I downed slugs of brandy and waited for sleep. I woke up in the morning to find the Bach record still spinning round. Nicky was yelping. From the bedroom, silence. I dressed Nicky and told him we were going for a walk. If we went for a long walk and played in the park, and ran around the cedar trees in the flower garden, if we could do that for long enough, then maybe I would forget. And, maybe too, when we got back they would be up, dressed, breakfasting, and I could forget a little that they were such passionate lovers and forget I was so excluded.

When Nicky and I got back, they were still in bed. Not long after, Aileen got up and came to sit by me on the sofa and held me.

If my reaction to all this was curious and clinging, so was Aileen's. Harsh as she was, she half kept me there. No guilt-tripping in the universe, no please, let alone 'you are my wife' injunctions would have stopped her from becoming Mo's lover. It seemed to me she revelled in the novelty and shock of being a lesbian. She was in love with Mo and, the more she thought about herself, the more she knew that loving women was a true part of her which had been long suppressed. But, for all that, Aileen didn't quite want to dump me. One night she said that she thought it would be nice to spend the night with me. This time, the sofa was Mo's who looked none too happy about it. Aileen let me hold on to her.

'I just have to do what I'm doing. If you love me, like you say you do, don't try to stop me.'

For the last few days of Mo's visit, I went to stay with some friends. I told them I had some research to do and, every morning, I would scurry efficiently to the Bodleian Library and sit there turning the pages of books without reading them.

My friends had married the year before. Aileen and I had gone to their wedding. The implication was that we would be two couples who were friends. They had settled into love and, in the evenings, played music together. I envied them, and felt shy.

What could I say to them?

I didn't feel like explanations and deep talks into the night. I envied them quietly and shut up. I spun unlikely tales of what I was researching and they were too polite or too kind or too bored to ask much about them.

My other hope in coming to Oxford was that I would manage to pick a girl up here. This was ideologically unsound, but I knew that I would cope better if I could 'have' a girl up here. On the train up, I started to talk to a small, dark girl who was reading *The Owl and the Nightingale*. She peered at me through glasses and told me that she couldn't really see me properly. I said that was probably all to the good. She told me that she was very bored with people who confused *The Owl and the Nightingale* with *The Owl and the Pussycat* which was a nasty piece of Victorian whimsy. She was only interested in obscure literature, and few ballads were more obscure than *The Owl and the Nightingale*, a medieval romance in which the Owl symbolized the male principle and the Nightingale symbolized the female principle. It was an allegory with Jungian implications, she said knowingly. She had a slight hunch. We fixed to have dinner two nights later and she did – for which I blessed her at the time – invite me back to her tiny room. We kissed passionately and tumbled on her single bed. Suddenly, she took her mouth away from mine and grinned sheepishly.

'I don't look like a virgin, do I?'

'Oh . . . I hadn't really thought about it.'

'I know I don't look like a virgin. Men tell me I don't feel like a virgin either, but I am. I have this problem, you see. I can't lose it.'

It wasn't for want of trying. A few weeks before, she had gone to a hunt ball with a Sandhurst cadet. She was fully determined; he was fully determined. They ended up, fully determined, in a barn. 'But nothing happened in the end.'

Nor did anything happen in the end between her and me.

When I got back to London, the fact that Mo would soon be leaving dominated everything else. Aileen did try to be nice to me. She told me she had actually missed me. 'It may not look like I missed you but I did miss you and I'm going to miss Mo terribly when she goes just in case . . .'

'Just in case I make any assumptions.'

'Oh you're getting sharp. Just in case you make any assumptions. But I did miss you.'

She gave me a hug.

The best thing to do seemed to leave them alone for Mo's last day and last night so I disappeared tactfully again. I went to pour my confusion out to a girl I had been with in Oxford. The next day, I went out with Aileen and Mo to the airport. They embraced passionately and Aileen cried all the way back home.

'I've changed,' she said, 'and I don't want to change back.'

'Your really don't have to be so fierce about it.'

'If I weren't so fierce about it, nothing would have happened ever.'

'Maybe.'

'Really.'

I nodded a little feebly.

She added that she made no promises about Mo. 'She's just gone. I haven't given her up and she hasn't given me up. There's a lull. You and I will have to see . . . I suppose,' she trailed off as if the prospect did not entice her too much. 'I need to rest,' she said finally pouring herself a large drink.

It is probaby a mark of our craving for new experiences, new insights that my feelings were so mixed. Obviously, I resented Aileen and felt tired, bitter, humiliated, and outraged. But I also admired her. She had allowed herself to be swept along so dramatically. She had become a lesbian. She had finally said she hated being a wife and a mother. She had been dramatically unfaithful. She had asked so many questions of herself and ignored anyone else in the process. She blasted off, a heroine about her own self discovery. Only safety makes us want to be the same person for the whole of one's life. A biography requires us to connect and integrate events in our lives. But why? Maybe future entries to *Who's Who* will say 0–30 child, wife, mother; 30–50, period of sexual adventurism, lesbian, prostitute; after 50, saint and wise person. But if half of me admired, the other half was tired and only wanted the old Aileen to love the old me.

After Mo left, some parts of our life improved. We wanted, of course, very different things. Aileen wanted to rest, to absorb what had happened to her.

'Give me time,' she pleaded.

She wanted time; I wanted proof that she still loved me.

And while I wanted proof, there were many times when I was too afraid to talk too much about what had happened. Grief at Mo being gone welled up in Aileen. The only way I could parry her grief was to repeat both how hurt I had been, how I still loved her and wanted to make it work between us. I talked as if we could get the magic formula right, then we would leap towards happiness. I managed to get a proper job for the first time and that meant we could have baby sitters so that Aileen could write. Wasn't that part of the magic formula, part of the growth that would make all the pain worthwhile? I didn't even ask Aileen for any total commitment.

But I felt sure I was acting nobly. Often, lest she forget, I repeated the story of that first night when I had wandered down to Greenwich, stared at the river and returned freezing only to be frozen out by Aileen's 'now leave us alone'.

For Aileen, this noble suffering was a bore, an irritation when she was trying to hack her way through to what she thought she really was. Once, watching an ad for a bra in the middle of *World in Action*, she said:

'I really think I'm a lesbian.'

'Don't you like making love with me?'

'Yes but . . . when I look at breasts, I really get turned on.'

'So do I.'

'Stop being stupid.'

I swopped her confusion with my pain. It must be worth something, it must say something about me as a human being, that I hadn't spoiled her time with Mo, that I had looked after Nicky so much. Didn't I deserve love for that? Didn't it show that I cared for her 'as a person'. It was not as my wife that I cared for Aileen, it was not for what she could do for me at all. Great feminist and therapeutic heavens, no. I only cared for her as a person. I was devoted to her unique essence, her real self-hood. I had let her get on with discovering herself.

Behind all this confusion, clinging, and piety, we were groping for *growth*. For me to grow, I had to become less of a man and to give up many male prerogatives and assumptions, most of which had to do with staying in control of situations. We now deride the Victorians with their mania of self-improvement. We mock their desire to educate and enrich themselves. Perhaps, fifty years on, we'll be derided for our obsession for growth as we preen our souls and ourselves to become better, more mature, more whole.

And despite my intellectual commitment to growth, to relinquishing control, I found it hard to begin to do so. Often, in the evenings, seeking reassurance, Aileen and I traded pieties about becoming more whole, and that meant more androgynous, and we tried to understand what was happening and what we might do to sort out our lives. We drank (too much); we talked; we fought. She said what she felt. Usually anger, pain, frustration. I told her that she couldn't really be feeling that way. Not *so* bad. She would get angry; I would sulk. Nights would end with her stretched out on the living-room floor adamant that she would not sleep with me, part of a compromised couple in a compromised bed. I would eventually sulk off to bed, sleep fitfully, wake up, and go back to the living room. Gently, I would nudge Aileen awake and coo that she would really be cosier and more comfortable in our bed. Sometimes she came; often, she shooed me away. Why didn't I leave her in peace to be herself? And, of course, because I couldn't leave her in peace to be herself, I had no chance of being myself either. I was reacting to her, not acting on my own.

The situations I've described were confusing and emotional enough. But for me, they also were fraught because I was being made to feel feelings that were not really 'appropriate' to a man. We are schooled to success – not to feel pain, abandonment, betrayal. In the next chapter, I want to argue that men need to learn to experience those emotions without shame. They are part of life – not the end of it. I didn't, at the time, have the wisdom to see that.

Chapter Four

TO ACT, TO FEEL, TO ACHIEVE

The image of the typical man still owes a good deal to that of the classic hero I described in the second chapter. A proper man, a good bloke, is active and strong. He is successful. He leaves emotions to women who are good at that sort of thing. Feminists have argued that society conditions little boys and little girls to fulfil completely different roles. From birth, male babies are encouraged to explore, to handle things, to be masterful. Boys' games are allowed to be rough. Little girls, on the other hand, are encouraged to care, to nurture. Pitcher and Schultz (1983), in a study of children's play, found that even when they gave boys girlish toys, they used them roughly. Dolls were kicked just as if they were footballs. Girls, on the other hand, did the very opposite. Given footballs, they cuddled them as babies. Cline and Spender (1987), in studies of the conversations between men and women, found that men talked far more. They expected women to listen – and women were good at that. Their conditioning had made them experts at nurturing. Women were good at helping men, who weren't usually even honest in admitting they needed help or grateful for the support they got. I want in this chapter to question some of this research and to ask where the stereotype that men are emotionless and achievement-crazed comes from. I have found some curious gaps in the research literature too.

If I hadn't gone through the experiences I described in the last chapter I wouldn't have raised such questions. But, oddly, one of my favourite books as a teenager described some very successful men who ran quite counter to these stereotypes.

In *The Age of Scandal* (1963), T.H. White described the emotional behaviour of a number of more famous characters of the period. Dukes, generals, authors and even admirals emoted in a way that seems most unmasculine now. Even politicians like Pitt wept.

Such men were expected to have 'bottom', which White translated as 'substance'. But being substantial didn't mean being cold. It certainly did not rule out what we would now call over-emotional behaviour. White described the behaviour of Admiral Byng, for example, and those of his peers who presided over his court-martial. During the hearing, many naval heroes were found to be weeping as the court pondered whether Byng had been guilty of cowardice or not.

Voltaire sniped that the British occasionally executed an admiral 'pour encourager les autres'. But White found that it was 'normal' for admirals and generals to cry and explain their feelings at some length. So, of course, did those in the lower ranks. This display of feeling doesn't seem to have done much harm to the fighting record of the Army or Navy, let alone to the expansion of the British Empire. The foundations for the Raj were laid by these apparently not so macho men, like Warren Hastings who wrote fulsome, loving letters to his wife. By the end of the Age of Scandal (which White puts round 1790) Britain had taken India and Canada and was preparing to colonize Australia. America was lost, but it seems extreme to blame the emotionality of British forces for losing a colony that geography made impossible to hold.

Were these sentimental soldiers an aberration? The evidence suggests not. Huizinga (1945) argued that medieval men had much in common with those emotional 'sentimentalists'. In literature, the Age of Scandal was followed by the Romantic period, in which men were supposed to feel intensely. Pastoral, spiritual, romantic feelings tumbled out. Wordsworth and Tennyson were poets who could hardly be described as restrained or macho. Victorian society certainly went on to repress men as well as women. It demanded increasing conformity to social conventions but, as Peter Gay points out in *The Tender Passion* (1986), there was much evidence that 'bourgeois love' was keenly felt by men. He makes much of the history of Otto Beneke, a minor Austrian bureaucrat, and the English writer Walter Bagehot. Beneke kept a detailed, obsessive record of his feelings, sentimental and erotic, about his beloved Maritta. Bagehot was not quite as obsessive about Elisa Wilson. In both cases, the courtship was quite long, Beneke's ridiculously so. Before marriage, there was much letter writing, which was frequent in Victorian courtship. The letters show the men full of feelings. Bagehot struggled for some months before confessing to Elisa that his mother was mad. Two months after he had made that confession, he proposed. He couldn't help it. He said, 'since the day in the conservatory the feeling has been too eager not to have a great deal of pain in it and the tension of mind has been very great at times.' It was not easy for Bagehot to make these revelations – not just, of course, because men were not supposed to discuss feelings but because having a mad mother was shameful.

Gay argues that the Victorian period was one of transition. A strict old order was giving way to a freer one. Marriages were arranged less frequently. Women were beginning to demand some rights. But his work and White's analysis of the emotional tone of the Age of Scandal prompts questions about how good the evidence for men's emotional inadequacy is.

By the end of the nineteenth century, men were seen as hard warriors as opposed to frail women – but did this reflect what men felt? It may well have been increasing industrialization, changing patterns of work, and the kind of alienation that Marx struggled to describe which made men appear so cold and repressed. In America, early industrial psychologists tended to see workers as cogs in the great business machine. By the 1920s, it was accepted by anthropologists, for example, that societies were divided into emotional women and feeling-dead men. The anthropologist, Margaret Mead, searched for places where this was not true, counter to Western orthodoxy. It is tempting to see the unemotional male not just as a product of Victorian industry but also of the desire of Victorian science to classify sects and races.

I am not a historian of ideas so I can't pinpoint the moment of change, but it is interesting that, from Darwin on, nineteenth-century science was interested in fixing biological differences. Galton, for example, 'proved' that non-white races were less intelligent. Could it be that our stereotype of the man as being unable to feel was created during this period – partly perhaps in reaction to early feminist writings?

White and Gay also prompt a further question. Is the male level of emotionality fixed or is it a quality which changes, both in men and women, from period to period? This is not such a far-fetched idea. The psychologist David McClelland has shown (1969) that our need to achieve varies from time to time and from society to society. It was very high, for example, in sixteenth-century Britain. Could the same be true of emotions? Do men become more or less emotional at different times? Psychologists have not really paid much attention to this question but it is worth studying especially if, as I want to suggest the evidence shows, men are now becoming more emotional.

The women's movement accepted the male stereotype. Bem, who first argued that we would all be better off if we were psychologically androgynous, claimed that men were emotionally repressed (Bem 1974). We accepted the stereotype that it was masculine to be aggressive, forceful, tough, assertive, decisive, and independent. Having feelings was irrelevant. It was feminine to feel, care, and nurture. This stark division reflected the kind of conditioning of boys and girls that play studies showed.

I want to ask how good the evidence for these stereotypes is and, in particular, whether men gain much by sacrificing their emotional lives for work. In some cases, I have had to speculate and extrapolate from less than perfect evidence. It is surprisingly difficult, for example, to find research which asks whether men and women feel different 'intensities' of emotion. Izard (1977) in her standard work on the emotions and in a later tome (1984) hardly raises the question of sex differences. John Nicholson (1984) in his book *Men and Women* points out that men also have hormones and go through cycles when they are likely to be more emotional. But he doesn't cite any direct evidence for whether men feel as much as women. Despite these gaps in the research, I want to argue as follows:

1 that men feel emotions as much as women do;
2 that men feel similar emotions in similar situations to those that women feel – the kinds of things that make men angry will make women angry;
3 that men are less skilled at expressing their emotions but that this is changing – moreover, men don't seem to be much worse than women at recognizing other people's emotions except when these are very subtle – sometimes, of course, men choose to ignore them;
4 that some emotions are much harder for men to acknowledge than others – these are particularly emotions of failure which make us see ourselves as powerless;
5 that men score higher only on some measures but not all of achievement motivation;
6 that the pressure to succeed is damaging.

It would be convenient if a solution lay in the development of psychological androgyny. It was fashionable to believe this in the seventies. Unfortunately, the evidence suggests that androgyny by itself is not enough of a solution. It is too psychological and leaves out crucial political issues. However much I 'grow', if society stays static my 'growth' will be of limited value.

That men are capable of feeling emotions

William James (1918) suggested that we felt things as a result of the state of our body. If I notice that I am sweating and running away – purely physiological measures – it tells me that I am afraid. I identify my emotion as a result of my aroused state. James's theory has been much criticized, but physiological arousal has remained a key concept in the measurement of emotion. The question of 'how much emotion one feels' is fraught with problems. Most contemporary theories argue there is a clear link between how physiologically aroused subjects are and how much emotion they feel. Arousal may be a crude measure but it is the best objective one we have. The only other method available is to get subjects to rate how emotional they feel. Psychologists accept arousal as some measure of how much emotion is being felt (Derryberry and Rothbart in Izard 1984: 148).

Generally, we measure how emotional we feel through measuring our state of arousal, and we measure that through some standard physiological reactions, mainly heart rate, pulse rate, and galvanic skin response. Eysenck (1969) argues that one also needs to measure the more elusive cortical arousal by mapping brainwaves. There are intense debates as to how effective such techniques are but little evidence of men having weaker or slower physiological responses to emotion-arousing stimuli. A few specialized groups (like bomb-disposal experts and meditators) are good at slowing down all their metabolism. In general, the basic physiology of emotions of men and women is similar.

In studies since 1970, Carol Izard has suggested it is possible to identify a number of key emotions. These include interest, distress, shyness, disgust, fear, enjoyment, anger, guilt, surprise, and contempt. Izard has constructed a number of scales to tap what makes subjects feel particular emotions and how these emotions are related. Typic-ally, subjects are asked to recall a real situation which made them feel emotional and to describe it. Then they are asked to recall and visualize it. While they do so, they fill in Direct Emotions Scales. In one experiment on 113 men and 116 women, Izard reported (1977) that there were some differences due to sex but only small ones. For example, men tended slightly more to feel contempt.

Other factors matter rather more than sex. McLean (1981), for example, read a highly emotional playlet to his subjects. He divided his subjects into males and females, and those good and poor at imagery. The quality of one's imagery affected average heart-rate response more than sex, he found.

In a more recent study of emotions and self-consciousness, Bromberg and Hartmann (1984) studied 66 persons who were shown a film called *Where is Dead*. The story deals with a young girl's attempt to understand where her brother had gone after he had died. Subjects, both male and female, had their heart rate, pulse rate, and the galvanic skin response measured, all the classic indicators of emotion. Subjects were also asked to talk about the film.

Bromberg and Hartmann found some curious differences. Men's hearts beat faster in the minute after the opening sequences of the film while women's heart rate was slower. After a minute, the women's hearts beat as fast. The average skin temperature of the men rose more after the early parts of the film.

In their classic study of the psychological differences between men and women, Maccoby and Jacklin (1974) analysed over 5,000 studies. They found little difference in the early development of emotions. Take crying. Three studies showed boys actually cried more than girls. Landreth (1941), for example, found that, in a group of 32 children of pre-school age, the boys cried just as much as the girls. The boys tended to show more frustration and to display more so-called 'negative emotion'. They yelled and wept more freely, perhaps, Maccoby and Jacklin suggest, because they could not say as well as girls of their age what was wrong. Studies of fear show no clear pattern of sex differences. The physiological evidence for boys being less emotional is 'inconclusive and thin', according to Maccoby and Jacklin (1974). 'Thin' seems specially true. Many of the assumptions about women being more emotional and more emotionally competent stem from somewhat indirect evidence – such as the fact that more women are diagnosed as depressed and seek help for it. But that reflects sexism in psychiatry and the fact that it is probably more socially acceptable for women to own up to their feelings of depression. Men hide it more, don't feel it less perhaps. Some psychiatrists argue that the symptoms which give rise to depression in women show up in men as alcoholism or petty criminal behaviour.

The lack of physiological and 'pure' psychological evidence for the lack of emotions in men is telling, given how deep the assumption is that men are like that. Improbably, the EEC provides some evidence that men are perhaps more emotionally aware than stereotypes allow. Scherer *et al.* (1986) tried to see how men and women reacted to emotional stimuli. They measured heart rate and galvanic skin response. The stimuli they used were intended to evoke joy, sadness, fear, and anger. There was no evidence that men were less physiologically aroused by emotional stimuli. The only major sex difference concerned *crying*. Women were more likely to cry when they felt angry and sad.

Traditionally, men are supposed to pride themselves on their lack of emotion. The survey evidence tends to reinforce the physiological evidence. There is certainly a cluster of men who deny feelings. But as 'early' as 1977, *Psychology Today* in a large survey of American men found that while men admired toughness, they also admired being able to express their emotions and even to cry.

I feel, you don't feel

Men may not feel less but both men and women attribute less feeling to them, according to Maccoby and Jacklin (1974) who highlight a number of studies which reveal that. Teachers judge girls as being more anxious and more timid, for example. Men are rated in many social psychology experiments as being harder and less likely to give way to their feelings. It is possible to understand where the attributions come from. Maccoby and Jacklin argue that there is good evidence that boys are less willing to discuss any emotional difficulties they have. Men learn early on to protect themselves against 'accusations' of being weak, incompetent, and less than perfect. If anything is wrong, don't show it. This defensiveness is revealed by work on the expression of the emotions. Here, too, the facts are odder than the stereotypes.

There are times, I have come to learn, when I don't show what I feel. Sometimes, I know I don't show. At other times, I don't show knowingly. I used to think that Aileen used this accusation unfairly against me. I showed nothing, was old rock man. To me, it seemed unfair because I felt I had many feelings, some of which I've tried to outline in the previous chapter. I was ashamed of some of them because I felt powerless and rejected. But there were other feelings that then, and now, I didn't realize I wasn't showing.

It is not clear that this hiddenness is wholly a male trait. Much sexual behaviour in women is about hiding, hiding what you want, hiding what you feel. Society doesn't encourage total truth-telling, which is considered something of a nightmare. Groups which self-consciously say all they feel often aren't really honest and can be manipulative. In considering the psychological evidence it is important to retain a sense of proportion. Men may show emotions less than women but it is untrue to suggest that men show no emotions while women are paragons of emotional honesty.

Studies of the expression of the emotions rely either on (1) self-reports (how emotional do I feel in different situations?) or (2) studies of facial expressions.

Studies of self-reports have found that men are more likely to lie and deceive but also that, in general, most men think they reveal most of what they are feeling.

If we are less good at expressing emotions, it will show on our faces.

For the past twenty years, the American psychologist Paul Ekman has been studying how people use their faces to show emotion. Ekman (1980) drew inspiration from Charles Darwin's famous *The Expression of the Emotions in Animals and Men* (1872). Darwin found, interestingly, very little evidence of different emotional expressions in men and women. Ekman has examined the anatomy of the face minutely and mapped the particular muscles that are involved in the expression of particular emotions. For example, if you use the muscle 12 of the risorious when you smile, the smile is not just friendly but a genuine one. Ekman came to these conclusions through years of research, much of which involved the study of photographs. Typically, he takes pictures of people in emotional situations. One of his articles has very evocative studies of people in anger, disgust, surprise, joy, and ten other states of feelings. Ekman shows these photographs to other people to see if they recognize the emotions expressed.

Sometimes, he asks subjects to show how they would use their faces if they were angry or surprised or afraid.

Ekman has found that different rules govern the ways in which men and women show emotions. In a number of cultures, it is acceptable for women to make a grander facial display of their emotions. Ekman has repeatedly found that self-reports of how much emotion women feel and how much they show correlate highly. With men, the pattern is not quite so simple. He also found that, as children got older, they became more adept at using their faces. In one experiment, he tried to teach children how to move a single muscle of their face at one time. Twelve-year-olds were much more skilled at this than 8-year-olds.

Ekman wasn't interested in testing how athletic children could be. For him, the study showed that, as we get older, we learn to control the expression of our emotions more. The evidence suggests that men get particularly good at this.

The EEC study confirmed that women do, indeed, use both their faces and their bodies more in revealing feelings. The researchers used a complex scoring system, but the trend was consistent. Women 'outscored' men in the expression of emotions. On joy, it was by 120 to 90; on sadness, 95 to 69; on fear, 73 to 56; on anger, 118 to 104. Men reported more general emotions but were less skilled at pinning down just what kind of emotion they were feeling or, indeed, were trying to express. This suggests too that the problem is not that men feel less but that we are less good at labelling those emotions.

Buck (1984) made his subjects look at slides of emotionally laden subjects. He found that, while the slide was being projected but before it was discussed, women showed more facial expression and gestured more than men did. Once the discussion started, however, that ceased to be true. Emotional expressions became equal.

Men are also supposed to be less skilled at recognizing how emotional other people are. In relationships with other men, this deficiency doesn't matter too much, feminists argue, but it means that women often feel short-changed. They often find men who are 'just friends' confide in them yet but the confiding tends to be one-way traffic.

Buck (1984) again casts doubt on this stereotype. He argues that communication is both verbal and non-verbal. Non-verbal communication has different degrees of 'leakiness'. The body is much leakier than the face. If I am crumpled up in misery and am sitting down, hugging myself on the floor, even the most insensitive male will divine that I am unhappy. It's hard to hide my 'leaky' feelings. Tone of voice is next in 'leakiness', according to Buck. If I am sobbing, it is again pretty evident that something is wrong.

Women are more adept in interpreting the least leaky forms of non-verbal communication. They do respond more accurately to shades of expression of the face. It is possible that they are sharper at spotting the mismatch between what a person is saying and what their non-verbal behaviour shows. They can recognize that while I am saying everything is fine, my smile is too stretched because I am using the wrong muscle. 'Feminine intuition' here may be sharper observation in the flux of everyday life. The more leaky the cues become, Buck found, the better men become at interpreting the emotion they see. To castigate men as emotionally illiterate is just polemical – and not true.

Some feminist writers will not be impressed by this line of argument. Buck's research was, like all laboratory projects, artificial. His subjects were instructed to concentrate on this one task. In real life, Cline and Spender (1987) argue, men just don't bother. We prefer to focus on what we selfishly see as the important things in life – like getting out of the house to go down to the pub or seeing the next customer. For them, one recurrent failure of men is that we are willing to drain emotional support out of women. The 'new man' is not shy about talking of his problems. He just wants women to listen. Coward (1987) wrote in the *New Internationalist* that she is very suspicious of men who say their best friends are women. To her, it means that they leech off them emotionally. It's all give and no take.

The research shows, however, that men are quite capable of giving as well as taking. We are neither unable to feel nor unable to understand feelings. We tend, as I shall show, to have been conditioned only to show certain kinds of feeling, and there is no doubt that some men like being mothered, cosseted, and listened to. The old joke runs true. You say to lots of women 'my wife doesn't understand me' not just because you want to seduce her but because you want her to listen to you.

But the research shows that men can change, and I am suggesting that we ought to choose to change. There are plenty of social skills techniques which show how to do it and, if you are part of a couple, it is much less painful to learn how to listen than to cope with the endless misery of being told you don't listen. Also, there is pleasure in listening as well as being listened to.

OK AND NON-OK FEELINGS

Late in 1986, I had to visit a shelter for the homeless in Manhattan. I took a taxi from safe Manhattan to the badlands of the Bronx. I had been warned that this was the most dangerous area in New York. The taxi driver demanded an extra 5 dollars to take me there. As I got out, I saw in front of me what had been an armoury of the New York National Guard. The building was forbidding. Outside, a number of men loitered. Some looked menacing. I could feel my stomach tighten as I walked up the steps. The security guards on duty blocked my way.

They yelled who was I, who was I coming to see and, anyway, I couldn't go in. They were not particularly big but they frightened me. Obviously, they were frightened themselves. There were twelve of them in charge of some 585 derelicts, many of whom had criminal records. The guards seemed to enjoy adopting their threatening posture. After a few minutes, during which I waited nervously, I was allowed in to see the director.

Some four weeks later, I returned with a film crew. This time the emotional intensity was higher. When the guards saw us approach with a camera, they formed a blocking scrum and took out truncheons. If you film controversial institutions, you often see very raw emotions in men. Those who are the guards in such places – high security hospitals, units for offenders, shelters – often radiate very open hostile feelings. The happy reverse is the kind of male triumphant joy you see at football matches when 'our side' wins. There has never been a block on men displaying emotions that are linked to aggression. I know myself the pleasure that I got when I did get past those guards to film or when I sneaked a camera into an Egyptian hospital where I had been told I could not film.

There is a high in getting through obstacles and succeeding in that. Studies of soldiers report, in a rather more extreme way, the fact that some of them do experience a kind of joy in action. In his *The Right Stuff* (1970), Tom Wolfe caught this kind of feeling very well. Wolfe described the acute competitive pleasure that the Americans felt when they lobbed their first astronaut, Alan Shepard, into space. Compared to Gagarin's flight it wasn't much:

> But that didn't matter. The flight had unfolded like a drama, the first drama of single combat in American history. Shepard had been the tiny underdog, sitting on top of an American rocket – and our rockets always blow up – challenging the omnipotent Soviet Integral. The fact that the entire thing had been televised starting a good two hours before the lift off had generated the most feverish suspense. And then he had gone through with it. He had let them light the fuse. He hadn't resigned. He hadn't even panicked. He had handled himself perfectly. He was as great a daredevil as Lindbergh and he was purer; he did it all for his country. Here was a man . . . with the right stuff. No one spoke the phrase – but every man could feel the rays from that righteous aura and that primal force, the power of physical courage and manly honour.
> (Wolfe 1970: 226)

Emotional stuff – and very masculine. Who can say that the right feelings aren't the right stuff for men to experience and be uplifted by? But, all too clearly, Wolfe is describing feelings that go with success.

Work into how emotions are expressed usually doesn't differentiate between different kinds of emotion. Ekman (1981) has argued that social conventions usually allow women to display emotions more openly than men. This may well be true, in the West, of sadness, fear and even tenderness, but I think it's hard to maintain that for emotions such as triumphant joy. Where do you see women behave as men behave on the football pitch? It has also been argued that many eruptions of street violence are a way in which men express their anger because they have never learned any other way of doing it. You fight, you drink, you assault. These aren't always meaningless or malicious acts but the only way men can show what they feel when it comes to bad feelings.

I'm certainly not justifying that kind of expression of triumph or anger, but anyone who argues that men have no emotions ought to watch such male 'displays'.

Our failure to deal with sadder feelings, with the emotions that come with failure, stems partly from our initial conditioning. Feelings of failure should not be admitted in a world where men are supposed to be always competent, always in charge.

Astrachan points out in *How Men Feel* (1985) that many American men who joined the male liberation movement did so as a result of failure. Sometimes, they admitted that to themselves; others dressed it up as exploring new areas of personal growth. There was a great difference between the men who admitted they felt guilty about how they had treated women and those who claimed no guilt. Those who owned up to guilt, Astrachan claimed, were often furious. Though they appeared to endorse many of the arguments made by feminism, they really were just bitter. They demanded the right to be as angry as women, as destructive in their relationships as women had been. Only through that could they learn. Astrachan believed that, though these men waxed lyrical about being caring and concerned, they were essentially furious because they had failed in their relationships with women. They felt powerless and, not knowing how to deal with the novelty of that, they said they felt guilty but acted furious.

It is not easy for either men or women to accept failure. But, for the past century, it has been easier for women to show failure. That has been of no advantage to women, as authors like De Beauvoir and

Rowbotham have pointed out. It just made low self-esteem, low self-confidence, low self-worth seem inevitable. For men, the problem is the opposite. We are taught to feel we ought to succeed and achieve. Yet we find ourselves in situations where we are powerless. In the chapter on work, I argue that one of the ironies of the market-place is that men often have to take orders and simply be obedient cogs in the great industrial machine. That causes stress, especially if you've been told that your biological role is that of leader. In relationships, something similar operates. Men are told they ought to be in control. Yet, often, we aren't. We feel powerless. Our response is to deny these feelings. Our expressions of any negative feelings get repressed. It's hard to accept them as part of life. Rather, they show us up as being less in control than society tells us we ought to be. It isn't that our feelings are less intense than those of women but that certain feelings are shameful. Triumph and success are splendid. If you have cause for any other feelings – misery, fear, worry – it's best to hide them. Put on the mask. Assume the stiff upper lip. How will other people, how will women like and respect you, if you show you're not a man?

The paradox is that we need to learn to show certain feelings more and, perhaps, control others. There's every reason to suppose that some male violence is linked to the fact that we have no inhibitions about revelling in triumph.

Ironically, the evidence shows that while men are conditioned to seek success and to express success, we aren't as motivated to succeed as legend and stereotypes suggest.

ACHIEVEMENT

In their survey of sex differences, Maccoby and Jacklin (1974) argue that boys do less well than girls in school. It takes longer to motivate them. They accept that achievement is best measured by David McClelland's methods. He gave subjects pictures and asked them to make up stories to go with them. This Thematic Apperception Test (TAT) allowed him to judge how high achievement needs were. For example, if a boy is shown a picture of a man playing a violin, a low achiever would make up a story where the player loved music. There was no purpose to his practising. A person with a high need to achieve would be more ambitious. The violinist would, for instance, be practising to get into the conservatoire which would please his parents. McClelland (1969) compared the levels of achievement needs between

85

cultures and between different historical epochs. The method has its critics but it remains widely used. Most of the studies Maccoby and Jacklin review employ it. Maccoby and Jacklin conclude that studies show that, for men, the need to achieve depends on the social context. They claim (1974: 138) that 'men show a high level only when aroused by reference to assessment of their intelligence and leadership ability'. Again, the evidence 'is thin and inconsistent' (p. 138) for men having a greater need to achieve than women. If so, why do men strive harder to perform? Are they being untrue to themselves in doing so?

Lunneberg and Rosenwood (1972) asked college graduates what made them happy or miserable. Points were given towards an achievement score if the individual said that happiness would come from success or a rewarding career or misery from 'doing badly on a test'. The differences were hardly extreme: 33 per cent of men gave fulfilling achievement as reasons for happiness. Women turned in a similar score: 30 per cent said that achievement would make them happy. An interesting recent study by Whitbourne (1986) looked at a number of families in the north-east United States. She interviewed in depth ninety-four men and women. Though her sample was not very large, the interviews were very revealing. In general, men did not see themselves as being driven by, or for, success. Work did matter to them because it offered them a chance to be competent. One of her chapters examined in detail the pleasures given by being competent. But most of her respondents saw this as just one part of their lives. To her surprise, a majority of the men as well as of the women put the kernel of their identity in love and the family. She offered one response as indicative of this change. Whitbourne wrote (1986: 69):

> Another area of common ground between men and women was the extent to which both sexes claimed to be experiencing a sense of personal fulfillment from their families. This man's statement expresses this sentiment very clearly:
> Q: How would you feel about yourself if you did not have your marriage and your family?
> A: I think that I would feel very empty: I think that I would feel very self centred: I think that I would feel I was missing a very big part of my life. I have a lot of friends who do not have children, number one, and some friends not married, and they just seem quite empty.

Whitbourne confessed to being surprised by what she had found. Men should not have been behaving so like women. Cancian (1987) in another study of American relationships, this time on the West coast, also found, in her small sample, that both men and women were committed to making relationships central to their lives. It's the theme of Woody Allen's films, after all, that we all are desperate for relationships, desperate to make them work out. Allen is recognized as being one of America's great contemporary comics, and his films touch a vein of popular feeling.

Findings such as Whitbourne's and Cancian's challenge tradition. The assumption has been that men and women seek success in different areas. Tasks matter to men: people to women. Maccoby and Jacklin (1974) studied the results of smaller and more precise experiments. They found that the evidence didn't support the tradition. Boys were not more task-oriented than girls, though when they were being watched they were more competitive and more energetic. Astutely, Maccoby and Jacklin pointed out that if men performed best when they had an audience, it argued a high degree of person-orientation in boys. Girls showed this need for people too but in a different manner. They noted academically that ' "social acceptability" arousal suggests person orientation in girls' (1974:149).

Other psychometric work whose appearance is more 'scientific' than Whitbourne's and Cancian's also indicates that it's wrong to suggest that men don't care about relationships and over-value achievement. Spence and Heimreich (1978) argued that achievement is more complex than often imagined. They devised a new scale called the 'Work and Family Orientation Scale'. They too saw that work was not the only centre of men's lives. They divided their sample into masculine, feminine, and androgynous men, using Bem's scale of androgyny. According to this you can judge which category particular men fit by their descriptions of themselves and their aptitudes. Subjects tick off a list of adjectives. If you say you are aggressive, you get one masculine point; if you say you cry a lot, you get one feminine point. Subjects were androgynous if they had high masculine and feminine scores. The weeping boxer was a model of psychological androgyny. Bem urged us all to work at developing our androgyny, for it would mean the sexes were more equal and more fulfilled. In Spence and Heimreich's work 25 per cent of the feminine men and even 12 per cent of the masculine ones claimed that a happy marriage was their first priority in life.

When they examined the achievement literature in detail, Spence and Heimreich (1978) discovered some interesting methodological points. It seems that the sex of the TAT figures in the stories McClelland used is crucial in establishing sex differences. When the stories dealt with women's roles, women scored higher. Much of the evidence for the greater achievement motivation of men is due to the fact that women react poorly when trying to imagine stories based on the success of men. Since all the work on sex differences is based on comparison, if women do poorly, then an 'average' score by men becomes a high one. With these key TAT studies, it wasn't that men were superabundant in achievement motivation; rather, certain kinds of pictures (and most TAT pictures, of course, used men) stopped women expressing their own need to succeed. Give women pictures with women in them to respond to and their achievement motivation scores rise.

With their Work and Family Orientation Scale, Spence and Heimreich found that attitudes towards achievement weren't just a matter of motivation. They identified six important factors: orientation, mastery, effort, competitiveness, and concern for the job of the spouse. Mastery meant taking pleasure in doing a good job; orientation being willing to go on trying 'and not goofing up but doing the best that I can'. The differences between men and women were again more subtle. There were few between women who had a college education and all men. On three of the factors there was little difference between the sexes. Men scored significantly higher on mastery, competitiveness, and work orientation. These are important factors, but what I find telling is that only one of them relates to pleasure in work. Mastery may be fun, but orientation seems linked to fear of failure. Competitiveness is double-edged, involving both. Certainly both orientation and competitiveness are stressful and, in the current economic climate when unemployment is still high, particularly so. Fail, and you may not just suffer in your ego but lose your job.

The evidence that men have more achievement motivation is far from perfect. It owes more to the bad performance of women rather than to the good performance of men.

Research on self-confidence and feelings of self-worth (many of them in this society associated with work) is also not clear cut. One often-cited study is by Carey (1958). Carey found that male students did have a more positive attitude to the future than women did. Men also tend to predict that they would succeed even in tasks (such as doing anagrams) where the evidence is that women are superior (Crandall 1969):

Other work has examined feelings of self-worth. One technique has been to show children a polaroid picture of themselves and get them to talk about the qualities, hopes, and fears of the child in the picture. Typically, researchers ask how he or she feels about appearance, academic ability, skill in sports. The assumption is that the subject will be honest. Boys tend to say they are generally better-looking, more intelligent, and superior when compared to girls. But is this what the boys really feel or what they think they have to say? A good man doesn't undersell himself.

As with emotions, it is an area where a complicated subject is made all the more complicated by social roles and expectations. The crude view that men are obsessed with achievement and too insensitive to be self-critical is hard to sustain in the face of varying evidence. Maccoby and Jacklin concluded that it was impossible to maintain that men have more self-esteem. In general, the results are neutral, and where there is a sex difference 'it is as often boys as girls who receive higher than average score'. Goldrich (1967:153), for example, found this to be true also of college women students aged 25 to 40. Maccoby and Jacklin noted, but did not elaborate, on the consistent finding that girls are more willing than boys to disclose and discuss their weaknesses.

I see in that finding about self-disclosure a link with the fact that men are afraid to admit and reveal failure. There is strong evidence that boys are more defensive. They get higher scores on lie scales and on psychological tests of defensiveness. Boys are far more concerned about their position in the social hierarchy (Goldrich 1967:157) and have to convince even themselves of their confidence. It seems plausible to suggest that that is why men will talk up their performance. To argue that macho is often bravado will not surprise many feminists. But I think it's important to recognize that this isn't usually individual wickedness but a response (not very bright, not the best) to social pressures and the anxieties they arouse. To accept that means to accept that men do not get as much out of 'patriarchal attitudes' as might be expected. It is understandable that the women's movement initially focused on the advantages men gain from ambition and self-confidence. In the next chapter, I analyse the relative earnings of men and women for work of equal value. But patriarchal attitudes exact their own price. For men, there is a penalty in having to be the confident one or, in sexual situations, the one who takes the initiative. You cannot afford to look weak or wimpish. If you feel unconfident, don't let it show. Perform your role and pay the physical and psychological price. Be a man.

ANDROGYNY AND ITS VICISSITUDES

In the light of this evidence and of feminist critiques, it's no wonder that psychological androgyny seemed such a miraculous idea. Teach men the most useful and sensitive of women's skills, teach women the toughest of male skills, and we would all attain instant nirvana. Like many writers on psychology, I was attracted to the idea. Yet for all its merits, it is a theory of only limited use. It overvalues what individual personal growth can achieve without any changes in society as a whole. It is bizarre that, given how frank Sandra Bem was in explaining her political position as a feminist, her theory lacked any political perspective. It said almost nothing about power and privilege. Two critiques pointed out the limitations of the theory. Taylor and Hall (1982) re-examined some 100 studies which used Bem's inventory. Most had looked at how well masculine, feminine, and androgynous subjects did on a variety of tasks and tests. For Bem, subjects were rated as androgynous if they were high on both masculine and feminine traits. Taylor and Hall pointed out that this meant that all the androgynous subjects had high masculine traits. They said, 'it is primarily masculinity – not androgyny that yields positive outcomes for individuals in American society.' Bem emphasized the power of personal psychology and the capacity of individuals to change. She did not, Taylor and Hall accused, examine social structures in any depth. Taylor and Hall pointed out that Bem had to adjust her scale of socially desirable items because too few feminine items were desirable enough. Instead of commenting that that reflected society's sexism, Bem fudged. Taylor and Hall (1982) added that this fostered 'a false consciousness that problems entailed in current sex role definitions have psychological rather than social structural solutions'. The personal might be the political, but the political was more than just the personal.

In a second critique, Spence and Heimreich (1978) complained that psychological androgyny was enticing but simplistic. There was a limit to what people could change by altering their personality style. You might be able to top up your masculinity with a bracing balance of feminine traits to be the perfect person. But you'd still have to operate in the real world. Bem didn't realize that masculine and feminine behaviour are the product of situations too, Spence and Heimreich suggest.

Androgyny was attractive because it was easy to understand and appeared to be possible to achieve. Stick the world in an Encounter group and we would all develop the insight to flower into miraculous creatures, our ying rapping with our yang. Mayne (1987) talks of 'Utopian heterosexuality'. We just had to bloom into the full splendour of our insights. It was naîve to suppose that radical personality and behavioural changes could happen so easily. The literature on groups and group therapy points to an interesting paradox. On the one hand, it is quite possible to use therapeutic techniques to learn specific skills. We can learn to be more assertive or to listen more sensitively to others. I have tried to suggest at points in this chapter ways in which men ought to change in such ways. Such limited, well-defined change is possible. It is much harder to achieve global change, to revolutionize my personality, to be something I was not before. Even if I want that to happen, can I do it? On the whole, the groups that set out to achieve such grand changes failed – and often failed in rather nasty, exploitative ways. Much literature on therapy organizations like EST, the Orange People, the Scientologists, suggest that members became either bullies or victims. Therapy and insight became devices for wielding personal power. Love, honour, obey, and grovel to the guru. This is not to be cynical about the possibility of changing. It *is* possible. Cancian (1987) cites a number of cases of androgynous love where marriages have flowered with changes in the behaviour of both the men and women.

However, such changes don't come easily within a couple. They need to be worked out. Aileen and I often battled round such areas. I was certainly willing to change and did determine to spend more time at home and not to take on so much new work. But, realistically, we needed money and I wasn't, in the end, willing to change my career drastically. I didn't have the power of a famous film maker to say I'd only work on certain projects which didn't mean working out of London or late nights. Often, Aileen remained alone – and angry about being alone. The fact that I would have had to make such a drastic change shows all too clearly that it isn't just a psychological question. The structures in which we work determine a great deal and are in-imical to the kind of androgynous development Bem was advocating. In recommending us all to develop psychological androgyny, Bem was being optimistic and, perhaps, a little naîve in a way that is frequent in

American psychology. The individual is all. The individual's change is not enough. As I have tried to show in this chapter, many of the assumptions about how men feel and react are societal or ideological assumptions. They aren't accurate descriptions of how individual people act or behave. Not surprisingly, though, the assumptions are powerful and affect the way that we see ourselves.

Men do need to change. It has to be a self-conscious decision. I don't think the self-consciousness is damaging. It is good for men to realize that most of us are, in political terms, 'the weak', as Astrachan puts it, and to recognize that we are oppressed as well as oppressing. In most cases, oppressors stand to lose much by way of power, property, and privilege. They stand to gain little except a feeling of decency. Men have, however, a great deal to gain by recognizing the way stereotypes oppress us. The most obvious potential gain is a sense of well-being and physical and psychological health. There is considerable evidence that bottling up feelings and focusing exclusively on work is bad for one's health. I know of few men who would care to describe themselves as unfeeling, insensitive and only interested in their work. There has been, incidentally, little research so far on how women react to men who do change in such ways. But one strand of anecdotal evidence suggests that women also have work to do in this field. A number of American newspaper reports suggest that when men do cultivate their feeling side and become less macho, women find them less attractive.

The problem of how to change – and how to react to that change – isn't just one for men. In the next chapter, I look at the part work plays in contributing to men's sense of both well-being and oppression. If patriarchal attitudes are so glorious, why historically, have men given work such a bad press?

Chapter Five

WORKING TO ROLE

In many countries, for a man not to work is a crime. The Soviet Union retains the right to condemn those comrades who are shirkers. In doing so, Communist Russia is following a long capitalist tradition. The Elizabethan Poor Law outlawed vagrants who refused to work. More subtly, the Victorians often committed to lunatic asylums those who failed to do their duty for the Industrial Revolution. Being work-shy was a sign of insanity. The Quaker Retreat at York had a very progressive reputation and also many patients whose main symptom was laziness. Not to work made you mad. In Egypt, India and in other Third World countries, psychiatrists report that families often call in doctors when a man becomes unable to work. Idleness is a disease. Poor societies offer little choice, but, throughout the world, the work ethic has become more triumphant than the Puritans would have dared to hope. Unemployment is seen as a plague, not just because it brings poverty but also because it robs men of the precious right to work. The Labour Party honours its name. Evidently its leaders believe that if they can convince voters they really will get the nation back to work, they will win. Everyone, and especially every man, will have his job.

This glorification of work is slightly odd, especially on the left. For many centuries radicals looked on work as a kind of slavery. Men, and women when they worked, did so out of sheer necessity. Rousseau, Marx, Engels, and many other nineteenth-century political masters would be a little surprised, I suspect, to see Work held up as a new God while not working is seen as a disgrace and a disease. The more cynical of these great but sardonic thinkers might wonder if this worship of work was not an ultimate triumph of capitalism. If men don't even see that a pattern of their lives oppresses them, then they really are its victims.

That last line of argument owes a lot, of course, to feminist theory. In the late sixties and early seventies, feminists pointed out that women were often so oppressed they didn't know they were oppressed.

The revival of feminism did not, fairly understandably, focus on the question of men and their work. Feminists argued that women had been denied the right to work equally. They suffered discrimination in jobs: society did not recognize that women who were 'just housewives' worked as hard as macho commuter men. Feminists claimed that many men and many male organizations (from big companies to trade unions) resisted, and still resist, campaigns for equal pay and equal opportunities. A woman pilot, bus driver, or prime minister still seems miraculous. The emphasis for feminists was women's right to the same work as men on the same terms. Few feminists questioned the primacy of work. Perhaps one reason was that they saw work as a means to economic power. Working-class men might be poor, but they were richer than working-class women and they used their relative wealth against women. Groups like the Child Poverty Action Group repeatedly pointed how deprived women (and children) were in comparison to men. The fact that many women worked part time for unequal wages made full-time work seem even more of an ideal. Given all these factors, it is perhaps not surprising that most feminists wanted women to work like men. 'Nice' new men accepted the justice of this; less 'nice' men fought against such progress but denied that they worked to oppress women. They, chivalrous souls, wanted to protect 'their' women from the sweat of the factory floor or the suburban commuting. When alternatives were discussed, it was usually a reaction to unemployment. Job-sharing was seen much more as a way of spreading the precious commodity 'work' like you might do with tasty biscuits than a way of evolving different attitudes to work.

Few asked fundamental questions such as why men work, why we work so hard especially when there is a lot of evidence that work is very bad for our health. In so far as men responded to feminism at all – and, in general, the response has been pretty meagre – we focused on how to cope with the 'new' woman in 'new' relationships.

An older tradition, however, asks just why men and women have to work. Not so long ago, in the sixties, scientific progress promised a high-tech world in which we would all have to work less. The dawn of a new era was at hand although theorists like Herbert Marcuse, who wrote *Eros and Civilization* (1968), warned that capitalism would find ways of chaining workers to work. Surplus repression would keep us at our jobs. Capitalism would weave a sinister conspiracy of Freudian and Marxist pressures to deny us all the pleasure that might come if we worked less and played more. Marcuse is credited with inspiring the hippies. One of the ironies of the sixties was how few hippies there were and how quickly they faded. You can shorthand hippie history: flower power; budded, 1965; bloomed, 1968–70; polluted by oil, 1973. One weird legacy of flower power are contemporary American high achievers. They dabbled with hippie ideals but they learned not to drop out but to turn on, becoming dependent both on work and on drugs. The cocaine addict who is also addicted to arriving promptly at his office every morning to play his part in the rat race is a peculiarly modern figure. T. George Harris, the founder of *Psychology Today* and now the editor of *American Health* explained to me that Americans (especially American men) live in a society where their performance is judged every moment of the day. They have to out sell, out-analyse, out-smart the opposition. Because work is so pressured, they turn to drugs and booze if they are destructive. Halper (1989), a San Francisco psychologist, has just published *Quiet Desperation: The Truth about Successful Men*. Forty-eight per cent of his middle managers questioned felt they sacrificed personal lives for careers. They felt 'empty'. The less destructive turn to what have come to be known as fitness rituals like jogging and aerobics. As women succeed more in the market-place, Harris told me, they are beginning to exhibit the coronary, vascular, and 'stress' diseases which have long afflicted executive British man. These various ills that come with over-work suggest that radical questions about how, and why, men work need to be raised. And they need to be raised in the context of feminism and post-feminism.

Feminist writers developed a new, interesting mixture of personal experience and political analysis. As a man, I could only read those texts as something of an outsider. But the technique feels both useful and natural in handling the issues of work, especially since many of my friends tell me I'm a workaholic. I don't feel like a workaholic, but, then, alcoholics are often sure that they only drink a little more than average. To be so 'invested' in work has become a very male trait. Orthodox thinking among both psychologists, sociologists, and political theorists suggests that boys are socialized to see much of their identity as tied to work. A good summary of this orthodoxy can be found in John Nicholson's *Men and Women* (1984). The psychoanalyst Viktor Frankl (1968) showed that American men, when asked to reply to the metaphysical question 'Who am I?', tended to start their replies with their jobs. They saw themselves first and foremost as 'an engineer', a 'tax consultant', a car worker', and so on. The arguments all tend to suggest that this is an ancient, biological truth. Man, the hunter, sees his job as the pivot of his identity. He will, therefore, sacrifice all to his work.

For me that was not wholly the product of my upbringing. I was certainly brought up to believe that achievement mattered, but my father and my uncles organized their work in ways that a normal company would not recognize. My father qualified as a lawyer but has spent much of his time as a businessman. My uncles were traders, dealing in ships, clothes, property, and money. Some didn't have offices and worked from home. Others lived on top of their offices. When we lived in Israel, most of them went home at lunchtime. There was no literature on organizational efficiency and occupational psychology to tell them how best to arrange their work. The uncle who carried this relaxed style to an extreme was Ziggy. Ziggy was a smuggler by love as well as trade. From an early age, he taught me that a trip (even a school trip) was basically an occasion for smuggling. It might be whisky, cloth, or, occasionally, foreign currency, but you couldn't cross an international boundary without contraband. I was rewarded, like my other cousins, with proper amounts of money. Not that Ziggy just smuggled for profit. The idea of defying official regulations delighted him, even though in most other respects he was a law-abiding man and believed the state should not be soft on criminals. Ziggy did exceedingly well and never left home without $5,000 in his wallet. Gold bars were buried in the flowerpots around his flat in case the Nazis should come again. Ziggy was not anxious despite the risks he ran, and led a peaceful life. He never rose before ten o'clock. He then spent an hour on the telephone before it was time for a stroll to give him an appetite for lunch. He and his wife had a pleasant lunch, after which Ziggy retired for a siesta. She did voluntary work in the afternoons. It was a crime to ring Ziggy before four o'clock, when his siesta ended. Then he would walk to a bank and, in the evening, they would go to a play or concert. He told me once that he had wanted to be a poet but poetry meant too much hard work. To me Ziggy looked like the ultimate pear-shaped bourgeois; he reminded me of Alfred Jarry's Père Ubu who was a monster of greed, intolerance, and prejudice. Ziggy had some of those characteristics but, also, unknown to him, unknown to me, he was a hero. He kept work in perspective.

And, though he loved money, he didn't let the pursuit of it obsess him so much that he didn't have a good time. Where my father-in-law, an American executive *par excellence*, never took more than a week off, Ziggy always took at least two-month-long holidays a year – one to swim and the other to ski. There was no point in making money unless you could spend it on yourself.

I wish, in many ways, that I had understood better quite how clever he had been. I assumed he was clever with money, not clever with life.

When Aileen came out of hospital with a baby, I prepared wine and delicatessen treats to welcome her home. It was a special occasion, after all, so I had taken three days off work. It would not have been difficult to take far longer. I was trying to make a career as a writer and film-maker. There was no regular job demanding that I turn up at nine o'clock. The jobs I did varied from the glamorous writing of film scripts, which might, you never know, take you to Hollywood though they never seemed to take you much further than restaurants in the King's Road, to the banal. For years, I wrote small articles on the latest research published in The *Lancet* or the more esoteric *Journal of Neurology, Neurosurgery and Psychiatry*. Getting 2,000 words in the *New Scientist* seemed a triumph. I could have interrupted all this for more than three days, but it didn't seem an option.

The first night when Nicholas didn't sleep, it was annoying but cute. Soon he'd settle to the rhythm of our life. The second night, we were more worried by his sleeplessness. The third, Aileen sat up with him far more than I did because, after all, I was going back to work. No one would have missed me if I had taken more than three days off or arranged things so that for two or three months I worked from home. But the idea just didn't occur to me or to her.

Aileen complained she had 'married someone who isn't there'. Once, when I got home, she was so tired that she just thrust Nicholas at me. 'I'd die if it meant getting a good night's sleep,' she groaned. My absences made Aileen angry but what was the alternative? It made me angry that it made her angry. Double anger didn't make me – or her – look at the problem in a fundamental way. What was the price of working? Was there a way of organizing work that meant we could share minding Nicholas rather more? A way of organizing it that made it easier for her to work?

After the Mexican play at the Roundhouse I tried to get TV work. It would be nice, but untrue, to say that I took a job to give us more time and less anxiety. After knocking at the gates of television for years, finally, I was offered a job as a researcher. A job promised a less frantic life. I would have taken it anyway, but I believed it might help. Working as a television researcher meant being at the beck and call of producers. Some were demanding and rational: others were demanding and irrational. One told me that as a researcher my job was to 'fetch and carry', though he never said quite what I was to fetch and carry apart from his whims. One initiation was to work on shows where you had to find the ultimate freaks – say, an Old Etonian who was a member of the Communist Party, and played competitive backgammon, or a rabbi who worked as a part-time barman. To become a director, you had to deliver these exotic or representative characters. No one cared if you had to hang around pubs, clubs, and the telephone till midnight to book the magic plumber who could confront a cabinet minister with Marx in a typical cockney accent and be not a bit intimidated. I often had to work till late, and often worried that I hadn't delivered the right characters and wouldn't ever get made up to a director. So, weekends were times to collapse.

Moreover, as both I and Aileen worked so hard, we competed as to who had had the more miserable week. She was exhausted by the children; I was exhausted by work. Both of us were resentful. Feminist theory makes it clear that she had every right to be resentful, an intelligent woman left at home with a child. As a result, I wasn't welcomed home with open arms and asked how I had coped with the frightening world where power-crazed producers might ask you, any moment, to drop everything in order to find the 1976 equivalent of Shaw's philosophical dustman, Alfred P. Doolittle.

We weren't quite blind in our resentment, but it was hard to translate our awareness that something was wrong into any positive action. I minded that she didn't cosset me when I got home, even though I realized she needed cosseting herself after a hard day with the baby. Despite all our reading, education, and experience, we didn't really organize any alternative. Once we thought of living in a commune but the others were in a wondrous sexual muddle because the husband of A was creeping into the bed of B and C after midnight: it looked like a recipe for disaster. So Aileen never, and I never, asked each other just why I was working so frantically. Neither of us ever analysed what working like that was doing to our relationship, or to her, or to me. Feminist theory didn't help much as it stressed that women suffered because they were stuck at home. If only they could work as well, then, equality and nirvana would arrive. In so far as

98

we saw the problem, we blamed it on Aileen's not working. Her identity had become that of a mother and housewife. The solution was to change things for her. Once there was regular money coming from television, we got baby-sitters so that she could write. Aileen might laugh at my working as hard as Sammy Glick, the hero of that Hollywood epic *What Makes Sammy Run*, but the pattern was natural. Her father worked that way, getting up at 6 a.m. to go to Wall Street. Every evening he got home quite late. It was hard for him to find much time for his children because work was such a priority. He was only doing what most men of his generation did. Dr Spock, in his *Baby and Child Care* (1970), urged fathers to romp a little when they got home from the office though he accepted that weary men might not have the energy.

It's easy for the radically righteous to snigger. For all that many feminists were Marxists, few remembered the misery of work that most nineteenth-century reformers had lamented. By the early 1970s, everyone seemed to gloss over the ancient radical literature which saw work as misery, alienation, and slavery. To blame feminist writers for this would be unfair. It was true of all the analytical classes. Take the 1962 edition of *Individual in Society*, a classic textbook of social psychology. Its impeccably pre-feminist authors, Krech *et al.* (1962) argued that as America grew richer and better educated, work would become more glorious. They conceded that, for the present, there were class differences. Thus, while for

> a member of the lower class work may symbolise an unpleasant but necessary means of securing food and shelter; work is neither interesting nor desirable. For the middle class person 'work' may symbolise a means to such goals as enhancement of one's prestige, realisation of one's talents etc. and for him work may be satisfying and desirable in itself. (p. 283)

In a long study of 600 steel workers, miners, salesmen and doctors, another psychologist, Argyris (1957), came to a similar conclusion. He found it hard to accept working-class critique of work and gave only one illustrative quote. In an interview, a retired industrial worker complained when asked:

Q: Was there anything you liked about the job?
A: No, I can't think of anything. It was hard, hard work and I wouldn't go through it again.

WIFE: Come now, honey, you couldn't have worked there all those years and not found something you liked.

A: There is nothing I can think of only the money – I couldn't think of anything else. (p. 505)

Professionals find it hard to accept that view. The one apparent challenge to the ideology of work – the hippie movement – was essentially a student and not a worker movement. Moreover, almost none of the texts, like those of Marcuse or Laing (1968), questioned doing work but rather questioned the kind of work you were doing. You ought not to sell out, not to alienate yourself. The objection was to doing conventional work, not work itself.

Many feminist writers for whom the urgent task was getting equal opportunities for women accepted that work was fulfilling. In accepting that, however, they also accepted the central place of work. It took a while for many to realize that this would give many women two careers, since all too many men did not easily take either to housework or to child care. Also, in terms of traditional male roles, that emphasis ignored the fact that a few writers were wondering whether men were not 'over-invested' in their work. An early advocate of that view was Viktor Frankl, the psychoanalyst. He made much in his book *In Search of Meaning* (1968) of the evidence that people identified themselves as engineers, tax accountants, or car workers. He mourned that most men had so little sense of self that they needed to weld their identity round work. Men almost relished the myth that casts them as hunter-gatherers. Heroic males go out to 'hunt' while women stay at home waiting for us to return with a tasty gazelle to fry. After grub, lust. Yes, it's a man's world. Desmond Morris's *The Naked Ape*, perhaps the most popular science book of the sixties, insisted on this view of man. Now that we did not roam the plains with our spears, males left home to wield their spears at the office. No wonder people spoke of the 'business jungle' or of 'making the killing'. It's in the ancient hormones to get on the 7.00 commuter train and hunt the gazelles on Wall Street. Morris questioned whether such ancient aggression was appropriate to the work men did now but not the central role of work itself.

Desmond Morris's popular book was reinforced by weightier, academic tomes such as E.O. Wilson's *Sociobiology* (1975), which argued that the divisions between the sexes were genetic and affected the minutest details of social behaviour. Morris, Wilson, and other writers were justifying the status quo scientifically. Not surprisingly, that made many people glad to read them. What is nicer than to find that the way you are behaving is really the way it's natural for you to behave? But their analysis of the evidence ignored the remarkable variety of ways in which work has been organized through the ages. Till the Industrial Revolution, soldiers, sailors, and the odd eccentric might lead adventuring lives, but most men lived and worked on the land. They did not leave home. Women may have served them but men were much more present to the family than they are now. There was no going away to work. The French historian Le Roi Ladurie (1978), in his portrait of the French village *Montaillou* in the fourteenth century shows a sexist society in which men and women nevertheless lived on top of one another. Women were unequal but not isolated; men did not leave for work. They oppressed women not by their absence but by their presence. Shepherds were the only ones who went to work, in the high mountains.

An interesting example of the presence of men comes from an unlikely source, the philosopher John Locke. Locke (1692) wrote a series of letters to his kinsman Edward Clarke on how to educate his son. The advice that the eminent philosopher gave assumed that Clarke would be usually present to answer the son's questions. Locke advised that Clarke should treat his young son as one might a traveller from Japan. All questions were to be taken seriously and answered with respect, because the child couldn't be expected to have any time of contemporary culture. Clarke was expected to be present to teach his son to reason well rather than to 'prattle'. Locke did not argue that Clarke ought exceptionally to stay at home as some early marvel of how to be a father. Rather, the pattern of life meant that he would be there. In Jane Austen's *Mansfield Park*, Sir Thomas's family is distraught when he goes on a business trip to Antigua. One son is bored so he arranges for friends to stage a play. Poorer men had even less opportunity to be away. The division of labour that Morris and Wilson see as being natural was very much the creation of the Industrial Revolution. The post-Industrial Revolution has succeeded in convincing middle-class men that if we find our work interesting and, even better, if it provides us with the odd delicious freebie, we are only doing what is natural. The biological 'myth' of man the hunter-gatherer who has to work to be whole needs to be put in its historical context. What we need to understand is how men of recent generations came to be educated so as to make work the central focus of their lives.

There is one paradox worth developing. The image of man the hunter is a noble, free one. You can't easily dream up a more self-motivated image than the hunter after his prey. Yet, of course, the reality of commuter life is the very opposite of that. Artists who analysed how men work since the Industrial Revolution – from Dickens in *Hard Times* to H.G. Wells in *Kipps* to Miller's *Death of a Salesman* to the marvellous Italian film *Il Lavoro* made by Olmi in the 1960s, found that work requires men to submit to authority. A man who did what a man had to do had, in fact, to obey. Someone told him what rivet to place where, what sales conference to go to, which customers to visit, and what to say when somebody complained. The structure of industrial life for men requires obedience, submission, often accepting insults. Before men can begin to re-evaluate their ideas about work they need to see through this myth of heroic work. Feminists complained rightly that women bought for centuries a patriarchal model which set them up to be wives and mothers. Women did not deliberately foster men's images of themselves as noble workers, but there is little evidence that women have helped men to question that view of their work.

Recently, the idea that work is good has been boosted by unemployment. In 1983, I interviewed Marie Jahoda for an American magazine that was doing a series on unemployment round the world. As a young social psychologist, Jahoda had studied the havoc that unemployment caused in the 1930s in the Austrian town of Marienthal. The men who were out of work lost far more than their wages. Their self-esteem, self-confidence, and, even, their love of life went. They could see no point in carrying on. Their sex drive often disappeared as well. They reacted much as victims of natural disasters or prolonged violence did. Looking back in the 1980s, Jahoda was appalled by what she saw as history repeating itself. Psychologists in Britain, America, Germany, France, and other countries had all come to the conclusion that men on the dole were especially likely to suffer psychological and, even, physical damage. Women suffered too but a little less dramatically. Jahoda argued in a short book, *Employment and Unemployment* (1981) that work not only filled time but it also provided a very necessary structure to our lives. Without it, people felt isolated from their society and had to spend too much time with their families. To work was a social and psychological necessity.

In the accumulating mass of 'tragic' research, only one study suggested that unemployment did not have to be crippling. Karen

Trew and Rosemary Kilpatrick (1984) compared unemployed men in Belfast and Brighton. A good number of those in Belfast (where unemployment is high and carries little social stigma) had reorganized their lives. They drove their wives and children to work: they spent a good deal of time with friends at their clubs; they did far more do-it-yourself work than before; a few even used the time to educate themselves. In achievement-oriented Brighton, the situation was very different. In theory, Brighton was a resort where people ought to be free to do nothing; in practice, though, it was a town hungry for success. Those who were out of work suffered all the usual reactions of grief, loss, and misery. Jahoda's book summed up nicely orthodox psychological views of our need for work. She did not seriously consider how not working might be freeing or that you could be happy without working in any kind of structure. In her theory, people like my uncle Ziggy who didn't even have the excuse of being an artist should not have existed.

In the light of all this, I am disappointed, but not surprised, that I didn't work out, as it were, a better solution to work.

I have no idea how willing I would have been to listen to Aileen. She complained that I was obsessed with work, but she also complained that she hated being just a wife and mother. She was a writer. As there were plenty of other tensions in our relationship, neither of us were particularly sensible and we were too proud to seek any kind of help. We aspired to be experts at modern living. The arguments became repetitive. She was lonely. If I didn't work so hard, I would be around more. Fine, I countered; why didn't she do some freelance writing too? Then I wouldn't have to try quite so hard to make money for us to live and for the baby-sitters. No, she countered, she wanted to be a writer. And writers wrote. They didn't spend their time churning out articles for *World Medicine* or the *Illustrated London News*. They wrote creatively. Neither of us really listened to each other and, when we did temporarily solve our problem, it was by accident. But it's not surprising that we floundered because the only analysis that we could look to was that which feminists were developing. And, understandably, that analysis was more concerned with women than with men. The last thing one could expect feminists to consider exhaustively was that work might not only make men oppress women but that it also made men oppress themselves. In the adversarial mode of feminist argument, that almost could not be. What was bad for women had to be good for men.

Today, there is evidence both that men enjoy their work and that they feel victimized by it. Until recently, psychologists did not ask what is a crucial question – how do we spend our time? But recently a new technique has been devised with the agreeably fancy name, Experiential Self Monitoring. Subjects are given an electronic bleeper which goes off a number of times every 24 hours. They have to jot down what they were doing and what they felt about it there and then. Two studies, one at the University of Chicago and the other carried out by psychologist, E.J. Dearnley (1981) on himself, make one hope for signs of rebelliousness that Marx would have relished.

Dearnley was jolted on 384 occasions by the electronic bleeper. Observation 87, which he shared with the British Psychological Society, was not untypical. At 12.41 p.m. Dearnley was sitting in the Railway Inn drinking beer with his friends; at 2.45 p.m. he was still drinking beer but he had moved to the Conservative Club. At 7.35, the self-aware psychologist was examining the cut of a new pair of trousers. At 11.00 p.m., Dearnley was back drinking beer with his wife and discussing the introspections of the day. (I ought in fairness to point out that it was a Saturday.) Dearnley was distressed to find that as much as 41 per cent of his time was spent on work, while only 31 per cent was spent on pleasure. He found himself doing distasteful things only 4 per cent of the time. In a different study by Csikzentmihalyi (1982) the subjects at the University of Chicago were asked to keep a diary of their daily thoughts. Work was not something most of them spent a great deal of time thinking about. The results showed that people were happiest dreaming of food, other people, and housework. Many noted that they felt very passive and resentful when they were doing their work because their time was not their own. With all the pro-work propaganda, it's not surprising that young men coming on to the labour market find that an unpleasant revelation. A recent American study of entrants to work (quoted by Astrachan 1985) found that after a week 50 per cent said they found their work most interesting. Within a few months of entering work boys had come to see that work was more structured, more limiting than they had expected. It was not the magic key to becoming adult that they had been led to expect. Astrachan did not comment on this at length but it is a very revealing result. I would suggest it confirms the analysis that I have been trying to develop. Men have been led to see work as the focus of their lives. When it fails to satisfy, they are puzzled and angry. And when the work is rewarding, as most of my own work has been, it becomes easy to imagine that it is the most important part of one's life. Nothing else matters quite so much.

It is perhaps this which makes men not act on the accumulating evidence that work is very bad for your health.

THE STRESS OF WORK

This devotion to work is surprising given how relatively new and far from natural the modern organization of work is. America has seen in the last 70 years the application of management techniques and psychology to industry. This revolution initially aimed to use psychology to promote efficiency. What were the most scientific ways to maximize the worker's output. This trend continues to this day. The Midland Bank recently announced that it had improved its graduate selection techniques by relying on psychological tests which could weed out those who would end up lending to all and sundry because they couldn't bear to say no.

By the 1950s, psychologists had begun to argue that work caused stress. A recent Japanese study has claimed that perhaps 10 per cent of its conformist workforce suffer from stress so acute that they need professional help (Kobuta 1984). Initially, only middle-class executives were believed to suffer from stress. But, recently, Cary Cooper, Professor of Organizational Psychology at the University of Manchester, has argued strongly for the concept of 'blue collar' stress (Cooper and Smith 1985). Factory workers who don't have major decisions to make don't just suffer from classic industrial diseases but are also subject to considerable psychological pressures. No one who works can escape stress. Men, the majority of the workforce, are clearly at risk.

Within the stress literature, deep debates turn on whether stress is objective – that is the environment does it to you – or subjective. Even those like Kasl (1984), who think that reports of stress are greatly exaggerated, concede that it can become a self-fulfilling prophecy. If you think you are under stress that becomes, in itself, a kind of stress. The allegation that work causes stress can hardly be dismissed as a kind of fantasy. Good physical and psychological evidence backs it – particularly for men, and, latterly, for women who are adopting a male style of doing work.

Perhaps the best-known psychological evidence concerns type A behaviours. Some fifteen years ago, American cardiologists began to notice similarities between some of their most frequent patients. Many of the men were high achievers and anxious. They were restless, anxious, decisive, and always rushing from meeting to meeting. They made tough demands on themselves and knew often that others expected them to succeed. They found it very hard to relax. In America, particularly, such men lived in a business culture in which (thanks to psychologists) performance was always being monitored. This cluster of behaviours and attitudes have come to be known as Type A behaviours. A well-documented link seems to exist between Type A behaviours and heart attacks, and with cardio-vascular diseases.

Many of the fitness rituals described to me by T. George Harris of *American Health* are conscious strategies to reduce the risk of succumbing to precisely those diseases. Recently, while in America, I eavesdropped on the conversation of two medical executives. As we flew from New York to Washington, they were discussing the dilemmas of their health. It was hard for them to be sure whether they were more at risk from (1) jogging, since the latest evidence suggested that addiction to exercise could develop; (2) not jogging; (3) eating too little bran, which drove up their cholesterol; (4) eating too much bran, which increased the risk of cancer of the colon. They were worried about which medical catastrophe to worry about more. I would have liked to crack a little joke to them about it, clearly, worrying was something to be taken very seriously. Furthermore, men are not just at risk from such intangibles as stress.

Jeanne Stellman and Barry Snow, two American occupational psychologists, have amassed a great deal of evidence on accidents and physical illnesses (Stellman *et al*. 1984). In America in 1983 there were one and a quarter million industrial accidents. The cost of these injuries was $30 billion. There are 62,000 industrial diseases. Hazards interact in certain jobs so that a health worker may, for example, be exposed to noise and vibration while they need to make very precise judgements about when to cut the wood. A mistake can lead to serious injury. Even the office which is free from pollutants is likely to offer an arena for stress. In a study of 2,000 office workers, they found that noise, air quality, extensive machine use, limited privacy and the feeling that work is meaningless distressed workers. The quality of the air was linked to upper respiratory tract distress. Stellman and Snow argue that men tend to suffer more such diseases since more of them work and that we know as yet too little about women's occupational problems.

Sceptics such as Kasl who believe it is hard to pin down specific links between stress at work and coronary heart disease or Type A Behaviour, accept that certain jobs do produce hardship. Saw-mill workers who have to make sure they don't saw themselves in half are likely to find the strain telling. Kasl (1984) concedes that where work consists of repetitive, boring tasks it does lead to mental problems. He suggests that there are contributing factors. Long commutes do not help: being able to unwind easily does. Is the good little wife there to help you unwind?

All these authors agree, too, that stress at work can lead to problems at home. Increasingly, many women are working at stressed occupations. Even less than before can men reasonably expect to come home every night to a cuddle and a cocktail. Many of my women friends grumble that they are so busy that what they really need is a wife. It's a joke, but it identifies a real need. If you do battle daily with a difficult world full of dangers, decisions, and rivals, not to mention the odd paranoid colleague or competitor, you want to come back to the safety and comfort of home.

Only, home, precisely because of the demands put on it, is not likely to be either cosy or safe.

The situation I found myself in meant that both of us had impossible expectations. I expected Aileen to support me while she had to manage a child and manage her own frustrations. She expected me to provide for all of us and even to provide extra so that we could pay someone to mind Nicholas while she wrote. But she would neither use her writing to earn money nor give me much by way of support, care, or encouragement. She said she was too furious to do that. This was not what being married and having a child had been cracked up to be. Neither of us realized that we could have found ways of dealing with what was a particular period of time while Nicholas was so small. I don't suppose that if we had done so we would raise ultimate questions about the nature of work, but we might have asked just what I was working for. Was there no other way of doing it? I had more freedom than most men have, and still we didn't do it till it happened by accident.

In 1973, Aileen and I went on holiday for two weeks to Tolo in Greece. The first night we got there, we ate on the beach. Little fairy lights were hung round the two cafés. There were fishing boats out. Two islands stood out in the bay. One was a prim little rock on which stood a church: the other was known as Aphrodite's Breasts, two huge scoops of hill on which goats ran. The place seemed magical. We had rented a villa for two weeks. After a few days, we asked if it would be available next winter and how much it would cost. They wanted £50 a month. We paid, then and there, three months' rent for 1974. It would be nice to say that this was a properly considered political decision to cope with the difficulties we had been experiencing. It wasn't anything of the sort. Tolo seemed wonderful: we had been having a nice holiday. Why not spend three months there?

After our two weeks' holiday, we came back to London and I returned to the treadmills of television. For a year, we lived with all the old tensions, which were made even worse by the particular producer I had to work for. He was determined to act the part of Bossman, Supermogul, and Office Tyrant all in one. By the end of nine months, for the first time in my life, I knew how people who have authority over you at work can make your life an utter misery. It didn't put me off work, though. Aileen and I decided we had better travel to Tolo separately. She would take Nicholas on a plane. I would come over six days later by train because I had arranged a series of interviews with psychologists all over Europe. My three months of not working started with me travelling to Marseilles (to interview the latest French radical psychologist), to Lyons (to interview a dream researcher), to Vienna (to interview Frankl and the then head of the Psychoanalytical Society), and to Budapest (to see what Hungarian science might have to write up). It took me six days to reach Athens with lots of material in notebooks.

GREECE

The next three months were, in most ways, the nicest I have ever spent. We had a little villa, called Villa Daphne, which was perched half-way up the hill behind Tolo. It had three rooms and a big kitchen. We divided work fairly equally. One of us worked in the morning while the other took Nicholas down to the beach. Nicholas was 4 years old and relentlessly curious about the sand, the sea, the jellyfish, the strange habits of the strange Greeks who were apt to come up to him, coo, and pull his nose. He put up with that indignity with four year old grace. At about one o'clock we had lunch. Then, we had a siesta. Then, round three, the one who had worked in the morning took Nicholas down to the beach. Both of us were writing during this period. A few times during the three months I went to Athens to research stories for the *New Scientist* and *Country Life* and on those days Aileen looked after Nicholas on her own. But for the most part, we simply arranged the day so that each of us worked for half of it.

There were not many problems – other than worrying about when our savings would run out. After about two months, we did rather hunger to talk to other people. The village treated us as bizarre outsiders, though we did get invited to one wedding. Apart from the lack of company, it was wonderful. We knew we had to leave after three months because Aileen was pregnant and we didn't want our child to be born in Greece. Three weeks before we were due to leave and I was just beginning to worry about work, I got a telegram. A man I had done a little research for was offering me a job. I bargained with him to be given two of the documentaries he was producing to direct. Thames TV agreed, and so I had finally managed to do what I had strived so manically for: I had broken into TV directing.

There wasn't a phone in the Villa Daphne, so all these negotiations took place from the Tolo phone box. When I had clinched the job, I walked up the village street happily. It was something for Aileen and me to celebrate. There'd be no worrying about where the new baby's nappies would come from. I didn't stop to think that, after being so happy in Greece, I had just chosen to go back to the very way of life that had made us both so miserable. And, if Aileen had any objections, she didn't say. We got amiably pissed and planned all the knick-knacks we could now afford to buy since we weren't going back to poverty.

And, of course, I did promise that I would be around more and that, with plenty of money, it would be easy to find the money for baby-sitters so that Aileen could write.

Both of us knew we had been very happy, simply happy, in Tolo. It had sun, sea, sex (proper marital sex with each other), and both of us were besotted with Nicholas. The day we left Tolo, we had to leave at four in the morning. The communal taxi picked us up and we squeezed in with three other people. The night sky was dark. I looked up at the stars and thought what a wonderful time it had been. I wish, in the light of what happened, that I had been more willing to learn what it was that had made it so wonderful. A different feeling about work, time with Aileen, time with Nicholas, a total lack of frenzy. I knew that I was lucky because my kind of work had made the interlude possible. But, as I tut-tutted to Aileen about our going, I was thinking of the films I was going to make. I didn't think properly, and, if it comes to that, nor did she. She said she was worried about not being able to write as much as she had in Tolo.

Within a week, normal work seemed normal again. Aileen had been seven months' pregnant when we left Greece. When our second child Reuben was born, I took three days off as I had done for Nicholas' birth. I was there when Reuben was born. The next week I had to be filming. Aileen was well; there were friends around; I would be gone at nine and back by five since we were filming in a school; we had arranged for Nicholas to spend the day with some friends. I was far too green and inexperienced a film director to risk putting the film back because I had just become a father again. Eleven years on, and because it perpetrated no particular disaster, I wish I had acted differently. At the time, I felt I had no choice.

I have tried to argue that one of the paradoxes of current society is that it has made us men feel that we have no choice. Not to perform is, somehow, to opt out. We, and especially middle-class men with interesting jobs, have allowed ourselves to forget that there are ways to organize our identity other than around work. Work can be absorbing; it can confer power, prestige, and money. But it also does damage if it becomes one-dimensional. Frankl (1968) warned that some of those who described themselves in terms of their work rate seemed to see themselves as nothing more. One of the disappointments of the last fifteen years has been the relative failure of leisure. Where is the fun-loving, work-left-behind society that we were meant to enter when we had robots and technology to do the dirty jobs? To have more choice about work means being willing to challenge how central it is. It means playing with a variety of ideas that would outrage the work ethic. For each man, I think it means calculating quite consciously what you gain and what you lose as a result of working the way you do. It also means being able to dream up alternatives. I am in a privileged position to do this since I work for myself. The personnel department of ICI might not be too pleased if you announced that, as a result of a re-evaluation of your values, you were only going to work three days a week.

But you could, if it meant enough, always change your job.

A calculation of the pros and cons of how work affects you would need to examine your individual situation under the following headings: gains, losses and alternatives.

Under gains, you would need to include, obviously, the money you earned, the pleasure you took in your work, the status and privileges it brought. I have many gains from my work. I earn good money, and, usually, I can pursue topics that interest me. If I weren't interested in work I wouldn't write about it. When I've had to work on things that did not interest me – I once produced a number of science programmes which had to be so relentlessly popular they couldn't be anything more than a box of tricks – I resented wasting my time on that. Being a television producer means that you travel, eat out a lot, and meet interesting people. As work goes, it has many advantages.

There are losses I am certain of, and others I suspect exist. When I started out, I worried frenetically. If the right cockney plumber wasn't available to appear on a chat show, it was a disaster. I was a good candidate for all the stress diseases. Drinking a bit much on expense account lunches didn't help. Slowly, I became less anxious. But, as I've written, my work put endless pressure on my marriage. It made Aileen unhappy and she retaliated by making me unhappy. I sometimes wonder that if I had been less frenzied, ironically, I wouldn't have done better work. I paid a steep price for failing to ponder what had made Greece so lovely. A year after Reuben was born, our marriage was back in crisis. Much of it had nothing to do with work, but if I had had a different attitude to work, I might have been more often present when Aileen needed it. Aileen often accused me of using work as an escape. It meant I could get away from the tensions of our marriage. I never deliberately did that – but, unconsciously, who can be sure? Certainly, as things got worse, I would dread getting back from work.

If you are self-employed, alternatives are easier than if you have to fit in with a large corporation. I did slowly learn to take on less work that always took me away. After making a few films, it became easier to do some work from home. By this time, it was too late, and there were too many other difficulties to save my marriage in any conventional sense of the term, but it did give me a much closer relationship to my children.

To explore the alternatives is crucial if you feel that your work is damaging a relationship that matters to you. There are a number of practical options like job-sharing and arranging to work more from home if that's possible. What is important is to keep control, not to let the problem seem beyond solution. One interesting exercise is to imagine how you would describe yourself apart from work. Do you have to be like Frankl's engineers who saw themselves, first and last, as engineers?

I have tried to do this for myself and I have to admit it requires a self-conscious effort. The following seems fairly true. I am a father who loves and is anxious about his children. I like the company of women and eating. I enjoy expensive restaurants but rather less than I expect to. I love cooking, and would like to spend time learning how to cook better. There are endless books I've never read and would like to read. There are things which I'm tired of not being able to do – such as decorating and mowing the lawn properly, which I would like to learn. Without work (for now we're in fantasy land where there are no money worries) I'd spend my days reading, having a long bath, going for walks round London, making love when possible, and making sure my children had treats for tea when they came home. It isn't an idle identity. Everything I have written is true of me but it does miss out that crucial element of work. I don't claim to have solved my own problems about work. But, at least, I know what some of them are and I believe that they are not untypical of those that bother many men. Becoming more conscious of those problems seems to me important if we are, each and every man, to make less driven choices.

Freud wrote that the task of psychoanalysis was to enable each person to 'lieben und arbeiten', to love and to work. The tremors that Freud lived through were very different from the transitions we are living through now. If men are to become happier and freer – and we saw in Chapter 1 the evidence of physical and mental ill health among men – then one of our main tasks is to challenge the role of work and to become more flexible and relaxed about it. That's easy to write but hard to do. It's also easy for men who want to avoid doing so to suggest that all this requires too radical a political shift. It does – to some extent. But it's the kind of shift that won't begin to happen till we are willing to change our own attitudes.

Workers of the world, especially the male ones, relax.

Chapter Six

SEXUALITY AND ITS MYTHS

SEXUALITY

Most of us spend more time thinking about love and sex than we like to admit. The philosopher Marcuse argued in the 1960s that capitalism employed surplus repression. It couldn't allow sexual joy to flourish. Today Marcuse is rather out of fashion. Yet it certainly remains true that most of us know we don't make the best of our sexuality or relationships. In this chapter, I use 'relationships' to mean one-to-one sexual relationships between a man and a woman. Other relationships, especially homosexual relationships, matter but I focus here on what is primary for most people: their heterosexual sexual relationships. They're troubled enough.

Sexual politics began to change before Kate Millett published *Sexual Politics* in 1970. Just after the 1945 war, Simone de Beauvoir gave a bleak exposé of the way men exploited women sexually. Women were often forced, and often disappointed in their lovers. De Beauvoir said that feminine sex 'is the soft throbbing of the mollusc. Where man is impetuous and woman is only impatient her experience can become ardent without ceasing to be passive; man dives upon his prey like the eagle and the hawk' (1949:407). Both birds are known for tearing their prey apart.

Later, there was more direct anger. Germaine Greer lambasted authors like Mailer and Fleming as typical of how men wrote about women. She said, 'the proper fate of the Great Bitch is death, either the metaphoric death of orgasmic frenzy and obliteration or actual death' (1970: 193). This was ecstatic for male writers, for 'Killing your woman is like killing a bear or a legendary monster'. No male author on whom Greer commented seemed to have liked going to bed with

113

women. Blood had to be spilled as well as semen. She projected a universe in which men and women were ultimately incompatible. Love was an illusion of the penny dreadfuls. Greer sniped at the start of her chapter: 'In love' 'as in pain, in shock, in trouble.' Very stylish, very false. What about 'in ecstasy' or 'in joy'?

Men were not just oppressive and brutal but also incompetent. In real life, women didn't get much 'orgasmic frenzy and obliteration'. Frustration was more likely because men could not be bothered to study what women needed. There was excitement as sexologists discovered first the clitoris, and then the famed G spot. The feminist case against men as lovers emphasized our deep-seated fears. Men were frightened of romantic commitment and proper, attached relationships. Others just wanted their mothers. Many argued that men were actually frightened and disgusted by sex. We were products and victims of the patriarchal Christian tradition which condemned women. Eve was evil. The first woman seduced the first man. And it was downhill to Sodom and Gomorrah from then on. Mort (1988) has examined attitudes to sex up to 1914. Women who were honest about their desires often risked being labelled mad. They were either madonnas or whores. Men needed sex and yet they felt ashamed of their 'animal' desires. So they hurried it, paying no attention to what women wanted. A touch of foreplay, penetration, climax. Wham, bang, thank you ma'am. Mort called his book *Dangerous Sexualities*.

Permissiveness and the pill appeared to allow many women to discover their bodies for the first time. But the climate in the late sixties made it possible for women to make public the failure of men. There was new academic interest in sexual behaviour. Michael Schofield (1964) studied the sexual behaviour of young people. He found that only 6 per cent of boys and 2 per cent of girls had lost their virginity by the age of 16. He also found that, for many, sex was a disappointment: 54 per cent of girls said they were disappointed by their early experiences, as were 36 per cent of boys. Yet both tended to persevere – often with the same partner. Schofield found that often boys got physical pleasure out of sex whereas girls got the pleasure of doing something for the person they loved. The frank nature of his enquiry, financed by official research councils, shows how much the climate had changed.

Less then twenty years earlier, de Beauvoir, a daring radical, had been very harsh about men but also a little coy and detached. We certainly did not learn if Sartre was a lousy lover. By the late sixties, the issues were treated more openly and women could be more direct. When permissiveness didn't lead to climactic bliss, they began to complain vocally. In print and in bed. Many men were just not good enough. The phallus was a fraud. Based on a hundred interviews, Seaman (1972) offered a selection of quotes which reveal different aspects of failure. Too often, men demanded love-making too forcefully.

'All men are just interested in is getting their rocks off . . . the great penetration and the big come.'

'They don't care whether a woman is satisfied and usually the sex doesn't last long enough.'

Many women complained of being 'receptacles for sperm' and that men couldn't find their clitoris. Other complaints included that men were too focused on the obvious erogenous zones, that they were 'still victorious at heart', that they lacked humour about sex, and that, in the desperate poverty of their imaginations, they insisted on making love in bed. Seaman's litany of frustration echoed Greer and de Beauvoir.

It wasn't just radical feminists who noted the poor performance of men. Ideologically neutral books, like Comfort's *Joy of Sex* (1968), started from the premise that men did not know how to use their bodies. Masters and Johnson in their pioneering work on sex therapy (1970) came to the same conclusions. The difference between these authors and radical feminists was that Comfort and Masters and Johnson didn't blame men or link poor sex with other gender deficiencies. Both were technocrats of the flesh. Give us the right recipe and we'll whisk up the best orgasm going, a soufflé of such sensuality it'll take hours to consume. Comfort wrote glowingly of the joys of sex once you had mastered the techniques.

Given such attitudes, it wasn't surprising that many women took flight into lesbian relationships. Women were warmer, more open and affectionate. Soon, some writers like Adrienne Rich and Mary Daly argued the superiority of lesbian sex. Women knew each other's bodies with an intimacy that no man could aspire to. When de Beauvoir had written, – very daringly, given it was 1947 – of lesbian sex she had made nothing like the same claims. The lesbian could be understood but de Beauvoir didn't recommend this as a path for all women to follow.

Radical feminism took a much more revolutionary line. Forget men.

115

After all, another woman would find the clitoris and the G spot since she knew what she was looking for. The idea that homosexual relationships are sexually better also surfaces in much male homosexual literature. This left feminist women who wanted to relate to men in a dilemma, as Hamblin (1983) explained:

Faced with this [male] oppressiveness and rediscovering our own spontaneous creative female sexuality, one of the first choices we confront is: do we really want to go on having sexual and even social, relationships with men at all? For a considerable number of women the answer to this question will be an unequivocal no. Some will choose celibacy, others will maintain social but not sexual relationships, with men. A number will reject all relationships with men. Their lives, their friendship and their love are for women and it is to women alone that they will make any future sexual commitment. During the past decade this has been seen by many as the politically correct choice for women within the women's liberation movement. (p. 119)

Hamblin notes that if heterosexual women, rather like drug addicts, suffer while they are about the task of weaning themselves off men, there is sisterly support.

But there has been less sympathy and support for women who have lived through these same agonies and conflicts and have ultimately made a different choice. Those women who have chosen to maintain their relationships with men and struggle to transform them are often seen as taking the easy way out, selling out on feminism or even as 'collaborators with the enemy'. (p. 119)

No man could be involved with intellectual women in the 1970s and not be confronted by these arguments or be alive to the anger and anxieties these feelings provoked. It was hard to know what to say or to do. How do you respond if you are told, angrily, that a woman would do this better than you or would cuddle for hours after making love whereas, being a man, you drift off all too soon into sleep? The film, *Manhattan*, in which Woody Allen casts a wry eye on such issues, skirted much of the experience, however. Allen retreated into cosy defensive humour, casting his ex-wife as a publicity-crazed harpy.

Being honest about sex isn't easy. The romantic novel might wallow in emotional self-confessions, but who knows what Rochester and Jane Eyre did in bed or the erotic skills of Scott Fitzgerald's gilded folk.

116

The earth might move for Hemingway but he wasn't too specific about the nature of the movements. To find descriptions of sexual behaviour one has to turn usually away from ordinary literature to pornography or to the recent rash of S/F (Shopping and Fucking) books that revel in Harrods and hard-ons!

The immodest exceptions include Ovid's *Erotic Poems* and a few of Donne's stanzas. Casanova was perhaps the first writer who believed he could write usefully not only of who he slept with but how. He even attempted to judge how much pleasure both parties got out of it. Casanova's memoirs did not appear in his lifetime and it took until 1822 for them to appear complete. D.H. Lawrence did try accurate descriptions not just of the acts but of the feelings that went with them. His 'honesty' made him a scandal. Considering how central sexuality is to human experience, our shyness in describing it is odd. It remains refreshing to find a novel like Alison Lurie's *Foreign Affairs* (1987) which, among much else, deals with sexual performance directly. Lurie's heroine, who is a middle-aged academic and not beautiful, actually needs lovers. She is surprised by the prowess of a fat American as outwardly unattractive as she is.

This silence owes much to official censorship but also something to our own awkwardness. It is hard to write about sex, for it is intimate and unknowable. How many of us really know for sure how it was for the other person?

This lack of a literary sexual tradition made it even more shocking when women began to write about their lack of sexual satisfaction. It was a revelation to many women and an accusation against men. Men apparently couldn't cope. American newspapers discovered an epidemic of impotence. Strong men on Budweiser could be found lamenting. Why had they been born into a generation when women, instead of lying back and thinking of England or the USA, sat up and thought of their orgasms? Usually orgasms they were not having. Masters and Johnson turned inadequate sexual performance into an illness. They claimed that men who suffered either from secondary impotence or premature ejaculation were sick. They had a proper medical excuse, much better than a headache, for not performing well. By medicalizing the problem, Masters and Johnson became a bestseller. It was a popular approach both because we are interested in sex and because they deftly avoided most of the new politics involved. Other experts suggested that it was no accident that men were showing more signs of impotence and premature ejaculation. Losing the certainties of their role and their dominance made men flop. Anger made some men brutal and others withdraw. Terror of the growing sexuality of women made many men seek gay experiences. Rather than face the insatiable demands of turned-on women, they turned to other men who wouldn't be so demanding.

In a time of change, a proper account of sexual behaviour and sexual attitudes is important. Unfortunately, psychology isn't really able to provide very adequate evidence from which to start.

Ever since Kinsey, behavioural scientists have tried to discover what we actually do sexually. Kinsey's legacy has in some ways been unfortunate because it led to intense study of the number of partners and orgasms. Kinsey was not at home with studying feelings or fantasy. The scientific literature tends, therefore, to be either physiological or therapeutic. Masters and Johnson have put forward a four-stage theory of sexual arousal. It explains well why many women take long to come to orgasm. Surveys examine how many partners people have had – and these appear to have increased considerably since Kinsey's time. Sex therapy has flourished, but one has to be wary of assuming that the study of people who feel so inadequate as to seek help reveals much about 'normal' sexual behaviour. Sexology has become a respectable discipline with chairs in universities and learned journals to its name. Yet, the scientific approach to sex leaves a great deal out. It usually ignores the sexual politics that feminists have put on the agenda. It deals poorly with emotions, and tends to treat sexual performance as mechanical. How to achieve an orgasm is a practical task like fixing a car engine. Perhaps sexologists have been more influenced than they would admit by Thurber and White's magnificent spoof, 'Six day bicycle riding as a sex substitute'. Sexology also usually treats fantasies as masturbatory devices. You wouldn't guess the emotional longing behind, for example, Erica Jong's 'zipless fuck' fantasies (1979) which stress melting together through clothes, desire breaking down all barriers. Even zips.

Feminists have of course written much about heterosexual sex but usually destructively. As Hamblin noted, feminists have offered little helpful analysis of heterosexual relations since many of them appear to want them to end. Bravely, Hamblin (1983) has drawn up a manifesto for heterosexual women. It is worth quoting in full, and men ought to pay sympathetic attention to it. Hamblin writes:

Men have no right to our bodies.

118

Being sexual/sensual/affectionate with a man does not mean we have
   agreed to have sexual intercourse with him.
It is a violation of our right to bodily integrity for a man to pressure
   us by any means into sex.
If a man has sexual intercourse with us against our will he has
   committed rape.
If a man subjects us to any kind of unwanted sexual attention he
   is guilty of sexual abuse.
We have no obligation whatsoever to meet men's sexual
   demands/needs.
In long term relationships (including marriage) we have no duty
   whatsoever to satisfy the man's sexual needs by providing him
   with regular sex.
It is not 'natural' for a man to initiate, control and determine
   everything that happens sexually between us.
We will only engage in forms of sensuality/sexuality which enhance
   our pleasure and do not oppress us.

There seems to me little to quibble with in this except that it is highly
defensive. Hamblin has presumably the problem of not seeming to
be too much on men's side. For a man, what is important about this
list is that seven of the items deal with women proclaiming (as much
to themselves as to men) that they have a right to refuse sex. Only
two items deal with pleasure. Hamblin's list usefully sets out the pitfalls
of heterosexuality for women who have clearly chosen to relate to men
at a time when for feminists it was 'ideologically unsound'. As a man,
I listen but I also feel I have a right to ask women to listen to men's
side of it.

   Hamblin notes that most men and most women 'carry around in
our heads' definitions of what is proper heterosexuality and its 'rituals'.
As in many of the other chapters, I want to deal with these issues both
personally and psychologically. I want to argue that there are many
aspects of contemporary heterosexuality which also oppress men. I
want to suggest that here is an area where men and women can make
individual commitments to change – and get a lot of fun out of it. But
for men to feel free to change, we need – and women need – to
understand some of the pressures we are under too. They may be less
overt than those Hamblin is guarding against, but they are no less
real. I want to look at the following themes:

1 the dynamics of the pass;
2 the pressure to perform;
3 the denial of men's need for tenderness;
4 the debate concerning male sexual violence which presents all men as violent;
5 non-penetrative sex.

I want to suggest that men pay a price for their role in normal heterosexual 'practice' especially during these confusing times. I also comment at a number of points on the language used by feminist writers to describe sex. They tend to report it in only the harshest terms. In feminist discourse, men *penetrate* and *fuck*. They never *slide inside you*. They never kiss but *crush*. It's the language of the battlefield. If men need to be open to women's feelings of fear, women need to own up to some slightly comic aspects of sex. How threatened can you feel when you are sitting on top of your man?

Men do need to confront how our behaviour oppresses women. But there is only a point in going through that pain if it's done as a way of being freer, to achieve a better relationship with women in the future. It can't be done as an act of penance and much of it can't be done alone. Rather like Hamblin, I want to suggest that it is a time of opportunity for heterosexual men and women. Men need to do much work – but we are not the only ones who need to do it.

THE PASS

Hamblin suggests that men shouldn't always be the ones to initiate. She doesn't ask, though, what the effects of always having to initiate are. You make a pass in fencing and you make a pass in love. The parallel use of the phrase isn't accidental. Sex has often seemed to be about conquest, and I suppose one could add that in fencing they use a rapier.

Most people remember their first sexual encounter. In 1961, I was 14 and I was sitting with an older woman, my 15-year-old relative who was a distant cousin. Her name was Laureena. We were in a flat in Mount Carmel. Outside, in the pine trees, the insects chirruped: inside, in my head and body, lust thumped. And something greater than lust. Terror. I had never been in a situation like this before and I had no idea when I might be again. No problem with the theory. Move closer to Laureena, stare intensely at her eyes, say she was beautiful (which wasn't hard, she was beautiful), and then aim my lips at her lips. I couldn't control my excitement or my anxiety. What if I did all that and she told me I was an animal. Or hit me? Or told my parents?

My sophisticated cousin Rita who had an Afghan hound and two husbands had given me the '*Art of Dating*', which had useful hints on how to order a pizza and make conversation with a girl. Neither of these was tricky. Whatever flavour pizza Laureena might have desired I could have ordered with plenty of *savoir-faire*. And I could converse about anything. Leaning forward for that first kiss required different oral skills. In the end, I reckoned it was now or never. My mother might be back soon. Summoning all my 14-year-old macho, I edged closer, looked into her eyes, and lauched my lips. Unfortunately I closed my eyes (which is what they did in the movies) before I moved so I missed her lips and my passion landed on her cheek. Laureena laughed gently, I opened my eyes. Then she presented her mouth. I pressed my lips avidly against hers. After a few moments she pulled back.

She was going to scream I was an animal.

'David', Laureena said, 'you open your mouth. Like at the dentist.' She had obviously made good use of her extra year.

In the intervening years, I have learned to aim better and that you don't open your mouth quite as you do at the dentist. But I haven't become a stranger to those feelings of anxiety. Flash forward fifteen years.

I am in love in Amsterdam. I have been in love with Hania since I saw her dancing on a table during the Festival of Fools. She was involved with someone else. I had to go back to England. Two months later, I am back in Amsterdam. Married for eight years, I am much out of practice at these rituals. We meet in a bar. We spend the evening wandering round the city. By one in the morning, she says why don't I come back to her place. I can sleep on the floor. We get to her room. She lights candles and we talk and talk. Conversation is as easy now as it was with Laureena fifteen years earlier. But again, I worry. If I lean forward to kiss her, she might look startled, sit up and complain we weren't having that kind of evening at all. At 2 a.m. in her room, that might not be logical. I point out to my id that she is lying back on the bed and that it was she who turned off the lights and put on the soft music. If I don't do something soon, we'll both be fast asleep. She might even think something is wrong with me. Or that I don't want to. Nervously, I stop talking; nervously, I lean forward to kiss her.

As I lean, I risk rejection. You always risk that when you make that move. Only men who are willing to use force – and know it – don't risk that rejection.

You never know, until you try, the reaction you will get. You may have every reason to suppose you will be welcomed only to discover differently. You may get pushed away or be met with affronted surprise. I have been met with both. In theory, sensitive men should be aware of cues – both in body language and in furniture language. For example, if someone sits across the room from you in an armchair, it is unlikely that they want to be made a pass at. Be very sure before you get up, cross a room, and either sit at their feet or bend down to kiss them while walking behind their armchair. I am trying to put this wryly because, often, I have been wrong-footed. Body language is, of course, more subtle than furniture language. Psychologists like Michael Argyle (1975) suggest that any competent human will be able to judge from body language just the precise fractions of intimacy desired or acceptable. In real life, it's not always so easy to know. The onus is on the man to understand the meaning and the intentions of the other person. For de Beauvoir that male power means that the woman is robbed of her individuality and becomes the Other. For me, as a man, it means that even if de Beauvoir is right, there is another perspective. The man is one who has to act and who risks the action being wrong, undesired, and embarrassing. Worse, we know it from the moment we begin to operate as sexual beings – witness my embarrassment with Laureena.

In societies in transition, where boundaries and conventions are no longer so clear, the dangers of embarrassing mistakes are worse. We touch one another more than people did in the past and more casually. But it isn't always easy to know what gestures mean – especially at the start. For example, if I am on a first date with someone and they let me take their arm, are they interested? Do I go further or are they being just 'warm'? If it's an old friend, or a colleague after a good lunch, a gesture doesn't have the same meaning. You know generally it's just friendly. Even more obviously intimate gestures, like prolonged eye contact and holding hands, can easily be misinterpreted. I am not sure 'misinterpreted' is right. It's a sign of our lack of clarity about sex that it is very easy for situations to be ambiguous because no one is quite sure what they want or mean. That can be quite funny. Among the anguished explanations and refusals I've had while holding hands are the following.

Everything in italics, by the way, is what I think but don't say.

'It's nothing personal.' *What can be more personal?*

'I'm in love with a man in Kashmir.'

'Frank and I have an open marriage but we always discuss it before anything happens.'

'After you leave your wife, not before.' *Ouch, touché, but why have you been out five times with me?*

'I thought we were friends.' *Do you do this with enemies?*

'I want to sleep alone.' *At the height of the new celibacy which, thankfully, didn't last long.*

'What with herpes and AIDS, I find it hard to trust anyone.' *Am I meant to bring a medical certificate along?*

There are, of course, the rejections that you get when you are having an affair with somebody – or, even, married to them – which are of a quite different sort. You do have a sexual relationship but things have become dicey. I'm not talking of the situation when you live with someone and, just that night, your partner has had a hard day and just wants to fall asleep. But when there is a relationship and it isn't going right and it might be petering out, I've been in receipt of the following:

'Why don't you stop fidgeting?'

'I meant to tell you before but I'm thinking of becoming gay.'

'Look, I don't want to wake the dog.' *Why have I let darling dog on the bed?.*

'No thank you!'

I only list these best rejections of the past few years because they do suggest that, in some ways, things haven't changed. They certainly didn't change much between the writing of Marvell's 'To His Coy Mistress' in 1635 and e.e. cummings *may i feel* in the 1930s. Marvell's message is clear enough:

> Had we but World enough, and Time,
> This coyness Lady were no crime.

Given the exigencies of time, though, it is a crime. Marvell having allowed that, but for time, she could 'refuse Till the Conversion of the Jews', adds:

But at my back I alwaies hear
Times winged Charriot hurrying near:
And yonder all before us lye
Desarts of vast Eternity.
Thy Beauty shall no more be found,
Nor, in thy marble Vault, shall sound
My echoing Song; then Worms shall try
That long preserv'd Virginity:
And your quaint Honour turn to dust:
And into ashes all my Lust;
The Grave's a fine and private place,
But none I think do there embrace.

Marvell's moral is clear. Since we're mortal, we can't be too moral
and his mistress should be less coy. Two hundred and fifty years later,
e.e. cummings was chasing much in the same vein:

may i feel said he
(i'll squeal said she
just once said he)
it's fun said she

(may i touch said he
how much said she
a lot said he)
why not said she

(let's go said he
not too far said she
what's too far said he
where you are said she)

may i stay said he
(which way said she
like this said he
if you kiss said she

may i move said he
is it love said she)
if you're willing said he
(but you're killing said she

124

but it's life said he
but your wife said she
now said he)
ow said she

(tiptop said he
don't stop said she
oh no said he)
go slow said she

(cccome? said he
ummm said she)
you're divine said he
(you are Mine said she)

In the 1950s, the anon couplet continued to circulate: 'She offered her honour/he honoured her offer And spent the whole night on her and off her.'

It may by now be clear why the honest pass made in appropriate circumstances is something that feminism analyses rather little. Men may not offer their honour but we do offer ourselves. You never know how someone will react when you offer a caress or a kiss. There is a moment in mid-air when you commit yourself to action. The woman may change her mind. Suddenly, as you get to within 2 inches, she may be put off by your teeth, your smile, the way you smell, what she has remembered about your past, what she has remembered about her past. She may recall that she did promise to be faithful to Frederick. In the wake of a failed pass come excuses and embarrassment. It's hard to really believe the kind of statements I detailed earlier. One friend of mine explained to me that she had rejected a man when she noticed, as he leaned forward to kiss her, that he had a touch of green scum on his teeth. But she couldn't say that could she?

What I feel as a man is that I am not good enough, that I won't do. Writers have long ago observed that rejections bruise our vanity. They bruise more. Many men deny that they feel such rejections and, as you get older, it's harder to be as badly hurt by the feeling. You become encrusted.

I am not suggesting that once women get in an intimate situation they don't have the right to change their mind. One of the most pernicious legal doctrines is that women somehow lead defenceless men on. Nevertheless, it would be nice to have some honesty about the power and the politics of the situation. Women do keep power. Men don't talk much to other men about this kind of plight, but I know that when I am rejected I feel rejected. I take it personally. I feel foolish and depressed. I feel frustrated and sometimes, of course, curious. What would it have been like? It isn't just my vanity which has been dented.

Interestingly, comment on current sexual attitudes claims that women are freer to make passes at men. Some sexual surveys suggest that within a marriage women make advances fifteen per cent of the time. By then, of course, it is different. You know each other. You can say you just happen to be tired or not in the mood. Sometimes, it can be even more difficult.

By the early 1980s, I was separated, free, and ready for this brave new world. On the love market women do make passes, but in my experience they are curious ones. Try them as a man and you're in trouble. I am in a country cottage with Nicola, a Home Counties heroine who flew for a living, had a berserk dog and an extremely fast sports car. It was our first date. We were sitting round her log fire. The logs burned; Bach trilled; armagnac aromaed. I was massaging her foot and pretending I had learned this technique of mystical massage from *The Tantra of Sex*. Suddenly, Nicola sat up, and said: 'Why don't we continue this conversation in bed?'

'Well yes,' I said, politely.

She put out the fire and Bach. We padded, rather chastely, to bed. There were no passionate embraces here. Only under the duvet did we peel off our tops and knickers. Then, we lay there nude and a little dumb. But although she had brought us here, I still had to turn round and make the first physical move. It would have been very odd if she had suddenly changed her mind. But that initial physical touch was my male, should I say, prerogative or duty.

This curious verbal pass wasn't an aberration. Some time later, I met again an old friend who had ended a date in the past with the romantic rejection that Frederick might mind. Frederick was living with her and had been known to employ private detectives to follow her, so she had to be careful. After sagas, Frederick returned to his wife who had always hovered uneasily in Twickenham and my friend made contact again. We had a drink in town. The next time we met, she suggested, perhaps we could meet in my sauna bath. And she wasn't coming just for the heat. But, again, through the steam, I had to make the first move.

The only time a woman took the kind of risk I feel I take as a man was after we had been filming on location for a week. We had just finished dealing with a difficult expert on Judaism who could never get his takes right because he felt the consumption of vodka was a religious duty. One evening, he insisted on being taken to the casino. The moment we had left him there, she looked at me and put her arms round me. She kissed me.

'I thought you'd never ask,' she said.

I had suspected she was interested. She knew I was already involved and I had done nothing about approaching her. In the middle of the pavement I admired her for taking the risk. I kissed her back.

'Your room or mine?' she smiled.

Since we were on unfamiliar territory, I settled for mine.

The drift of my argument concerning the start of relationships is simple. From youth, boys learn that they have to make the first move. Sexual politics have affected sexual etiquette. Women do ring up (very occasionally) to ask if you would like to go out. But the passes they make, if made by a man, would seem too crude. I once tried the 'shall we continue this conversation in bed?' line and was told off, quite rightly, for lack of finesse. Words are invitations. A rejection can be graceful, even witty. There is nothing witty when someone turns away, or presents their cheek or meets your lips with a firmly closed mouth.

It has been claimed that men couldn't cope with women who make passes at them. I have to doubt this. The evidence for this proposition is suspect simply because the kinds of passes women make are so different. Hamblin (1983) quoted one woman who claimed to have learned to make passes at men and that it had now become easy. Taking the initiative meant that sex started off on a different, non-ritual basis, and even sexist men were willing to try things they might have not done otherwise. Hamblin did not comment on this woman's experience but it seems perfectly plausible to me. It seems easy to exaggerate men's need to initiate or conquer. Men who are driven to cock conquer are seen as somewhat bizarre. Casanova was funny and outrageous enough not to be labelled pathological. But Georges Simenon, the creator of Maigret, was seen as a classic 'case' or Don Juanism. He said he had slept with 10,000 women – most of whom were, of course, prostitutes. Freud described Don Juanism as a pathological condition. It was an illness due to lack of attention as a child. It carried no glory.

In reality, most men are far from being such sexual adventurers. All surveys point to a few men who have had perhaps fifty sexual partners, but these are exceptions (Luria *et al*. 1986).

Surveys suggest that the average man has some three to six partners during the whole of their lives. Women tend to have fewer partners. The rampant phallic conquest that Scruton (1986) argues for is for the elect or the especially decadent.

It is, of course, possible to argue that that is what men in their secret hearts of hearts desire. Gay literature occasionally suggests this, but other studies of sexuality suggest that it isn't so. Luria *et al*. (1986) report that 'college men' now have fewer sexual partners than in the 1940s but offer them more commitment. Further, the sexual behaviour of men and women is becoming more similar, 'converging', they claim. Male sexual behaviour is not that rampant and conquest-centred. There are, of course, fantasies like that in Fellini's film *8½* where the film director hero has a harem of mistresses, but even studies of fantasies show that men often seek quality rather than quantity.

The cultures in which men habitually have harems are traditional ones in which rich men buy sexual favours. There is little evidence that most men feel triumphant if they have to buy sex. If I had ever had to do it, I would have found it very humiliating. It would mean I had become too ugly, too dull, too charmless for anyone to want me for myself. Whores can seem glamorous in very repressed societies where they represent, in Kinsey's phrase, the only 'outlet' outside marriage. Then sexual conquest isn't really sexual conquest but financial conquest. It lacks all the stuff and charm of desire and seduction. It's a business deal. Men do have the power and women are the victims, but it is not a question of sexual power but buying power. Cynthia Payne in many interviews about running a brothel in Streatham claimed that the majority of men who visited were slightly pathetic and unable actually to get a woman for themselves. This is not to justify what men do to prostitutes but it hardly shows that most men seek to be unfettered studs.

Generally, most men and most women enjoy the dance of seduction with its variety of rituals. Asking someone out, flirting, beginning to feel that it might be possible, are lovely experiences. They are ruined if you feel you are taking advantage of someone else. Key to the pleasure is the fact that the pleasure is mutual. You both conquer the other.

I give another bit of personal histories. I met Elisabeth when I was filming in Japan. She was translating for us as we investigated psychiatric hospitals. We had to work closely together. During the first two days' shooting we had to talk and plan a great deal. She was my only way of getting through to most of the people I was talking to. By the end of the second day, I knew that I would like to sleep with her before we left Japan. I had no idea if she was married or living with someone or deeply committed. I didn't want my film crew to overhear me asking her out for dinner. We sat next to each other on a train heading out of Tokyo and I thought I better take the opportunity. I had no idea what she would say. She was delighted. It was Thursday. We'd have dinner on Saturday. The next day, when we finished filming, I had to meet a publisher. Elisabeth insisted on taking me through Tokyo to his office in case I got lost. Saturday morning, we had to film outside a hospital that was refusing us access. Sitting in the taxi together, I very much wanted to take her hand. Our hands were perhaps 3 inches apart. I felt my own tension and desire very strongly. But we were working, after all and she might feel pressured or put off. The cab ride was, luckily, not too long.

That evening, we met. Both of us knew I was flying to New York the next day. We wandered down the narrow streets of Akasaka and eventually found a restaurant. We established that we were both free that night though both of us played down other ties. Halfway through dinner, Elisabeth smiled that she thought one should take one's chances, however brief. We finished our meal and, then, in the street, I took her hand. Japanese hotels are (or I imagined them to be) very formal. I couldn't invite her back anywhere. We had a coffee in a coffee bar and, then, in what I thought was a deft turn of phrase, Elisabeth asked me if I wanted to see where she lived.

We found a taxi and I leaned forward to kiss her. When we got back to her small room, we fell into each other's arms.

I had a similar experience in London. I went out to dinner with someone I hardly knew but who had useful information about conditions in gaol. She was a friend of a friend and I had met her twice before. We discussed conditions in prison, began to talk about how our marriages had collapsed and, at eleven, we left the restaurant in Charlotte Street. I put my arm around her (the first physical move) and asked if she wanted to come back to Lewisham. I had no idea what she would say.

She said yes.

When she said yes, she didn't surrender and I didn't win a famous victory. We agreed to start something – together.

To say that I seduced or conquered or won seems to me to falsify the experience. It wasn't something done against someone but with them. Both times, these evenings led to proper relationships, but even if they hadn't – and I've had 'one-night stands' (a weird phrase) which have led nowhere – it doesn't mean that the language of battle and conquest is the right one. It is heady and exciting to go to bed with someone for the first time but it doesn't leave me with a feeling of triumph. Perhaps the best way I can distinguish it from that is with the feeling I have when I have outdone a rival, or got and broadcast a story before someone else. That is triumph. There's a lot of adrenalin and, though you tend to deny it, there is also a less than generous delight in having done someone down. When you sleep with someone the first time, there is pleasure but the pleasure is mutual. And the more pleasure I feel I have given, the more I have. When one-night stands are embarrassing or fail, there isn't much delight. I don't think that the sex might have been lousy, but it was 'mannish good' to have conquered her.

It's worth paying some attention to the language that men and women use – especially now that women feel able to express their own sexual interest more. Words like 'fancy' and 'seduce' imply mutual desire, not men imposing our phallic will.

One woman friend who as far as I know hasn't read Hamblin's manifesto distinguished sharply between the experience of being harassed (after an evening's drinking in a bar at a conference, men bother you, 'Why don't they just go and masturbate?') and what happens when two people want each other. Desire isn't one-sided, she claims, though it is a sign of the very different experiences of men and women that she was surprised when I told her I felt the risk of rejection each time I made a pass.

PERFORMANCE ANXIETY

The Yerkes-Dobson law in psychology states that individuals do their best when they are motivated but not too much. The student who is fearfully anxious will be crippled during the exam; the one who doesn't give a damn will not do too well either. The successful student will be the one who cares enough but not to the point of anxiety or fear. The experiments that established the validity of this law weren't carried out in the bedroom but there is every reason to believe it applies there as well. Men who try too hard seem to suffer from a variety of sexual problems, mainly premature ejaculation and lack of a hard erection. Masters and Johnson (1970), Kaplan (1974), and Luria *et al.* (1986) have all come to this conclusion. But why do men try too hard?

Historically men have made the first move. We are the ones who declare the first interest, make the first invitation, and, as I have tried to show, make the first physical move. True, we expect to do it but women also expect it of us. Once or twice, during a period of some confusion, I didn't make passes at women in situations where I was fairly sure they were also attracted to me. One asked me ten years later why I had done nothing. How could I expect anything to happen if I didn't make the first move?

The first move is expected to be competent. De Beauvoir (1949) claimed that many women were disppointed because their lovers did not make them enjoy the experience. It was clearly the responsibility of the man, the active partner, to lead. On the dance floor, you are supposed to lead the waltz: in the bedroom to lead to orgasm. The ballroom has changed more than the bedroom. Thirty years after de Beauvoir, Hamblin (1983) complains that many women experience men as poor lovers. Men want to make love often, usually more often than women, but then they don't want to experience pleasure to the full. The women's movement allowed women to articulate the ways in which they were not being satisfied. Men who were the lovers of feminist women were often told that there was not enough foreplay, not enough caressing, not enough sucking, not enough time. Making love easily became an examination in all these skills. Did you pass?

The kind of agenda that Hamblin sets out entirely ignores (and why shouldn't it?) the effect that this had on men. While women weren't expected to enjoy sex, men did not have to feel pressured about how well they were doing or guilty if they failed. Feminism affected post-sex etiquette deeply. Often, it's perfectly clear if someone has come, but not always, and readers of feminist books knew that many women faked orgasms. Cartoons of the late seventies and early eighties show men asking, almost before love-making is finished, 'Was it all right for you?', 'Did you have an orgasm?' Quite often, feminist women who had spent years suppressing their frustration felt they had a right to complain if they didn't come. One lover of mine would get quite accusatory when she didn't come or when she had an orgasm that wasn't quite as perfect as the one she had had the time before.

The last thing I am saying is that women are wrong in this. Good sexual relationships depend on people being able to say what they want and feeling free to find it. But, for men, this sudden release of pent-up sexual frustration that women had long endured meant pressure. You had to make love well or you were a failure.

The statistics of sexual dysfunction show clearly that the 1970s and 1980s saw many men afflicted with sexual problems. In the past, it had been assumed that it was mainly women who were 'frigid'. A number of studies began to reveal a very different picture. Frank *et al.* (1978) studied 100 volunteer couples. Their average age was in the mid thirties and twelve of them had had marital counselling. Of the husbands and wives 83 per cent rated themselves as happily married. Yet 36 per cent of the men reported problems in ejaculating too quickly, and 16 per cent reported problems with maintaining erections. Among the wives, 48 per cent reported difficulty getting excited. In a study of older men (average age 59) who were already being seen for physical problems at the Minneapolis Veterans' Hospitals, it was found that 34 per cent had erection problems. In 14 per cent of cases, the origins were psychological; in 11 per cent they were unknown. Luria *et al.* (1986), reviewing the literature, conclude that, in the wake of the work of Masters and Johnson, it had been shown that a surprising number of men had sexual difficulties.

The problems that Masters and Johnson had identified and other researchers followed up were essentially technical ones. Men did not know how to stop themselves coming or they could not get an erection. The late seventies saw a quite novel problem. Zilbergeld and Evans (1980) reported finding men who had disorders of desire. They just didn't want sex very much. Helen Singer Kaplan (1978) has also identified this group. She has found both men and women to be affected by chronically low desire, and claimed that during their lives 20 per cent of Americans would suffer this. Historically, this decay of desire in men is peculiar. Men were supposed to be aggressively randy and neither Kinsey nor Masters and Johnson found much evidence of a low level of desire in men. What had made them go off sex?

It cannot be entirely accidental that this period saw a great shift in sexual etiquette. For the first time ever, men were judged on how good they were in bed. Moreover, women were now expected to have some experience of different men to judge their lovers by. We may not like to think of it but, often, when you first start sleeping with someone, you discuss your past relationships. This is always a rather delicate procedure since you don't want to make it seem that your exes were too dreadful, and yet, if they were so good, why aren't you with them now? Into these conversations there often creep revelations of what they were like in bed. As part of your romantic psychosexual c.v. which has got you here with Emily, you do say that Judith nagged or Jemima kept on asking you to pay her bills or that Frederica actually was not too keen on sex and didn't really know how to caress you. I have listened to lovers explain that Frank came too quickly though his equipment was wonderful, that George never knew his lover didn't come, and that William preferred his ladies to dress up in black knickers but that it was likely he lusted after young boys.

This leaves men, has left me, to wonder:

How do I compare with Frank or Bill?

What did he do that she liked that I didn't do or don't know about?

It's very hard not to feel that sense of pressure. Women may also feel that they are under pressure to be the seductive siren, but it is still possible for them to retreat into passivity. Men have not been able to do that and now can do so even less, though couples do experiment with the man 'acting passive'. In the past, women had less to compare since they were supposed either not to have any other sexual experiences or to remain quiet about it. It was, true, easier for men.

For men who were involved with feminist women, the problem was worse since there was the possibility (wielded at times as a threat) that actually they might go off with another woman. If you don't give me better orgasms, I'll become a lesbian. The kind of anger I described in Chapter 3 made women feel they had a right to be assertive and aggressive. Wasn't it what men had been doing for centuries? Perhaps, but that didn't make it easier to deal with. Mass-market magazines like *Cosmopolitan* and *Options* urge women every month to get the most out of their sex lives.

I am not suggesting that women should not judge their lovers (we all do, inevitably) or that men should not learn what it is they like. But for men, the need to prove themselves as good lovers has been a new source of anxiety and one few of us have been sure how to deal with. You have to be the demon lover who is unflagging, full of stamina, imagination, and all the tickles that will make it a memorable experience. The first time I went to bed with one psychologist, she sent me a note saying that she had enjoyed the dinner we had together and the dessert. Her experience of me was yet another 'life event' on which she had every intention of casting her critical eye. So far, on date 1, I had come up to scratch.

Feminists may say that women are only behaving as men have behaved in the past. I'm not sure that's entirely true. Women may have been judged as objects of desire or on how beautiful they were but they were rarely judged on how good they were at making love. As long as men could come with them there was no problem. As women have come to understand their own sexuality better, they want more out of men. That can be a delight. It's much better to make love with a woman who is proud of her passion and wants to give and take, use and be used, than to make love to someone who lies there for you to bang away at.

But while women needed to be able to make these sexual claims, it is clear that this has had its impact on men. It can lead to better relationships but only if men are (and are allowed to be) honest about their anxieties (we have headaches too sometimes), women are also ready to listen, and, as I shall go to suggest, couples talk about what they like in order to try new things.

Some writers have suggested that anger at women's growing sexuality explains male violence. This doesn't sound anything except unpleasant special pleading. There is obviously no justification for any personal violence. I think it's important for men who write about sex to condemn all kinds of violence against women. But feminist writers seem to emphasize violence to such an extent that it seems that every man is brutal and that sex is nothing more than violence. This seems to me extreme. It also seems to me a view that depends heavily on the very selective analysis of the language used to describe sex.

PENETRATING EXPERIENCES

Writers like de Beauvoir (1949), Greer (1970), and Coward (1984) see penetration as the crucial aspect of female sexual experience. Non-penetrative sex isn't real sex. It's a form of petting. It's not going 'all the way', and unsubtle men will see women who just do that as holding something back. They're not giving themselves fully. De Beauvoir and others come close to arguing that penetration is, of necessity, violation. Writers cite instances of horrific injuries inflicted by men and, less dramatically, many cases in which men want either to make love when a woman doesn't or when they want to 'penetrate' before the woman is ready. It would be presumptuous for me to claim to describe better what is a female experience. But this requires some analysis.

Let's start with the language. The use of the word 'penetration' is odd. Does anyone say 'I'm going to penetrate you!' Exciting, eh! It certainly isn't a word that I have ever used in any love-making with anyone. It's a word out of medical textbooks. It was used because it sounded impersonal, which made discussing sex scientifically seem more respectable. But penetration has militaristic echoes. Tanks and armies penetrate behind enemy lines. Needles penetrate the skin. The word implies that you penetrate across a natural barrier which has to be breached to be entered. In sex this just isn't anatomically true. The word doesn't feel true, at least to my own sexual experience. I have said to women 'Can I come inside you' or more aggressively, 'Shall I fuck you?'. But the word 'penetration' is curiously impersonal.

A man can't question the experience of women, but I can describe what this conquering penetration feels like to a man. It varies tremendously from feeling aggressive and thrusting to being gentle, pushing, melting when you are taken inside someone. Technically, of course, you are penetrating but it could also be said that you have been led in by the hand. That doesn't happen to tanks. Coward (1984) makes much of the natural boundaries sex trespasses over. In fact, in good sex, you conjure up a space between you, an erotic space where it's not quite clear where you end and the other person begins. You are joined. Injections penetrate the skin and hurt. It feels better when the needle is out again. Clearly there are times when women are glad love-making is over. But all the time? Surely not.

Penetration is also a matter of position. A good thesis should be written on how the increasing use of a variety of sexual positions has affected views about sex. There is little research on this subject but it seems likely that the emphasis on penetration stems from (1) the fact that until recently most love-making was in the missionary position, and (2) that the phallus was compared to a gun or sword. This is a rather poor metaphor: few weapons change so magically in size or feel.

While the missionary position was the main position for love-making, it isn't surprising that women felt passive. As a man, I know there is a great difference in what you feel and what you do in different positions. When you are on top, you are the active one and, on the whole, you control the rhythm of love-making. It's you rubbing against her, your weight against her. You can make active, even aggressive love with a woman on top, but it's much rarer and, incidentally, harder. The only way I know of doing it is if she crouches forward so that, bending your knees, close to her buttocks you can thrust inside her. It can be very exciting, but you need good back muscles and stamina. The more comfortable position is if the woman really sits on you. Then, she controls the rhythm. She is rubbing against you. You are the relatively helpless one. Technically, you still penetrate but, as a man, it feels utterly different. Girls on top are on top.

In their first book, Masters and Johnson (1970) recommended women on top precisely because it allowed them to determine the speed and rhythm of love-making. So did Comfort (1968). Luria et al. (1986) report that the position is now widely used in the West. To me, the preliminary to coming feels quite different in these two positions. It's only when you ejaculate – 'ejaculate' belongs to the same stiff linguistic usages as 'penetrate' – that it feels the same.

Also, I'm not sure sexual behaviour between established couples is quite so one-sided. Men may usually initiate love-making but, once it starts, I have often had lovers say that they wanted to come on top of me. Usually, they've said either that they want to *come on top* or *sit on me*. The intention 'I'm going to sit on you' can be made to sound very menacing. You are not about to be pleasured but to be crushed. Most times, of course, it is sexy and friendly. But it could sound menacing.

The woman-on-top position is interesting since very obviously it suggests a shift in dominance. Luria et al. (1986) think that this position was considered the advanced form of love-making ten years ago. Now, it's widespread. I find this hopeful because couples have to realize it's important for women to get as much pleasure as men out of sex, and research repeatedly shows that, for many women, it's the most effective. Further, if most men are happy to give up being the controllers on top, it does suggest that we're slightly less obsessed with proving who is the sexual boss. A good sign. Incidentally, the 1983 *Playboy* survey of avant-garde sexual practices now reserves pride of progressive place for rear-entry position. Still, books tend to retreat into overly scientific language, so while human beings say things like 'Will you come in me from behind?', books refer to *ventral dorsal entry*, which sounds like something that dolphins, or skeletons, do. I harp on the language, because it is important. It remains surprising to find how feminist texts have adopted medical usages – jargon designed to keep sex sounding as cleanly scientific as possible. The description of what men do feels skewed and one-sided – to me as a man, at least.

I don't deny the evidence of the violence of men and the impact this has on all women. But it is possible to exaggerate and lapse into describing all sexual encounters as sado-masochistic.

Earlier, I cited Hamblin's (1983) account of how hard it is for heterosexual feminists to press their case. *Men in Feminism* (see Jardine and Smith 1987) contains interesting examples of how feminists have come to equate male sexuality with violence. One of the essays, by Judith Mayne (1987), comments on the success of films like the *Dirty Harry* series. She offers a somewhat sympathetic analysis of another Clint Eastwood film, *Tightrope*. *Tightrope* deals with a sexual killer, and is certainly fascinated by the violence of men towards women. Mayne argues that is pornographic, and notes that writers like Buddy Rich demand that if there really are legions of feminist men out there, they should analyse why men like porn and films like *Dirty Harry*. Their success argues the truth of the radical feminist axiom, 'Porn is the theory, rape is the practice'. But Mayne also notes that one of the stars of the film is a flawed feminist who runs the local rape centre. A key part of her essay focuses on a question asked by the 14-year-old daughter of the detective played by Clint Eastwood. The girl asks, 'What's a hard on, daddy'. Mayne writes:

> The daughter speaks from a position not unlike that of the feminist, a position of detachment (innocent in the daughter's case; critical and theoretical in the feminist's). The film has no answer for the question she asks. Wes Block (the detective) sleeps with women and the murderer kills them but what indeed is a hard on. Is it the desire to kill or the desire for sex, and is it possible to resituate the polarities of violence and sexuality in any but either–or terms?

Mayne seems to accept that it is a little extreme to claim 'rape to be the very paradigm of male sexuality'. She points out that some feminists have argued that rape is not a sexual crime but a crime of violence in an attempt 'to rescue sexuality'. But it is hard to rescue sexuality when men have so brutalized and debased it. For many, Mayne comments, that has meant that the only valid sexuality is lesbianism. Others have dreamed of 'a utopian heterosexuality between free and equal agents'.

I find Mayne's short essay depressing and disturbing. She is not unsympathetic to men or to male feminists. But her arguments highlight the extent to which feminist debate now accepts that all men either are violent or fantasize about violence – we are all the characters mean Clint Eastwood plays at heart – and that any attempt at an equal sexual relationship between men and women is 'Utopian'. The word 'Utopian' is depressing since, by definition, Utopias are dream worlds. We have, and do, make love in the non-Utopian real world where we flirt, touch, stroke, fuck, sometimes penetrate, and sometimes get sat on. These are many varieties of experience. Yet Mayne writes as if it is perfectly normal to equate sex and murder, rape and desire, the juices of the body and the tearing apart of the flesh.

I want to suggest for many men, this equation is very odd. It just doesn't correspond to what we feel or think we do. Perhaps, other men are so vicious. I have to admit that part of the problem may be in understanding the boundaries between violence and aggressive but 'safe' play, boundaries which men and women may see very differently.

Teasing is 'play' but it is not always fun. It is not fun when you are not sure if someone will go to bed with you. But once you are making love, teasing is enjoyable. Clearly, it isn't violence. No one is hit, threatened, or intimidated when you caress them and say you won't come into them just yet. But teasing does have something aggressive in it because, as you caress, as you nearly 'penetrate', you stay in control. They get hot: you make them wait. Both of you know it will happen. I have also been in the reverse position when I have been excited and told, 'not just yet'. The aggression lies in the control, in the fact that one partner makes the other powerless, reducing you a jelly of desire and not finishing you off. Whenever I've done this, the teasing has been just a delaying delight but I can see that women might feel more vulnerable. Will the impatient man just throw himself on top of them to get his way? I don't feel in control when someone is teasing me like that but I have never done it with a woman I didn't trust.

Clearly, sexual violence is a major problem. But not all men are intimidating and brutal even on the most pessimistic reading of the statistics – and it is wise to be pessimistic, since women tend not to report rapes, domestic crime, or sexual abuse. With all proper caution, it's still hard to maintain that sexual violence is something most men are guilty of.

Consider the evidence for (1) the nature of sexual fantasies, (2) the circulation of pornographic materials which many feminists see as violent *per se*, and (3) the statistics on rape and assault and sentences for them.

A number of studies have examined fantasies. Barlow (1984) asked adults to monitor their sexual fantasies every day for several weeks. He found that on average men and women had seven to eight sexual fantasies. Heterosexuals, male and female, tended to fantasize about normal sex. Only 25 per cent, mostly men but not exclusively so, fantasized about variations such as homosexuality, group sex, and sado-masochistic enterprises. Schwartz and Masters (1984) studied 120 men and women: 60 heterosexual, 60 homosexual. It was a small sample. For both men and women, the favourite fantasy was 'replacement of established partner'. We are more faithless than violent. The second favourite fantasy for men was 'forced sex with a woman', while for women it was 'forced sex with a man'. Next for both sexes was 'watching sexual activity'. Men then dreamed of sexual encounters with men while women dreamed of idyllic encounters with unknown men, Erica Jong's zipless fuck. The fifth favourite fantasy was group sex for men and, for women, sexual encounters with women. Neither of these studies suggest a massive trend towards violent fantasy in men.

Figures for the circulation of pornographic materials paint a rather similar picture. Surveys reveal that the majority of people of all sexes had read pornography. Consider the figures. A study for the 1970 US Commission on Obscenity and Pornography found that 80 per cent of men and 70 per cent of women said they had seen erotic material before the age of 18. Sixty per cent of the married readers of *Redbook*, a very middle-market magazine, had seen an adult movie. Readers of *Psychology Today* were the most debauched: 92 per cent of men and 72 per cent of women had read pornographic materials (US Department of Justice 1970). It is hard to maintain that pornography is exclusively a male problem. Woman use it too, often with their partners. Is that always forced on them?

The surveys showed that, although many people had been exposed to pornography, not many were regular consumers. Monthly buyers of magazines tend to be male, but it is only a small minority of men. The circulation of *Penthouse* in the UK now is uncertified. The 'men's magazines' market includes less intellectual products such as *Fiesta* (circulation 307,000), *Mayfair* (circulation 331,000) and *Knave* (circulation 116,000 – it usually only writes about nudes, cars, guns, and wines). The advertising rates on *Penthouse* are £1,600 a page – the same as *Mayfair*'s – which suggests a similar circulation. In all, it seems that this market might sell just over one million issues a month in the UK. It is unlikely there are a million individual porn buyers;

it seems probable that fewer individuals buy a number of magazines each. This market has been static of late. There hasn't even been much growth in more downmarket products such as *Whitehouse*, which emphasize women's breasts and buttocks in a very ugly way. It is clear that the pornography trade is nasty and exploitative. Some magazines degrade women. But the evidence suggests that both men and women occasionally read pornography – and that only a small group of men are regular users. To claim that most men use it and to use that as proof of a general, dark wish on the part of all males to degrade women isn't born out by the evidence.

The popularity of page 3 girls in the *Sun* and the *Daily Mirror* has also been used as proof of men's love of porn. Clare Short, MP, has argued that such images exploit the girls. But again these papers are widely read by women. When papers run material that is too overtly sexual, as the *Daily Star* did under the editorship of Mike Gabbett from David Sullivan's group, women do reject them – and so do many men. It has been estimated that during Gabbett's editorship, the *Daily Star* lost close to 20 per cent of its normal readers. Others (on the whole, men who didn't usually read a paper) did replace them. But the *Daily Star* sacked Gabbett after eight weeks because major advertisers found they couldn't stomach its crudity.

RAPE AND CRIMES OF VIOLENCE

Current rape statistics reveal nothing like the total amount of rape in the United Kingdom. It is difficult for women to complain of rape. Even now, after much publicity, many police forces do not handle complaints sensitively. In some cases judges condemn victims for colluding. If a woman hitches a lift or invites someone to have a cup of tea, it is 'leading men on'. Often, the rapist is known to the woman or is part of the family. Over the years the rape statistics show a rise. The US Bureau of Statistics in 1985 noted that 70 in 100,000 women were raped as against 25 per 100,000 in the 1950s. Since 1980, there has been a steady rise in the number of rapes reported in the UK. Women's groups and magazines like *Cosmopolitan* and other hardly radical periodicals have made violence against women an issue. *Cosmopolitan* asked its readers to write in with their own experiences. Many complained that it was hard to get official action. Often the police intervene but don't prosecute. An unpublished study by Dr Gill Meezy at the Institute of Psychiatry found that, in Brixton, the extent of unreported violence was very high. Many women were frightened to report the men who abused them. Others just accepted it as part of a relationship. They didn't expect any better. There is now more official recognition that violence against women is a major social problem. Mrs Thatcher, hardly a feminist, even encouraged the research for a report on the subject which was launched at 10 Downing Street. It called for better protection, stiffer sentences, and far more awareness of the impact that violence can have on every assaulted woman (Cabinet Office Papers 1985).

Men cannot be frightened in the way that women are when they walk down a street and hear footsteps. There are also positive things a man can do in that kind of situation – like cross to the other side of the street so the woman in front of you will know you're not following her.

But while it's important for men to see that women do often feel at risk, it is important to get a perspective on the problem. What matters and what you can control is whether you are violent. If you are, seek help. If you're not, don't feel guilt-trapped into admitting that all men are violent. Our genitals don't make us brutes. When people write of the penis as a club, sword, rapier, or gun, it is a metaphor. And metaphors have their limits. Many men see the violence of other men as a problem.

For me, the issue became complicated when I woke up to the fact that violence didn't have to be crude. To control and bully someone – endemic games in all relationships – isn't like hitting them, but it's hardly the mark of an equal relationship.

I asked a number of my women friends about their own experiences of violence and, which sounds daftly self-conscious, whether they had experienced me as violent. Did I see what had happened between us so differently that I thought I was sensitive while they thought I was a brute? Three of my friends did spend years involved with men who were violent. One had her arm broken. All these women were outwardly successful, and, indeed, two of them were professionally involved in helping people. Give them a patient in trouble, a battered wife, and they knew how to handle it. In two cases, the violent relationships lasted a very long time. One friend said that she had never experienced anything like it before and that she felt fascinated, and held, in its web. She and her boyfriend lived together. Often, he would spend days in bed or watch television. He expected her to supply all the money they needed to live. They lived on her Social Security money since he refused to sign on. He hated authority so he couldn't take its money. It was more than his integrity was worth. As a result, they scraped by on her benefits and a little money she made from running self-help groups for women. He could be verbally vicious too. To save money, she would buy the cheapest cheese in their local supermarket. He would yell inside the shop, swearing he didn't want to live like a pauper. Why did she have to remind him of that? She knew it was a terrible relationship. She was frightened of him, but there were many friends she could have gone to, as, indeed, she did in the end. It took her two years finally to throw him out.

We had been lovers years before. I experienced her as sensual but quite tough. She was a woman who had a clear will of her own. She could argue for hours. In other words, I saw nothing in her of the classic victim. She did not have a history of other violent lovers. She did not find the violence sexually exciting though it did make her curious. Trying to explain her own behaviour later, she emphasized how magnetic it had been because it was so unusual for her. She was amazed that someone could have that kind of hold over her and I was amazed she would put up with it.

Two of my other friends were also bemused by the way they tolerated the violence. Neither of them allowed the relationships to continue a long time but they too said this was something they had never experienced before. I wasn't able to talk to the men in any of these cases. These stories are interesting because, for all these women, this sort of violence was an exception. It happened to them once in a series of relationships. Usually, their men were not like that.

For myself, I believed that I had never used violence on a woman either in a sexual or a non-sexual relationship. The only incident in my marriage I could remember was when I threw a saucepan at Aileen after one of her lovers had left to go back to her husband. I thought I should check if other people had experienced me as violent if I was to write this. There's something ridiculous and self-conscious in this exercise, of course, and it's possible that people lied to me. Nevertheless, how else do you try to touch an area where there seems such a gulf between the experience of the two sexes?

At first I thought my own experience was confirmed. No one said that I had been violent. But it was not quite so equable. Two of my ex-lovers said, to my shock, that there had been times when they had felt intimidated or frightened. One said that I had used sex brutally, as a means of controlling the relationship. Another reminded me of a time when we had gone away on holiday together. It had started off well enough but, after two days, she stopped wanting to sleep with me. I didn't accept this with much grace. I didn't, she said, menace her physically. I sulked, though, or, as she put it, 'huffed and puffed'. It made her feel under pressure and the more under pressure she felt, the less she felt like sleeping with me. For the next few days, she didn't want to touch me, made it clear, and we spent an appropriately frigid five days in Helsinki. When we got back to Britain, she wanted to end the relationship though she later changed her mind.

In another case, someone said that she felt that sometimes in our love-making what I saw as teasing she didn't see as fun. It wasn't that there was any active violence. It was just that I was enjoying controlling her and she didn't like feeling powerless. I appeared to revel in the power. She accepted that I did not mind being teased back. Women do, after all, tell you to wait till you can come inside them, too. It's a kind of foreplay recommended by many sexologists. To me that has seemed playful, not menacing.

When someone has stopped me coming into them for a long time, I've experienced that as them exercising power. It has not felt frightening or made me resentful. It seemed a way of mutual pleasure. If you trust the other person, if you know that in the end she will let you inside her, the waiting is good, on the very boundary of the pain/pleasure divide. Yet, when a man is teasing, the feelings can clearly be more frightening for a woman perhaps because I never dreamed that the woman on top of me would turn nasty and suddenly pummel me. Women perhaps don't feel so secure even with someone they trust and so are more afraid. I have to admit that I wasn't aware of that till I started asking about it.

Comfort (1968), like many good writers on sex, suggests that anything can be tried as long as you ask your partner if they really want to do it. And listen to what they say. It's good advice but it demands more honesty about our bodies than comes easily.

The emphasis on male violence performance and conquest means you would never suppose that men too needed tenderness and could love it.

TENDER LOVING CARE

Feminist critiques of male sexuality leave no room for some male sexual needs that have nothing to do with violence. Research by a number of psychologists, including Masters and Johnson (1970), shows there are important differences between men and women. Masters and Johnson developed a four-stage model of sexual arousal. There was initial excitement. After some stroking, kissing and caressing, women reached what they called the plateau phase. This was a period of sustained, intense sexual excitement. Many women liked this phase tremendously and could stay in it, not quite coming, for anything up to an hour. To make love to someone like that is a curious mixture. On the one hand, it's very exciting because they stay at a pitch of delighted passion for so long: on the other hand, it can be frustrating because you feel constantly that they are just about to come, to flood if you keep doing what you have been doing. Then, mysteriously, though you think you have been doing what has brought them so close, they 'lose' it. You either give up or carry on. One lover of mine would take sometimes the best part of an hour to come and she could only come by being stroked. Often I did want to give up but I very rarely did partly because she used to love it so much when she did come. It was no good, though, rushing sex with her. As a couple, you have to want and trust each other a great deal to carry on so long, to laugh through the moments you lose it. If you can't do that because you are both too anxious about performing, you become bitter.

For men, the plateau is different. It isn't usually so exciting. Robinson (1981) suggests that some men bypass the plateau phase completely. They career straight from excitement to orgasm. This is a minority, however. The evidence suggests that although most men are apt to want to go for orgasm more quickly than women, it's a habit that can be changed. Men also enjoy the foreplay, the mounting excitement, touching and caressing. We do not have less of an appetite for sensual pleasure than women do. The problem is that while we know at least that it takes a long time to arouse women, women often assume that men don't want more. They can come, that's enough. Climax – end!

There's some evidence that women who have become much better at understanding their own sexual needs have continued to assume that all men really want to do is to get inside as fast as possible. I know that, for me, it isn't so. But it's actually hard to tell a lover that you like being stroked for ages, that even if you are quite erect enough to enter, it would actually be more fun if you waited. To claim that men dislike foreplay or can't learn to take longer over it is false. But these are skills that can only be learned in a couple.

Sex remains a thorny subject. Our culture teaches us to be ashamed of it and of our genitals. One of the reasons why oral sex is considered so daring is that you actually see what is going on. You show yourself and, of course, you show yourself off. Though we are supposed to live in far more open times, having passed through the joys of permissiveness, shame about many aspects of sex and intimacy persists. It's not easy to be so close, so vulnerable. We are far from having become fully liberated. Sexologists who advocate liberation, from Wilhelm Reich (1942) to Masters and Johnson (1970), always risk being seen as slightly crazed evangelists of the body. The orgasm is all. Men and women are sometimes defensive in different ways about sex. Men tend to be too quick and too obsessed with 'penetration'.

Some feminists argue that men need to learn to enjoy non-penetrative sex. That would feel less oppressive. They often doubt that men could manage anything so subtle. Certainly, non-penetrative sex needs to become one of the ways of making love. You don't always, necessarily, repetitively, have to come inside your lover. But there are ways of getting there. Couples can talk about it. It shouldn't be imposed as the only way of making love as a kind of penance of the sort advocated in Adrienne Rich's poem 'What will you undertake?' (1974). That is just reverse oppression. Imagine saying you can only make love to me in one way. Or else. That's no way to sustain a relationship. But I think that it's important that couples learn to play with the techniques of non-penetrative sex and that men learn that you can make love 'fully' and come without having to go inside your lover. For short periods, I've done that when it mattered to someone I was with and she talked about it. I felt very differently about it when I was told you either make love this way or not at all. What could be exciting, novel, and a wonderful form of long-playing foreplay became a kind of – it seems right to use that familiar word – oppression. And while I think it's very important for men to understand how they are sexually oppressive, I don't think that the answer is for women to oppress us back. As anything else in a relationship, it needs to be talked about. The problem is that it's only when things are going well that it's easy to talk about sex. When a relationship is fraught, when someone is trying to withdraw, there is too much anger and anxiety. But, at a time when heterosexual men and women need to consider what each of them needs sexually out of a relationship, non-penetrative sex is useful. Practise it. See what you and your partner like about it. It does offer a chance to discover, and

145

linger over, sex in a way that men are apt not to do.

I have tried to suggest that it is possible to exaggerate the evidence for violence and male use of pornography. I've also tried to indicate some areas in which men are oppressed. Undoubtedly, men are the ones to make passes because, in patriarchal societies, we were the ones to propose, to choose our partners. But in the very different social structures of today, the fact that it's always up to you to make the move carries its own burdens. So does the fact that, despite fifteen years of research, men are still supposed not to care about physical tenderness. How many men do you know who, if their partner strokes their back after love-making, snarls in fury? Heterosexual sex could be a lot better and I think feminists tended for a variety of reasons (as Hamblin (1983) explored) to deny the possibility. For that to happen, men need to learn a lot. But so do women, too. And we need to learn together – preferably with many laughs on the way.

Ironically, many of the 'improvements' that heterosexual feminists want are very similar to those recommended by experts in sexual behaviour. Spend more time. Express more tenderness. Talk about what you both need. *Never* impose sex on your partner. Do not use it as a form of blackmail. No one is obliged to make love to you at any time. Conjugal rights are out of the Middle Ages. Men – and women – have nothing to lose but the chains of habit and laziness that make most of us less sexual beings than we dream of being.

Relationships aren't just about sex, of course. In the next chapter, I examine some of the difficulties men have about relationships and the misery they can cause.

Chapter Seven

ONLY RELATE

Traditionally, men wanted sex without the commitment of relationships. Feminist writers like Chodorow and Dale Spender claim that men are bad at making relationships for a variety of reasons. We are frightened of showing feelings, do not listen, and do not admit we need love. Selfishness rules. Such authors remain sceptical about the new man with his much-vaunted sensitivity. This creature is a myth. He pays lip-service to feminism. He preaches equality to exploit women all the better, aping the antics of the big bad wolf. For women relationships become a losing battle.

I want to argue that such views are at best only partially true. Contemporary relationships, like modern heroes, are under novel pressures. Bombarded by often contradictory information and expectations, we are no longer clear what we want out of them.

In the past, there was little doubt. Love led to marriage and marriage provided love, sex, security, and children. It was for life. Dominian (1968) was only one of many social psychologists and other experts to discern a shift in the nature of marriage. During the century, it has changed towards being far more 'reciprocal', with power being shared between the partners – a great departure from 100 years ago. Since 1968, change has quickened: even in that year of liberation rhetoric few people argued that a good marriage was one in which both partners could 'grow'.

Feminism has added to the pace of change in relationships, a process that has left many of us sceptical, self-conscious, and confused about those relationships. We talk endlessly about them but are less clear than ever what they are for or how to judge whether one is good. Which of the following statements is true for you and how definitely?

I want to have a relationship:
    To have a good time now?
    Not to be alone too much?
    To see if one might develop into an old-time marriage?

A recent episode of *Moonlighting* caught brilliantly how baffled we remain by relationships. In it, Maddie kept pushing away David because having a wonderful time in bed wasn't a 'real relationship'. He asked to know what a 'real relationship' might be. To prove he wanted one, he offered to move in a toothbrush and a few shirts, even to take her to dinner. Maddie cared for him and desired him but also desired a proper relationship which, maddeningly, she couldn't define. Except that she thought this wasn't one.

It's evident that it isn't only men who are perplexed. Maddie, like some modern women, seems to have acquired the once-male trait of being afraid of relationships. To claim that the problem of heterosexual relationships is the problem of turning emotionally frigid and fearful men into human beings is simplistic. It's about as subtle, sexist, and true as saying all women drivers are bad. Francesca Cancian, Professor of Sociology at the University of California, argues, 'men are not as uninvolved and unskilled in love as the feminist perspective suggests' (1987:78).

Statistics confirm the confusion. One marriage in every three ends in divorce in the United Kingdom and in the United States. In Britain, *Relate*, which used to be the Marriage Guidance Council and other helping agencies claim to be overwhelmed by demand. The psychoanalyst Christopher Lasch said in *The Culture of Narcissism* (1980) that we have become so used to preening our egos that we can no longer love or commit ourselves. Marriages are temporary, till a better significant other turns up. We change partners much as we change cars.

Like Cancian, I think Lasch is too pessimistic but it is certainly true that, for all our self-conscious psychological expertise, we are perplexed. Old cultural ideals persist and the romantic couple, much like the old hero, is still one supreme fantasy. To be together forever is love, fulfilment, happiness, and success, according to songs, books, ads, and many other cultural products. Melt into a couple and share everything. No more lonely dinners, lonely nights, or vigils by the unringing telephone. A study in Singapore showed that teenagers on their first dates hoped their partner for the evening would blossom into the great, forever love. AIDS has given this romantic message a less romantic twist. If you're sane, and don't have a death wish, it's best to lay off casual affairs.

The feminist critique of marriage has added to the confusion of perspectives. Once, women wanted marriage and men tried to avoid it. The ancient bargain was that women 'gave' sex for security. Sexy men didn't have to get hooked to get laid. Then, feminists argued that the idea that women wanted marriage more was another piece of sharp practice on the part of patriarchy. When women got married, they lost their name, their identity, the right to control their property, and the right to determine what they did with their bodies. They became chattels. Some bargain. Men might joke about escaping marriage but it was men who did best out of it. We got a home, a confidante, children, sex, meals, and someone to boss. As long as women didn't question the unjust status quo, men were happy. The feminist critique made many women reject marriage as oppressive.

As men, we need to examine our relationships (and our selfishness) critically, but it is wrong to expect us to do it in a vacuum. Everyone is confused as to the nature and purpose of 'good relationships'. In Chapter 4, I claimed that men weren't as emotionally illiterate as we are sometimes made out. I now want to argue that:

1 Our idea of love, and its expression, has traditionally been a feminine one. Men are judged bad at relationships because we fail to conform to a 'feminized' definition of love.
2 Just as men are not so emotionally inept, many men say they need relationships, value them, and are willing to change to improve them.
3 Men who do not manage to make relationships are seen less and less as glamorous batchelors. Rather, people ask just why they've failed to settle down. What is wrong with them?
4 The psychological research shows that, though men and women have different fantasies about the perfect partner, both sexes use very similar criteria in judging whether relationships work, and claim to find almost identical satisfactions. Women like a good sex life too, and men want a partner they can confide in.
5 Though this area is little studied, I would speculate that the changing attitudes of women to work mean that the 'romantic' feminine definition of love is no longer adequate – for men and women.

FEMINIZED LOVE

The idea that love was a feminine activity is not a new one. The sociologist Talcott Parsons argued that it was the product of the nineteenth-century division of roles between men and women. It could be argued that it goes back even further. It was the troubadours who defined love for Western civilization back in the twelfth century. The rough knight was miraculously transformed by his devotion for the damsel fair. He cast aside his sword for a bouquet of flowers. He wooed his beloved with essentially feminine tricks. It's interesting that men have traditionally given women they love flowers. The code of love required the man to be respectful and attentive. He had to restrain his desire, going in for couplets rather than coupling. To be too dominant or too demanding was not acceptable.

Feminists have criticized this code as patriarchal. It reduced the status of women, and, anyway, once he won her hand, the lover-turned-husband was in control, demanding his conjugal rights. That may have been so, but the definition of love was one that was very unmasculine. To win women, men often put on very unmanly airs. They sang, wrote poetry, were humble. Through the centuries, this has remained the classic version of love.

Women were, of course, often attracted to strong, brutal men who scorned this code. Nevertheless, what counted was an adoring courtesy. Cancian (1987) in her essay on 'Love in America' notes that there has been insufficient analysis of this tradition. Briefly, it has meant that we judge lovers by how well they fulfil certain feminine ideals. This has not altered much. It means that, to fulfil these roles, men have to act in a way that is not very masculine if one accepts a conventional definition of the masculine.

There was a time when the man who rejected this was seen as glamorous. That is no longer so.

LONELY FAILURES

The status of single people has changed. Once the batchelor was glamorous. Smart enough not to be trapped, he was delectably free. Young men wanted to get laid; young women to get married. There were always a few committed spinsters who were seen as bizarre or weird but most women sought marriage, its security and status. Germaine Greer (1970:198) sniped at attitudes to spinsters: 'In the common imagination, nuns are all women disappointed in love and career women are compensating for their failure to find the deepest happiness afforded mankind in this vale of tears'.

Jane Eyre resigned herself, for example, to a loveless existence since she could not marry Mr Rochester. Till the fire freed him. A century later, Barbara Pym wrote of outwardly less passionate spinsters who consoled themselves with safe, but inappropriate, passions for curates and vicars who could be smothered in cream teas rather than kisses. In both cases, women without men felt incomplete to others and themselves. Greer argued that it was men who created such complexes. Today, however, that need for a man attitude has changed and is perhaps most evident in the attitude of many women to work. A career is not seen as second best to marriage, a compensation for personal failure but as an end in itself.

Hollywood has tried to create a new heroine to fit this trend. Judith Williamson identified a new genre, the single woman alone picture like *Jumping Jack Flash* with Whoopi Goldberg and *Black Widow* with Debra Winger. These heroines focus on work. A relationship would be nice icing but, if Mr Right doesn't happen by, life carries on, interesting and challenging. These films portray women in a quite different way from the women looking desperately for love as in *The Glass Menagerie* and the later *Looking for Mr Goodbar*.

Williamson argues that Hollywood is trying to handle feminist issues but cannot quite cope. The films compromise, for the women are not wholly happy without men. Williamson ignores the cultural differences from the Bronte's or Barbara Pym's time. Then, love was an imperative. Find a man you cared for and who cared for you, zoom to the happy ending. Both films Williamson describes also reflect a fear of failure. Both heroines have had too many relationships go wrong to risk optimism about a new one, much like Maddie in *Moonlighting*. It's a familiar anxiety. For many people, their emotional c.v.s are a narrative of involvements that didn't work out, if working out means lasting forever, which seems to be what most of us mean by 'working out'. The recurring failure is a pattern acutely (and cutely) shown in Ken Pyne's cartoon book, *Where Is He Now?* (1982). It traces wryly how we repeat the cycles. We fancy, we flirt, we fuck. We hope, become disenchanted, quarrel, break up, and wonder, a year on, what old Janet or John is doing now – and with whom.

Dr Johnson observed long ago that a second marriage is a triumph of hope over experience. Yet many people today still see marriage or a permanent cohabitation as the only happy end. Divorcees often try again and, usually, fail again. Second marriages end more quickly than first ones. Third marriages are even shorter.

One lover told me that she didn't want to break up our affair because she couldn't face starting again. Another, after a long period of celibacy, concluded that life is a lot tidier without sex. To be involved was, for her, to be frightened of what she might lose. Being involved wasn't worth the gamble. She pined for a relationship and yet defended herself against it superbly. Her defensiveness is similar to the defensiveness of some men.

I know some men who think of themselves as free glamorous bachelors, but they seem less than happy with their lot. They protest too much that freedom is what they want.

When Fred was 14 his mother left home and he lived with his sister and his father. Though Fred was clever at school, he played truant often. He passed exams without much effort but refused to enter higher education. Fred was 25 when I met him. He gloried in his solitude. He was physically attractive and often moaned that women pursued him. The poor harassed man had to flee women who wanted to bed or wed him. Fred drank heavily. He would sometimes go out with someone, sometimes female, sometimes male. But these affairs were always short-lived. Fred avoided any further involvement. Once, he went on a sailing holiday with a young man but their boat capsized and they ended up wet, cold, and ratty. By his mid-thirties, Fred saw himself as a man who could get along without intimate relationships. Only the weak needed them. He didn't make vast demands of his friends though he was always glad to be invited for lunch or dinner. Slowly, his isolation cramped him. He drank more and became more shabby. His work became his life and his work was always stressful. He seemed more unhappy, more desolate, and less able to change. Yet whenever I asked him if he didn't miss having a relationship, he'd always shrug that you were better off on your own. You didn't have to compromise that way.

Andrew is a ginger-haired man in his fifties. He is a painter. He too drinks heavily. Unlike Fred, he has remained good-looking and has many women friends. But when he was young, he was jilted by his fiancee. Since then, he has distrusted close relationships. When I first knew him, he was in his late thirties. He radiated a certain glamour which made me quite jealous. Women loved to talk to him. But, like Fred, he wanted to be alone. As I got to know him better, I began to see that he paid a price for this isolation. He has become depressed and eccentric. He often provokes people without meaning to do so. He offends when he thinks he is teasing. He becomes stubborn and rude, and then quips that no one should start arguments if they can't stand the tensions. He is surprised and upset that people are upset. Drink makes him become more stubborn. Yet he's a kind man. It's just that isolation has made him angry in ways he doesn't admit and very unskilled at handling conflicts.

Perhaps a more honest loner is Tony, who has long wanted to have a relationship. He used to be in a mental hospital but was released. He lives in a small room in London and, occasionally, he finds someone who will share it with him. A few years ago, he was very happy because of a girl who came to stay with him. But she left. He was very upset though he agreed that she had probably been right because he had so little to offer her. He was out of work. He was moody. Some nights he couldn't sleep and drew through the night. Given what he understood women wanted of men, he would smile sheepishly that he had so little to give. It was a true assessment. Self-awareness didn't help him and he still craved a partner. Without his drawing, he said, he would go mad in his loneliness.

Few of those who know these three men envy them or their isolation. Pretending to be free and happy now tends to sound hollow. Fred and Andrew, in particular, sometimes seem a little pathetic as they protest that they are really content. In a world in which the couple remains the social ideal, failing to make a relationship is a stigma. Ironically, it has become more of a stigma for men. A woman who chooses to be on her own can now say that she has decided to focus on her career. For a man, it suggests failure or pathology. The male hermit is no longer a saint but someone who needs a social worker. He doesn't have any ideology to back up his situation.

DO WOMEN GIVE MORE?

Feminists argue the spinster is smart because women give far more than men. The evidence for this tends to be rather literal. Gavron (1966) showed that women were saddled with the bulk of the housework, child care and domestic drudgery. Ann Oakley (1980) found that men still let women do far more of the housework. Hill (1987) found some progress but said that many men exaggerate their contribution to housework and child care. It is the same with the emotional side of relationships, according to Cline and Spender (1987). Men sponge support, security, and love off women. For some women, the need to give is almost pathological. Robin Norwood's *Women Who Love Too Much* (1988) claims that many women from disturbed families love cold, violent men who love to exploit them. For such women, to love is to be punished. Masochism rules. Spender, Norwood, and other writers like Chodorow are sceptical of men who say they want to change. The values that society teaches boys reinforce, and glorify, coldness. Feelings are weak. Those with the right stuff never reveal emotions or vulnerabilities. Women suffer in the pursuit of an impossible dream, a good relationship with a man. Separatists claim that it is pointless to try heterosexuality and that women would be wise to imitate Lysistrata. The non-separatist Rosalind Coward, author of *Feminine Desire*, argued in the *New Internationalist* (1987) that men might become more fit for relationships with women if we all had a homosexual spell. That would reveal to us the true awfulness of our sex. Coward fails, however, to acknowledge that expectations of relationships have changed. We have become more demanding and less dutiful. Once divorce was a total personal disaster. Today, it's an acceptable option if I'm not getting what I want out of this 'thing'. I can leave you quite honourably if I feel I'm not 'growing'. Paradoxically, although we accept that it is OK to end relationships easily, we still see success as permanence. Our conventions are confused.

If the desire for more total relationships is hedonistic, the hedonism creates novel pressures. Victorian couples didn't keep on monitoring how their marriages were faring. Today, we ask questions that can be dismissed as neurotic but that do reflect our growing awareness that there are other choices:

How was it for you?
How is it for you day after day?
Are you happy with me?
Are you bored with me?
Would it be better with someone else?

Remember, the dominant sexual fantasy for both sexes is making love with someone who is not their regular partner.

Constant reviewing doesn't make life easy for anyone, but for men, the alleged clumsy gorillas of personal relations, it is perhaps especially difficult. Who brought us up to aim for perfect relationships, the zipless fuck, the seamless coupling in the ultimate orgasm that's the climax of the ultimate relationship? Moreover, often we question relationships when we are angry, which adds even more tension. If relationships are more changeable and fragile than before, it's too glib to pillory men as being unskilled at them. Coming together, and growing together, is something of which both sexes have little experience. Patriarchy may have done that, but many men suffer from it too.

When you begin to study male attitudes to relationships, a paradox soon becomes apparent. Women are fairly consistent in explaining what they want out of relationships. The views of men seem to alter between the start of the affair and its becoming permanent. Men begin with a clear and powerful fantasy of the perfect mate. This is what attracts them – and sex is very much to the fore. As relationships 'mature' – and I use 'mature' to mean age – men seem to like qualities in their partner which are very similar to those that women want from the outset.

Let's first examine the animal side of male attraction.

THE PERFECT MATE

In 1972, Centers asked a sample of college graduates what would go to making their perfect mate. He found telling differences between the men and the women. For the men, what counted initially was sexual attraction. The perfect mate wasn't quite a 'Playmate' but she wasn't far from that. She would be physically attractive and have 'erotic ability' above all else. After that, it was necessary for her to have 'affectional ability' and to be socially skilled and understanding. Men also wanted their perfect mate to have dress sense. The girls looked for a man who had 'occupational ability', 'economic ability', 'entertaining ability', 'athletic ability', and 'leadership' qualities. They wanted commonsense too. They didn't even mention that he should be good looking and it wasn't crucial for him to have erotic ability or even to be very romantic. Centers was studying a young sample whose experience of relationships was rather limited. Nevertheless, the differences were telling and receive some support from work such as that of Duck (1987). He found that men are much more apt to say they have fallen in love quickly. This reveals, Duck hints, not that men are great romantics but that we are mesmerized by good looks and the hope of sex. If you love someone, they should love you and sleep with you. Eysenck and Wilson (1982) also suggest that men seek partners whom they desire physically while women seek less physical qualities. The only doubt I have concerning this evidence is whether women subjects felt free to acknowledge their own desire. It is only recently that it has become acceptable for women to speak of men as *hunks* or *well-hung*, to cast men as sexual objects too. There is no way of knowing if that was a factor in work like that of Centers.

Fantasies of the perfect mate may be different, but what people hope for out of relationships seems quite similar. Unfortunately, most research has focused on couples in trouble, in therapy, or where one partner is absent. We know more about the loss of relationships or extreme trauma than about 'middling', ordinary relationships. So we have less than adequate data. I want to suggest that such data as we have shows that the sexes want similar satisfaction out of love and identify very similar factors as being critical to the success of relationships.

Argyle (1985) found that happily married couples say they like the following things about being married: being told nice things; being given non-verbal 'strokes', such as a kiss, and help with chores; an enjoyable sex life; spending a lot of time together; agreeing over finances; and taking a problem-solving approach to decisions and difficulties. Argyle summarized thirty-one rules for a good relationship, which included being faithful, asking for advice, joking. There were only six rules which didn't apply to both sexes, and where wives and husbands ought to act differently. These 'men-only' rules were that model husbands should look after their sick wives, show an interest in what his wife did every day, look after household repairs, and offer to pay when they went out together. The model wife ought to show her anger openly and stop nagging. Most rules for a happy marriage required similar behaviour from both partners. Both men and women acknowledged this similarity. The rules differ less than the roles.

Much research makes it obvious that men value relationships. Campbell *et al.* (1976) asked more than 2,000 American subjects to rate how good, or bad, their lives were. They gathered information on basic details such as age, job, income, level of education, and also on more complex factors such as their emotional state and how happy they were. Among the 8,000 current psychological tests, the Bradburn Scale of Affective Balance claims to test the well-roundedness of emotional life. Using that and a number of other tests, Campbell *et al.* found that twelve factors make, or break, 'life experience'. Income was not paramount. Health mattered most. Marriage and family life came next for both sexes, followed, improbably, by the quality of the national government. Friendships and the quality of housing preceded both job and income. It wasn't that Campbell's subjects didn't care about money. There was a correlation between the level of income and the quality of family life. Poor people tended to be harassed by money worries, which made their family life stressful. However, much as Whitbourne (1986) found in her more qualitative work, the results showed how both men and women say that they judge success or failure very much through the state of their relationships. The lack of materialism surprised the researchers and some who have commented on their work, like Steve Penrod (1983) in his *Social Psychology*. He noted: 'This research definitely contradicts the idea that happiness can be bought. Although American society has been dominated by the belief that economic satisfactions directly determine human welfare, psychological research suggests that life is more than a bank balance.'

Flanagan (1978: 137 ff.) attempted to identify the precise formula, over and above a bank balance, that made people feel good about their lives. He interviewed 3,000 people of all ages. He asked them to say what had been critical incidents, high points in their lives that made them happy and low points that made them wretched. Subjects were asked when they last did something 'very important' or to 'tell me about a source of continuing pleasure'. Flanagan collected over 6,500 'important' incidents and then divided them into groups. Again, health and happy relationships outstripped money as the root of the good life. Both men and women ranked being healthy as vital. Jobs were an important source of satisfaction for 90 per cent of both sexes. Yet there was again evidence that men acknowledged the centrality of personal relationships. At the age of 30, 68 per cent of men and 83 per cent of women ranked visiting relatives and sharing things with them as important. Eighty-four per cent of men and 93 per cent of women ranked having and raising children as important. Caring for them mattered. Ninety per cent of men and 94 per cent of women said that relations with a husband, wife or a person of the opposite sex was important. Seventy-one per cent of men and 79 per cent of women ranked close friendships as critical.

At the age of 50, the pattern was similar except that fewer women saw their marriage as key. Eighty-eight per cent of men now considered it important, while only 83 per cent of women did so. By the age of 70, women had become even more dismissive. A mere 46 per cent thought of it as crucial to their lives, while 85 per cent of men did so. Relationships other than marriage mattered to these women. Certainly, 87 per cent of them valued their close friendships. Men were less convinced of the value of friendships. I'm not sure that this finding indicates how cynical or callous elderly American women become about their husbands. Rather, many of the sample had lost their husbands. Such survey evidence confirms that personal relationships matter to men.

Surveys are, of course, not the most sensitive technique. Can you really judge the quality of marriage by the answers people give on questionnaires? It's sane to be sceptical but, equally, it's the best evidence there is to date. Such work has shown that men are more satisfied with their marriages than are women but there is very little difference in the things about marriage which make men and women happy. In a study of 2,190 Canadians by Rhyne (1981) men and women were found to have similar sources of satisfaction. Rhyne asked subjects to rate on a scale of 1 ('not very satisfied') to 4 ('extremely satisfied') what they liked about the married state. The mean score for men and women fell between 2.70 and 3.51 on all the following scales:

	Men	*Women*
Love shown by spouse	3.14	3.09
Interest shown by spouse	3.00	2.86
Help given by spouse in the home	2.70	3.30
Treatment by in-laws	3.08	2.92
Time spent by spouse at home	3.32	3.11
Spouse's friends	3.07	2.98
Spouse's time with children	3.33	2.98
Friendship	3.28	3.13
Sexual gratification	3.39	3.51

Source: Rhyne 1981

The technique is crude. Do men and women mean the same thing by 'love shown by spouse'? A man may feel his wife shows him love by ironing his shirts or cooking his favourite meal. A woman may feel love is when her husband brings her flowers. The research doesn't raise such questions. Further, there are obviously subtle differences, such as the difference in the time spouses spend with children. But

Rhyne's work, like that of Argyle with other techniques in another country, shows that, though fantasies about perfect mates may be very different, what matters over time is the same for both sexes. Similar bonds, feelings, and events seem to spell happiness or contentment for men and women.

More qualitative research, such as that of Whitbourne (1986), reinforces this view. Interviewees said that family life gave them personal happiness, personal fulfilment, and pride. 'In each case, moreover, the feelings are ones equally shared by men and women' (p. 69). Whitbourne carps that some of her male subjects used work as an excuse to justify spending less time with their families. She was not convinced that work was always so pressing. Still, Whitbourne agreed that men tended to see the kernel of their identity in their marriage or their family nearly as much as women did. She was slightly sceptical. Were the men in her sample really so caring or did they just say it to be socially acceptable?

There has been very little research so far into how women who have demanding jobs change their own expectations of men. Usually, when men take on the role of looking after the home and caring for the children, it's the subject of detailed negotiations. It is seen as a special move usually for a set period of time. Such 'contracts' are still unusual. When women take on the bulk of housework and child care, the assumption remains that that is normal. It may well be that, in the future, many couples will negotiate the terms on which they live together and have children together. Research data would be very useful.

In *The Psychology of Happiness* (1985), Argyle reported a 'meta analysis' of 58 studies which showed that married people are happier than unmarried people. He found a correlation of .14 between being married and well-being. Long ago, Durkheim argued that single people were less bound to society and more likely to commit suicide. Isolated people, especially if young, are more likely to try (Kreitman 1977). For men and women, the end of a relationship is usually traumatic.

Young women are more likely to attempt suicide after a romantic failure (Stengel 1961; O'Brien 1986). Brown and Harris (1975) suggested that an important trigger to depression in women was the lack of a confiding relationship with a partner, usually male. Mental health statistics show that women are more likely to suffer depression and that they often attribute that depression to problems with their partner.

Men suffer less while relationships fare badly and more when they end. Divorced men are more likely to succumb to mental illness and alcoholism than either divorced or single women. It may be that, once men don't have a close relationship, conventions and conditioning make it harder for them to talk to people to whom they are not very close. For example, Gove and Hughes (1980) noted that men find it harder to live alone or with parents because they find it harder to confide in anyone they are not having a sexual relationship with. You can talk to a woman you are close to but not to anyone else. With drinking buddies, you stay positive and never show vulnerable.

But the differences are small. Troubled relationships remain traumatic for both men and women.

It is possible to use this evidence of what people seek in relationships to frame a list of needs that men and women have. Psychologists accept that we all have similar biological needs for shelter, sleep, food, and, probably, sex. Some psychologists, like Henry Murray (1938), also tried to define a set of non-biological needs. Usually, those who create such lists assume that needs are timeless. Human beings have always had them and always will. I want to suggest that the evidence in Chapter 4 and in this chapter suggests either a subtle change in the needs of both men and women or, at least, a new willingness to acknowledge such needs. We may still, as men, be less good at expressing some emotional needs and at giving support and succour. At least, however, we are more aware than before that these failures create problems. The following list is not intended to be exclusive but is a basic set of non-sexual needs that both sexes seem to have. The expression of those needs is, however, different in some cases – a difference that needs to be realized and discussed.

The need to be loved   No one questions that both men and women need love and that, for most people, the crucial kind of love is that of a partner. A study of blue-collar men in the 1950s showed that 64 per cent of husbands had no confidantes other than their wives. Only 24 per cent of wives were as isolated. Daniel Levinson (1978) studied an upper-middle-class sample and found that American men were as lonely. Feminists tend to argue that men don't seek out friends to be close to. But that dismissive note ignores the fact that, for most men, the pressures of work (often competitive pressures) make it hard to be close friends with many other men. It may be realistic to feel too scared to show our weaknesses to colleagues. Hence we are more likely to dump on the woman to whom we are closest. If men begin to see this, we can at least begin to realize the demands we are making.

The need for a home Murray (1938) spoke of a need for a home or a base. In his day, there were no debates about housework. I've accepted the data of Gavron (1966), Oakley (1980), and Hill (1987) that women do the bulk of the house care. Their analyses leave out one crucial element of creating a home: do-it-yourself. There is little academic research on DIY, but the work done by companies who sell the products reveal the following trends. On the whole, it is the women who choose the decoration and the men who actually carry out the work. One of the leading companies in the field, W.H. Smith, which has a large chain of DIY centres told me that the bulk of goods they offer are sold to be used by men. Women make the choice of colours or patterns – which is why DIY ads often focus on things like the soft touch of pastel shades – and then leave it to the man to actually do the work. Doing the work is seen by men, perhaps, as a way of expressing their care.

Interestingly, such an idea is not totally new to social science. In a study of love in 102 couples, Margaret Reedy (1977) found that men tended to see themselves expressing love in a practical way by giving help. The researchers tended to see this as 'instrumental behaviour' rather than as a form of love. But, for men, this kind of activity is a kind of loving.

According to market research, many men list DIY as one of their main hobbies. An analysis of the way that men spend their time during the day suggests that an average of two hours a week are devoted to what is, in effect, making the nest or embellishing the home. Trew and Kilpatrick (1984) in their study of unemployed men in Belfast found that the men spent 21 per cent of their time on such 'domestic' chores, far less than most men would spend at work. Nevertheless, it was both a way of consuming time and of expressing their need and care for a home.

The need for intimacy and tenderness as opposed to sexuality This speaks for itself. Penetration is not a panacea.

The need to be part of a couple I've argued that the glamorous bachelor is rather a dated figure. Certainly, there is evidence that men as well as women like to see themselves often as part of a couple. It affirms their identity. Murray (1938) spoke of a need for affiliation. Maslow (1968) noted that for many men peak experiences related to just the kind of romantic togetherness as it did for women. Studies of men who have been divorced suggest that many of them miss being part of a couple. It is too glib to dismiss this as being another proof of the fact that men can't cope with domesticity and want someone to warm their dinner and their bed. Most men, as Whitbourne's research suggests, report some of their best experiences as being part of a couple.

The need to show love According to the feminist perspective, women are brought up to give love. They often choose to give love to inappropriate and ungrateful men. Boys are taught, on the other hand, to repress their need to love. Men become deliberately inexpert at showing love. It could be argued, however, that traditionally men have shown love in different ways. Cancian (1987) argues that in the nineteenth century love was feminized. Men acted; women felt. The definition of love became feminine. As a result, the ways in which men show love are not accepted as being proofs of love. An interesting example is the study by Reedy (1977), which showed the researchers denying that what men said was loving was so. Helping with chores or mending a fence didn't square with the more romantic conceptions of passion, yet men said they did that as a way of showing they cared. Reedy in her study, Cancian in her analysis, and Duck in his book (1987) all find evidence that men are more romantic and as aware of their desire to love as women are. Men admit more than feminist writers allow that we want to love. But the way masculine love is expressed often doesn't seem loving because of our conventional definition of love. There is a need here for both sexes to analyse the way in which perceptions of love mismatch. Men need also to be honest about the way in which some expressions of love (like fixing the car) can look like giving your partner access to resources you, as the man, control. But essentially, I would claim that men need to love as much as women do and that we know it. To suggest otherwise is to be remarkably hostile.

The need to parent There is some research which suggests that a minority of both men and women do not want to have children. But it is a minority even with men. In Chapter 8, on fatherhood, I report much work on how men enjoy being fathers. Often, they find that surprising, and often it is not easy for men to learn to be good fathers because very little prepares us for the role – especially since that role has been changing radically.

The need for power and control   Murray did not speak of a need for power but many feminists accuse men of being excessively controlling. The male role has entailed, for centuries, that men have taken the initiative in most aspects of personal relationships. The classic male for this is Stanley Kovalski, the hero of Tennessee Williams' *A Street Car Named Desire*.

Stanley Kovalski loves his wife, whom he sees as something of a slave. She has to feed him, love him, and provide beers when he and his friends play poker. None of this stops Kovalski lusting after her brittle sister, Blanche and, in the end, making love to her while his wife is giving birth. In a splendid assertion of male power, Kovalski has the sister and then has her carted off to a lunatic asylum where she has to rely 'on the kindness of strangers'. Is Kovalski a typical man? How many fathers-to-be seduce their sisters-in-law while their wives are giving birth? Men, like women, do seek power over others, but it does not have to be destructive power. Nor is it the only male need. The others I have listed are not overwhelmed by this need.

OBSTACLES TO A BETTER RELATIONSHIP

I have argued throughout this chapter that men and women need to negotiate relationships in a period of rapid social and psychological change. Old patterns are breaking down and yet remain strong. In such a confused period, it is particularly easy for mismatches to occur, for men and women to fail to understand one another. Though I have argued throughout that men are not as unskilled at intimacy as feminist writers suggest, it is still breaking with traditions for men to disclose their weaknesses and vulnerabilities. And though women want to assert themselves more in all kinds of ways, that too is breaking new ground. None of this is impossible, especially as we have become more self-conscious and self-relevatory about how we are with one another. But such talk can bring about both closeness and clashes. The clashes tend to be particularly difficult because the shifts of the last twenty years have unleashed two forces. Feminists sought to arouse and channel the anger of women at the injustices they suffered. That anger often cut off men and, perhaps, more than anyone realized, it cut off men who were trying to change in positive ways. Second, but much less recorded, is the anger of men.

The anger of men

Some psychoanalytic writers like Chodorow have suggested that men are angry with women – mainly their mothers. This initial anger dominates all subsequent relationships with women and is reinforced by social learning. Men are brought up to exploit women sexually and emotionally and to feel no guilt about doing so. Some men deny their fury by acting withdrawn, but many others glory in violence and anger. Such generalizations don't seem to fit all men very easily. Surveys tend to show that men are as ready to commit themselves to relationships as women are. Reedy (1977) found, for example, that 64 per cent of men would not marry a person they were not in love with but 25 per cent of women would. Duck (1987) has shown that men tend to say they are in love long before women say they are in love. Duck found no reason to suppose that the men who said so were insincere. Schofield asked his sample of young people back in 1964 what the men wanted out of marriage and he found that the majority of young men hoped to get married. There were a few who saw a rosy future in which they went out with lots of women and maintained a precious, promiscuous freedom. But these were exceptions, and Schofield wondered if it was bravado in the face of the interviewer that made them trumpet such an attitude. The loners like Fred who refuse to become part of what they scorn as bourgeois marriage are statistical oddities who often become social oddities. Their patter often masks depression, as they feel unable to make relationships. Feminists may suggest that such data shows that men know quite well that they will do better out of marriage. But the data also show that men acknowledge a need for relationships too.

There is, however, a different kind of anger, which is partly the result of the success of the women's movement in putting women in touch with their anger. One consequence was to make women angry with the men they were involved with. It has taken men a considerable time to respond to this, but there are increasing signs now that men are beginning to be angry about the anger of women. On the whole, this doesn't concern the very young who have grown up in the late seventies and eighties. Those worst affected by the anger are slightly older men who started relationships with women at a time of little questioning and then found themselves in a radically different situation.

164

The reaction to such anger – and the guilt and desire to retaliate that it provokes – is covered a little in Astrachan's *How Men Feel*. A more recent American book *Men Are Pigs and Deserve to Die* (Steinem 1988), is more strident. Reacting to such vitriol American men are fed up with being portrayed as sadists, sexual failures, emotional cripples, or wimps. Men too, Astrachan argues, have their hang-ups, their weaknesses, their own sense of being oppressed. Men have put up with being put down for long enough. It's time for the male versions of Greer, Millett, and de Beauvoir to pen their own liberation.

I accept there are perfectly good historical and personal reasons for women to be angry with men. But there is a reverse case. Men have their reason for their own anger. I don't think that the way to better heterosexual relationships lies through a backlash. I don't want the pendulum to swing to men now exploding with anger at women. But the chances of men and women coming to a better understanding – Utopian heterosexuality, if you like – depend on both sexes recognizing and respecting the reasons why we are angry with each other. This isn't easy to do, as I have found in my own life.

The anger of women

The danger is that, instead of using a historic opportunity to negotiate better relationships, the theoreticians of sexual politics will abandon hope. Women were angry with men. Now, men are also angry with women. Give up. Men have to understand why women in general and women they are close to and desire are angry. It will be interesting to see, however, if feminists take seriously men who in good faith also seek to explain their own case, their own anger. There is no sign, as far as I can see, of any major feminist writer accepting that the women's movement now should seek alliances with men, as many of the conditions and traditions that oppress women aren't really to the benefit of men. Cancian, who comes closer than most, still remains deeply suspicious of men. She writes (1987: 78):

> Men's power advantage over women will decline if they adopt an androgynous style of love and become more expressive, vulnerable and openly dependent while becoming more androgynous will increase women's power. Therefore, men probably resist a change towards androgynous love. The hostility of men towards the human

potential movement and talking about their feeling may be part of that resistance: they may sense that if they become more aware of their feelings of dependency and their need for care, their power over women will vanish.

It is not going to be easy for both sexes to accept mutual angers. These two barriers can be overcome within couples if couples want to work on these problems. The third problem is more intractable because it is political. I return to that in the last chapter.

MY OWN ANGER

In my own case, as I described, I initially suppressed my own anger. Rather than confront Aileen with what she was doing in our marriage, I colluded with some of it. I made it possible for her to come back to me – often when I think I should not have done. The fact that we had children was one reason, though I suspect I tended to use that in order not to make a final break. She did not make it easy or acknowledge for many years just what she was doing. One story perhaps illustrates better than anything else the sort of disadvantage at which I felt myself to be. In 1978, I went to Holland to make a film on the after-effects of being hijacked. It was the first big film I had been commissioned to make. I was alone with a crew who were not too friendly. Two days into the shoot, I rang Aileen. She told me triumphantly that she was a lesbian. She had been having a marvellous time in bed with her newest friend. Men were so inferior. I was in a phone box in Holland. Outside, there was a tough camera crew, all men – all older than I was – whom I had to direct. I ended the phone call very upset. She knew quite well what she was doing in choosing that moment to re-announce her gayness. I had to end the conversation, put down the phone, compose myself, face my crew, and discuss what we were going to do the next day.

I left the hotel early the next day and sent her a very long cable. I said I was hurt, frightened for the children, frightened for myself, frightened for our marriage. I made no threats of divorce or of taking the children away. I waited for her to ring or respond to the cable. She didn't. When I next talked to her, she told me that the cable had made her angry. I had no right, it seemed, to complain or, as it happened, to express my feelings.

It would have been better if I had gone then or we had thrashed it out. In the event, and in time, I took revenge and justified much that was not justifiable because it was my turn to be angry. My revenge was to hurt her and when, in 1983, she suggested going back together, in neither rejecting the possibility nor in giving it a try. I kept her dangling for far longer than I should have before trying for a reconciliation. I didn't do it deliberately or maliciously but I have to admit, looking back, that I justified my behaviour then to myself on the grounds that her behaviour had made me so angry.

If we are to get better relationships, both men and women need to know more about their respective angers and try to work through them. That isn't easy personally or politically. In the last chapter, I want to draw together some of the themes of the book and examine how political structures make the kinds of psychological bargaining I've talked about even harder than it is likely to be. But not impossible!

Chapter Eight

BEING A FATHER

To many men and women who have not been involved with the debates that feminism provoked, some of the more personal chapters in this book may well have seemed peculiar soap operas that happened on another planet. I don't think that is the case with this chapter. Much suggests that men are becoming far more involved as fathers than they have ever been before. If you walk along the street in London, you often see men pushing push-chairs, which would have been considered weird or wimpish fifteen years ago. Hill (1987) in a survey of child-care practices has found that a sizeable proportion of men (25 in the 62 families in his sample), spend one or two nights a month looking after the children so that their wives can go out. Hill is also critical of the difference between what fathers say they do and what they do, but his findings are revealing. Whitbourne (1986) found that many of her interviewees, American men, said they were a 'father first'. In terms of the psychological literature, this suggests an important shift. In studies in the fifties and sixties, which asked men to describe themselves, they tended to identify themselves by their profession, saying, 'I'm an engineer' or 'a car worker' or 'a bank clerk'. Very many women described themselves as a wife and mother first; almost no men described themselves first as fathers. Whitbourne, like Hill warns against totally trusting male subjects, who may be apt to over-emphasize their commitment to care but, even if it isn't wholly true, it's telling that men should want to be perceived like that. Fathering is in fashion – and that can be built on. Popular culture accepts that fathers do look after their children more, though, interestingly, the men who seem to do so are usually divorced. They come to discover quite how much their children mean to them. The seminal film was *Kramer v Kramer* in which Dustin Hoffman battled for custody, but it's interesting that films which are not specifically about children increasingly show the man caring. In *Jagged Edge*, for example, the female lawyer is separated. Her ex looks after the children regularly; when she wins her case, he takes them off so she can celebrate with her new lover. Hollywood hasn't yet majored on a working marriage where the father is the main 'caretaker' but films like *Parenthood* are paving the way.

Becoming a father was always crucial for men. It showed you had reproduced. It was genital success, but men weren't expected to take much part in the rearing of the child. Or that is accepted history. Later in the chapter, I question just how true that has been and for how long. It was true, I suspect, for most of the twentieth century in the West partly because men have had to work further away from home and partly because two wars took so many men from their homes for long periods. Few studies of the break-up of traditional communities have focused on how that affected fathering, precisely because fathers were not seen as crucial. The psychological literature from Freud on has contributed to downgrading the role of the father. Freud's Oedipus complex put fathers and children in a situation of rivalry. The child took over the mother's emotional and erotic attention. Bowlby (1981) later argued that maternal deprivation was crippling for children. If father was there – fine; if he wasn't – well, it wasn't ideal but mothers were the 'key worker'. Bowlby has said that this is an unfair reading of his texts but it was how his texts were interpreted in the culture. Feminists criticized him for guilt-tripping them into perpetual child care.

Charles Lewis in *On Becoming a Father* (1985), an analysis of psychological studies on fathering, has tried to argue that it is naïve to claim that the new emphasis on fathering is novel or owes much to feminism. Psychology has always been interested in fathers. As Lewis himself shows, there were many early studies involving fathers, but most of them didn't examine what fathers did or how much time they spent with their children. Rather, they tried to see whether the total absence of the father had an impact on the child. The motive for such research was clear; in the Second World War, millions of American and British children grew up without their fathers being present. Biller (1982) in a comprehensive review of the literature, suggests that the absence of fathers did affect boys especially. They became less good at maths and were older when they started to play masculine games. But Biller also poses a very telling question. In reviewing studies of juvenile delinquency, he claims that for many delinquent boys, the presence of the father in the home was far from an unmitigated good. Fathers might actually damage their sons' prospects for they often created conflict.

The question is telling because it is inconceivable that any psychologist would ask a similar one about mothers. Imagine Freud or Bowlby asking whether mothers were actually good for children? But fathers were seen as peripheral and potentially harmful. Lewis' attempt to reinstate the father in psychology's history is academically intriguing but rather bizarre, especially as he doesn't make any attempt to explain why certain kinds of studies were sponsored after the 1945 war.

A far more realistic assessment comes from Anthony Astrachan. In his book *How Men Feel*, he paints a dismal picture of the relationship between fathers and sons as adult American men now remember them. Only one man in six recalled their father as being there. The absent father was the typical father.

I can hardly claim that the psychological literature influenced my own attitude to having children. But nothing prepared me for the joy that my sons have brought me. Like most men, I believed that having children would tie me down. It would mean responsibility and a loss of freedom. I was afraid of accepting either of them. If it hadn't been for Aileen's determination to have a child, I would have put it off and off. I had no idea then what I would have missed. I had no idea, because my own relationship with my father hardly led me to suppose he enjoyed it. He was certainly proud of me when I did well at school but I didn't see very much of him and, like many children of unhappy marriages, I felt guilty because my parents seemed to be staying together for my sake. Both of them said as much on a number of occasions. My mother, indeed, told Aileen when she was pregnant that she didn't realize what being a mother meant and that she would regret having a child when she was so young.

My father was typical. He was often absent. There were always pressing 'business opportunities' which obliged him to roam the world. For the first nine years of my life, he often wasn't in the same country as my mother or me. When we were in France, he lived in India: when we were in Israel, he was in India. He never came on summer holidays with us though, whether this was because he had to earn a living (his version) or whether he had to pursue floozies (my mother's version) I'm unable to say. Even when he was in the same country, I didn't get to see him often. Usually, I was in bed when he got home. He complained he had to slave because we had 'estomacs luxieux', stomachs in search of luxury. On Friday evenings he made a special effort to be home in time for the sabbath meal which is a focus of Jewish family life. At sundown on Friday, the mother lights the candles and the father blesses the wine. The week's troubles are set aside for a precious twenty-four hours in the bosom, and bliss, of the family. My father, however, was often late. My mother would not be sure whether to light the candles at sundown, the proper religious custom, or to wait till he got home which she felt was more correct. If she waited, he would carp she had been sacrilegious. The sabbath waits for no man. She would carp back that he didn't care for his family.

His absences seemed normal. I only resented them when my mother got in a state about whether or not to serve dinner before he arrived. She often sniped that men weren't to be trusted. The world was full of temptations and sirens. I slowly came to realize that she didn't really believe he worked at all. For years, I accepted her suspicions, and it wasn't till I was working myself that I realized that 'business opportunities' do need to be pursued and that the pursuit takes time. People come late for meetings. Meetings go on too long. It's difficult to say you have to leave now to get home. In most businesses, it is an unacceptable excuse for a man. To give it makes you sound either bizarre or as if you are in some kind of fraught situation where you are not 'being enough of a man'. The way home isn't easy either. There's too much traffic on the roads, and trains, tubes, and buses relish being late. I spent more of my life than I care to remember in phone booths ringing Aileen to say I was stuck on platform 8 in Doncaster, that British Rail had failed again, and that I wouldn't be able to take over looking after the children until . . .

Often she was icy.

I can't help it, I'd plead. Did she think it was ecstasy being on Doncaster station?

It wasn't ecstasy dealing with the kids on her own. It wasn't ecstasy having to change her plans.

As she was angry, she didn't often point out the obvious. The children were missing me too, and I was missing out on them. For her the problem was that all this echoed her own past.

Her own father was often absent. But he accepted it as perfectly normal – as did his family. No one really saw that it was making him at times a virtual stranger in his own house – the house that his money had earned and that his wife had designed, kept up and rendered beautiful in the ornate style she found beautiful. My father had been erratic in his comings and goings. We had always lived in the centre of cities. It wasn't clear to me how much strain commuting put on men till I went to New Jersey in 1969. Aileen and I had become engaged. I had met her father before and he had seemed to like me but he knew that his wife didn't. It took him a few days to warm to me. He then asked me if I wanted to come in to work with him. I would be introduced to his colleagues at work, a sign that I was accepted.

We woke up just before 6 a.m. The rest of the house was asleep. He made himself a cup of coffee and some toast and, twenty minutes later, impeccably dressed, drove to the railway station. The drive took fifteen minutes. We waited five minutes for the train. The train journey took fifty minutes, and, on bad days, he had to stand. We got off at Hoboken and then took the PATH under the Hudson River. Then we changed on to a subway which finally spewed us out on Wall Street. William was rattled unless he was in Wall Street by 7.45. In the competitive world in which he had to succeed, he couldn't afford to let colleagues steal a march on him. He did the journey every day, leaving before his children woke up and getting back just as the younger ones went to bed. As he became more successful, business trips took him out of New York more often. He could, of course, have chosen to live differently but it would have meant far less prestige and, also, a huge cut in his family's standard of living. He was victim as well as an oppressor and he was no isolated phenomenon. Astrachan, writing of American men, noted how many understood that kind of dilemma. William Isaac La Tourette had three heart attacks, and died at 50, in Texas – working. It takes a determined effort against such economic pressures to make men spend more time with their children. The truth that both men and women pay for that has been obscured by strange political alliances.

The conventional, conservative assumption is, of course, that it is the women's job to look after the children. Ideally, the father works and the woman cares. This has meant that efforts by men (and feminist women) to get some concessions like paternity leave fall on stony ground. Even in 1981, for example, only one organization in ten granted paternity leave, according to an Alfred Marks survey. The position of the Department of Employment is that there is no political momentum for change. The Department has a point. Over the years, the TUC has not campaigned for better paternity leave or for a more flexible pattern of working that would allow couples to vary who would look after the children. It has been assumed that it is normal for fathers to spend little time with their children and to concentrate on work.

Have fathers always been like that? The historical evidence is mixed. On the one hand, much social history suggests that fathers have been more absent than present. The care of the children has been women's responsibility. Nevertheless, in pre-industrial societies, men were not as far away for as long. Men worked in villages, on the land, close to where the children were. There is some evidence that suggests that fathers were not as excluded from child care as we have thought.

HISTORICAL FATHERS

The French essayist Michel de Montaigne wrote on the duties of fathers. Montaigne had very little to say about whether fathers should look after their children, though. He wanted to persuade fathers not to be so domineering and to demand exaggerated expressions of obedience. Recently, work on the history of childhood has been dominated by Philip Aries (1962) who claimed that childhood is a nineteenth-century concept. Before that, children were too apt to die young for parents to devote too much love to them. It was counter-productive. Not surprisingly, in Aries' view, fathering didn't exist.

The British historian Linda Pollock (1984) has countered Aries' argument. She concentrated on mothers but also found many interested fathers from the sixteenth century on. John Dee, for instance, included entries in his diary on children's play. William Jefferay believed his children were 'a comfort'. Pollock reports on Dee, Jefferay and five other diarists who nursed their children through illness. The notion that the father was some grand absentee wasn't true. Fathers were expected to play a key role in education. John Locke, the philosopher, addressed advice on educating their child equally to Edward Clark and his wife. Both should be involved in the daily routine of parenting. Locke recommended that Edward Clarke talk to his child as if he were a traveller who had just landed from Japan. To the child, everything would be new and interesting. The child shouldn't be palmed off with patronizing explanations. Locke did not much believe in play, but he did recommend to Clarke a game he had invented for teaching children the alphabet. Cakes had to be baked in the shape of letters. When the child recognized a letter, he could eat it. Clarke, as the father, wasn't expected to bake – that was woman's work – but he was certainly expected to feed his child these literate sweets.

Locke was not an eccentric exception. Linda Pollock found that many texts that gave advice to parents on how to bring up children were addressed to both men and women. She also quoted a number of eighteenth- and nineteenth-century diaries kept by fathers writing of the development of their children. These often record the father being there when the child did something of note. Moore (1779–1852) described, for example, how his ten-month-old daughter learned to walk. Pollock quotes him:

> Our little Barbara is growing very amusing. She started yesterday in walking: that is, got up off the ground by herself, and walked alone to a great distance without anyone near her. Bessay's [the mother] heart was almost flying out of her mouth all the while with fright but I held her away, and would not let her assist the young adventurer.

A number of other fathers observed the progress of their children, which suggests that, whatever their shortcomings might be, some fathers must have been around to observe.

It is possible, of course, to disagree on what constitutes paternal involvement. In *On Becoming a Father* (1985), the psychologist Charles Lewis singles out D.H. Lawrence's *Sons and Lovers* as an example of the aloof father. Lewis claims that Walter Morel wasn't involved. Morel was perhaps aloof, but even he usually came home from the pit. Young Morel complains with proper Oedipal feeling of the presence of Morel because he got in the way between him and his mother. Walter Morel is rejected by his wife and his children partly because of his violence, but even Lawrence concedes that their rejection, squeezing him into a corner of the home as something of a lesser being, helped provoke his violence. Walter Morel might have been insensitive, depressing, and a poor father, but he was not an absent one. Commuting fathers may have more sensitivity these days, but they are more absent.

Advice on parenting has not always played down the part of the father. John B. Watson, the founder of behaviourism, argued in his best-selling book, *The Psychological Care of the Infant and Child* (1928), that fathers and mothers should discuss what had happened during the day before bedtime. Watson offered a somewhat too precise programme for the growing child and was perhaps unduly worried that mothers would kiss infants to death and, thereby, produce a generation of sexually inadequate children. But the father played a far more central role in his 1928 book than in the well-meaning work of Spock. When Nicholas was born in 1970, Aileen and I bought Spock's *Baby and Child Care*. It said that father ought to play a little with the children when he got home from work but father mustn't tire himself out. Romping was fun but father had to have his rest. Spock has since admitted that his ideas on the role of fathers, and the burden of mothers, were rather inadequate. But Spock was seen as the authority on child care.

Spock did not sense or hint how much his ideas were a product of a particular period. Lummis (1982) took oral histories of Norfolk families, and found that father played a far more active part in family life than was supposed but, in dealing with children, they tended to discipline and entertain, rather than change the nappies. Still, they were present to tell quaint tales of rural life.

Nevertheless, Lummis' work points to an obvious conclusion. The absentee father is, in great part, the product of economic changes in the recent past. Work forces men to spend less time at home. On the face of it, we spend less time working than Victorian men did but we spend far more travelling to and from work. Many British and American men spend hours travelling to work. In the UK people commute to London from as far North as Peterborough. Travelling to work is no longer restricted to middle-class commuters, as it once was. It is becoming much rarer for people to live close to their place of work. The result is that fathers leave early, soon after the children wake up, and return late, not long before the children need to go to bed.

It could be argued that men have not agitated for a change in the structure of work because it suits them to have women burdened with the care of children. After all, the evidence shows that most men spend the greater amount of their leisure time either in pubs (often without women) or doing DIY. With more leisure, tney could spend all of it on children.

There's some justice in such an argument, but I want to suggest that men tend not to know what they have been missing until they become active fathers. There is, moreover, no tradition of men campaigning for more time with their children. The battle for equal rights for women, for the vote, for entering professions, started during Victorian times. It took between 50 and 100 years for most demands first to be articulated, then to be debated, then to be fought for, then to be won. The idea that men might stand to gain by being equally (or indeed more) involved with the care of children is very new. Neither the Labour Party nor the trade unions show any great inclination to pursue it. A private study by the TUC shows how complacent official union attitudes have been.

In 1985, the TUC asked its affiliated unions what arrangements there were for paternity leave. Britain, unlike other EEC countries, gives men no legal right to paternity leave. According to the TUC, the British government has been blocking the EEC's wish to give all fathers a legal right to such leave.

The 1978 Employment Protection Act protects women against unfair dismissal on account of pregnancy and provides for time off for ante-natal care. They receive maternity pay and can return to their work for up to one year. Men get no government guarantees. Camden Council's equal opportunities policy is telling. Women have 16 weeks' maternity leave on full pay and 24 weeks on half pay. They are encouraged to return to work part time. They have the benefit of a 'career counselling scheme' to deal with problems. Men? Men get ten days' paternity leave and Camden is a 'right-on', progressive council.

The TUC survey found that the very best paternity deals provided for ten days of paternity leave. These were in middle-class, white-collar or 'creative' unions. The survey concluded, 'the bulk of agreements provided for either 3 or 5 days off around the time of confinement'. Many unions, however, had far less generous deals – of only one or two days off. The survey found that most men actually took between five and ten days off, but usually this had to come out of their annual holiday entitlement or had to be wangled by their reporting in sick. Often there were discretionary arrangements. Many union officials thought their members did better with these informal arrangements, but 'most discretionary arrangements were less generous than average in the duration of leave permitted'. Somewhat oddly, the survey went on to examine leave for 'family reasons', which one might expect to include the need to look after a child. But 'family reasons' meant bereavement. Most industries gave between one to three days off for the death of a spouse. The idea that men might need to have long periods off to look after their children did not seem to register even as a possibility to the unions replying. In such circumstances, it's not surprising that many men find it hard to be fully involved fathers – even today.

A study for the Equal Opportunities Commission (1983) found that 217 men out of 260 did take time off at the birth of their child but that they had to be careful not to take too much. Typically, they had to use up holiday time and other credits, otherwise it might jeopardize their promotion. It's a classic instance of how the organization of work makes it hard for individuals to make alternative choices. You and your partner have to be willing to make extreme changes in order to alter traditional patterns. To be an equal parent, a father who takes as much responsibility as a mother, requires a very conscious commitment. I write that as one who has made something of a commitment to do it but never quite enough to alter things really profoundly.

Paradoxically, unemployment ought to offer a golden opportunity to change. But long-term unemployed don't automatically give their time to their families. In a study of how unemployed men in Belfast and Brighton behaved, Trew and Kilpatrick (1984) found that some but not all devoted more time to their children, taking them to school. They spent 50 per cent more time with their children and roughly 50 per cent more time fixing up their house or flat. At the weekend, their use of time was much more similar to employed men's. Smith (1987), in a review of health and unemployment, found that few men spent the time they used to spend working looking after their children.

Even where men have made a commitment to more child care, there is some evidence that we have been very choosy in what part of the care we get involved with. Feminists have complained that women still get left with the more arduous aspects of child care – the cleaning, arranging meals, and, surprisingly, often the discipline. When men do spend more time with children, it centres on playing. That may be good for the children and for the men, but it's unfair for the mothers. Astrachan (1985), in his interviews with a number of full-time American fathers, notes that many men who take on full-time child care get to a point when they complain that it's not fun but, often, boring, stressful, and hard. The justice of the feminist complaint does not mean, however, that fathers benefit from not being involved. We have been excluded from our children for too long. There are some signs that it's changing, but it isn't easy to achieve as it means making sacrifices.

Going to Greece while Aileen was pregnant was a very deliberate

177

attempt to be less intense about work and be closer to her, to Nicholas, and to our child she was carrying. When we came back from Greece, we were poor and she was about to give birth. I had suddenly been offered a job I very much wanted. As she prepared to give birth, both of us were too excited to wonder if that had already sown the seeds of future trouble. We had learned something from the experience of having Nicholas in hospital. Though it wasn't easy to arrange in 1975, we insisted on her having the baby at home. It would mean we would all be together.

There were some unexpected problems. The first one was the midwife, Miss Church, who saw men as something nature had required for conception but not for much else. The second problem was what to do with Nicholas. We took fright at the complexes it could create if he was at home while his mother was screaming in a room he could not be allowed to enter. It would make him delinquent in later life. So, we fixed a special treat for him – his first night away from home. We prepared him for it and set it up as a special, grown-up occasion. He was to stay with friends of his whose parents would pamper him on that night.

The next problem was the light. The midwife came and said, meaningfully: 'It's dark in here.' Aileen bought a 200-watt bulb which made the bedroom so bright we seemed to be in hospital. Months before the due dates, the midwife also delivered a mysterious-looking plain brown box that said 'Not to be opened . . . except in the presence of a midwife or doctor'. She never said it contained all her sterile materials so we wondered what lurked inside as we secreted it on top of the cupboard.

Well before the time, Miss Church came to examine Aileen at home. She had been trained before the Second World War and liked to reminisce. In her days, you had to pay to study to be a nurse; you were made to scrub floors. You could never go out. Now nurses expected to have a social life. And, as for money, she recalled that when they were given free tickets to plays or films, they could not afford the bus fare. She had delivered the children and grandchildren of babies she had delivered.

As opposed to the hospital where I felt, as a man, a complete interloper, at home, I had to be included. The closer the dates came, the more the midwife handed out useful titbits of information. She would need jugs, bowls, and jars. We had to have the phone numbers where she or the duty midwife could be contacted day or night.

Unlike the hospital, which disapproved of false alarms, she said we weren't to hesitate to ring at any time.

A week after one false alarm, Aileen's waters broke. She rang me and I raced home. The midwife had already got there and had made Aileen comfortable. I was told firmly to 'get my meal' by her and, when Aileen, in the middle of a contraction, asked where I was, she was told I was eating. It hadn't occurred to me to argue with Miss Church. Aileen waited on our bed which was covered with a rubber sheet. Contractions came and went. From decades of experience, Miss Church said she thought it wouldn't be long. She hoped Aileen would delay a little, she grinned, because then she might be able to force the doctor to give her his home phone number. Aileen obliged. By the time it was polite to ring him, Miss Church didn't need to, she stressed, but medical etiquette required it.

It was too late to get him at his surgery. She called him. 'Remind me to pay you for that,' she said.

Aileen had another contraction. I held her hand. I suddenly wondered if I shouldn't be wearing a mask or a white coat or something. No, said Miss Church, as long as I washed my hands. And put a kettle on. I could do that in between contractions.

Waiting while Aileen went through the first and second stages had a wonderfully surreal feel. We were entertaining the midwife. It was like a party. In the middle the doctor, an amiable middle-aged man, arrived, and complained that this might be the last baby he would deliver at home. It made him sad. To have nothing but hospital deliveries would be boring.

The contractions became more urgent. I sat down by Aileen's side so that she could grip various bits of me. The midwife asked if Aileen would like to have gas to breathe when it became painful, just to take her mind off it. She placed the gas at her side and offered it without pressing her in any way. Towards the end, Aileen took it. There was no insistence.

One of the things she had regretted about the birth of Nicholas was that she had not been able to see him come out. She had prepared a mirror, and when Reuben began to emerge, she asked me to hold it up. As I couldn't hold the mirror and be there to be gripped, the doctor took it from me and, sitting at the end of the bed, he held the mirror. She could see Reuben's head coming out through the film of blood and mucus. It was amazing how quickly it happened. Within ten minutes of the head starting to appear, he was born and screaming.

The differences with the hospital were telling. Aileen got to hold the baby. I got to hold the baby before he was washed down. I went to the kitchen to get the bottle of champagne we had bought to celebrate. The doctor and midwive seemed to be delighted by this extravagance. We all sipped our champagne and admired Reuben, whom Aileen was holding. The doctor dipped his finger in his champagne and put it to Reuben's lips. It would make him sleep better, he said.

It did. For the first two days of his life, Reuben was a model sleeping baby. After the shared drink, medical efficiency reasserted itself. Within thirty minutes, the bedroom was transformed back into our bedroom. Reuben had been washed, changed, and put to bed in his cot after screaming enough to convince us all that his lungs were in perfect working order. We were given the phone numbers we should ring – 'Don't hesitate, day or night' – if we wanted the midwife to come. They all left and we were left with a new baby. The immensity of it didn't sink in at all. Perhaps because it was so casual. That was one of its pleasures. At the same time, Aileen always felt it was secure and safe. So did I. And from the father's point of view, there is one great advantage. He is not excluded from what happens after the baby is born. When Reuben woke four hours later for his first breast-feed, I was there. I changed his second or third nappy. Then he went on howling a little and I walked him around. He howled so much that the woman downstairs rang, and said: 'I expect congratulations are in order.' If you believe that the first few hours after a baby is born are crucial just not for the baby, but also for making the parents attached to the child, there are obvious advantages if the father can be there after the baby is born.

Luck designed it so that our child was born on a Thursday night. I took Friday off. Then there was the weekend. I also took Monday off. By the time I went back to work, I was totally used to the routine of caring for the baby and felt pretty responsible for him. I don't think I managed to feel equally responsible but I certainly felt much more responsible and competent than I had with our first child. I didn't shiver with fear at the idea of so small a living thing in my arms. I didn't treat him as a jelly or gelignite.

It was important for me to be so closely involved with Reuben's birth. It didn't make for magic solutions. I still had to go back to work quickly. But I didn't suffer the feeling I had when Nicholas had been born – that all this was marvellous but far away from me.

THE STATISTICS OF EXCLUSION

Ironically, given his argument that it is unjust to accuse psychology of having neglected fathers, Lewis (1985) has shown that fathers are often left out from the start of the pregnancy. His study of a Nottingham general practice showed that in 80 per cent of cases doctors excluded the father as a matter of routine. He was relegated to a lowly part of the 'delivery' team. Lewis refers a little oddly to these fathers as 'sturdy oaks'. Unfortunately, he doesn't examine what impact being excluded had on their view of themselves and on their sense of competence as fathers. Did it, for example, make them lose confidence in their ability to look after their children? Feminist writers have shown that being discriminated against in certain areas, such as high-powered jobs, destroyed women's self-confidence. Is it fanciful to suppose that men suffer in parallel ways, especially as the psychological literature turns the father into a marginal figure? Some authors (some, admittedly, men) go so far as to argue that the father will be hostile to the new baby since both compete for the mother's attention.

The ways in which doctors, nurses, and midwives behaved towards me at the birth of our children meant that I was not surprised by Lewis' findings in Nottingham. It is telling that often the medical professionals had no embarrassment about 'sidelining', as Lewis put it, the fathers. That was normal. As a result, however, something quite abnormal occurred. Fathers were not allowed to take a full part in the pregnancy, the delivery, or the care of their child. Much evidence on the formation of the bond between mothers and children emphasizes how crucial the period just after the birth is. Mothers have to touch and hold their new infants. Some research suggests that if they are not given the chance to do so it becomes harder for them to love their new baby and that the risk of post-natal depression is greater.

It seems likely that fathers also need that initial contact with their child in order to create a bond. Given that our culture assumes that fathers will have less to do with babies, such early touching is perhaps specially needed. Lewis found that new fathers were likely to be nervous about their role. Fathering was unfamiliar and they needed encouragement. Instead, doctors and hospitals say that you are in the way and, really, a peek and quick cuddle with your baby is all you need.

Feminist critiques suggest that men themselves, or patriarchal institutions, are to blame. They have erected the structures that ban men or deny them much access to babies. Men didn't want to cope with the messiness of birth and, in earlier times, with seeing the dangers that women ran. It is true that some institutions involved, such as the medical profession and hospitals, are dominated by men. In the nineteenth century male doctors took obstetrics and gynaecology over from female midwives. In an excellent article, Wertz and Wertz (1977) show how male doctors triumphed over less specialized women. In the seventeenth century, the family Chamberlen, for instance, discovered how to deliver difficult babies using two spoons. This was the origins of the forceps delivery. Cleverly, the family kept their discovery secret and became accoucheurs to the British royal family. Their success as technocrats of birth helped confirm men as specialists in delivery. Poor hygiene in the home made it sensible to shift births to hospitals, an environment that male doctors controlled. Wertz and Wertz tend to ignore the powerful roles of nurses and do not examine an obvious paradox. The professional men who excluded other ordinary men from the process of birth saw themselves as experts. They did not identify themselves as men but as doctors. They did not think of the consequences for men who were now barred from the process of being in at the birth of their own children.

Professional men were not the only group responsible for this exclusion. Powerful female professional groups such as nurses collaborated in keeping men away from births. Feminists shouldn't find the idea that men are excluded by medical professionals too outlandish since they themselves argue that hospitals often treat mothers as annoying presences. The medical miracle of birth could be performed so much better without the all too lay presence of parents.

Hospitals saw it as natural and uncontroversial to exclude fathers from birth onward. No movement fought for fathers' rights to be involved as they did for women to be allowed equal opportunities for jobs. Men didn't understand what they were missing, perhaps because it isn't easy to articulate what you learn and gain when you begin to take fathering seriously. It involves precisely the sort of emotions – and they include being frightened for your children – that men are traditionally encouraged to suppress.

A father knows, of course, moments of triumph. When Reuben was 3, he was 'interviewed' in order to go to a smart kindergarten. He did all the jigsaws perfectly, recognized the letters they asked him to recognize, chatted intelligently, and, when asked to give the names of a variety of objects, commented: 'Ah, this is my exam.' When Nicholas was eighteen months old, he laughed for long minutes at his first sight of the sea. It was wonderful. But most child care isn't a sequence of highs. It's ordinary, requires a lot of patience and attention, and it isn't obvious what you get from it as it is going on.

I know, however, that I enjoyed being with my children from when they were little as much as I have enjoyed anything I have ever done. Slowly, men are beginning to understand what we have generally lost, though all too often it is pitched in terms of guilt.

Whitbourne (1986: 67) records one father who said that he had spent far more time with his son after the age of 5 than he had done before. The man admitted:

> Those years were important to me anyway. But like I said I couldn't be home and run a business at the same time. Today, I got help, it's different. In those days I didn't have no help, I was all by myself. You know, in other words, I wasn't home but I used to call him on the phone, you know, and 99 times he was sleeping, I have guilt but no regrets. . . . I feel bad with guilt because I wasn't there. Those growing years. But in other words, I wasn't doing anything for myself. In a sense it was for myself.

But he added that if he had been employed by another company he'd have had to do overtime.

Whitbourne's subject records the classic conflict between the demands of work and children. It is not a conflict that is easy to resolve. That is especially so if the work you do is apt to be unpredictable. I didn't give up my career but I did try to enshrine one or two routines.

The most regular commitment I took on was to take Nicholas and Reuben to play school each day so that Aileen could write in the mornings. The play school was in Greenwich. Nearly every day at 8 or 8.15 we left, and I walked Nicholas through the park to the play school where he stayed till 12 o'clock when Aileen picked him up. I can't now remember what we talked about, but we chattered during the whole half-hour walk. Over the three years I did this, we tried all the different routes through the park. When Reuben was born, we moved to a different house and it was too far, and less pretty, to walk him to the play school. I still took him in the mornings since Aileen needed the time to write, but it was very different travelling in a cab.

Taking your children to school if you can't drive has its comic moments. After two years at his first play school, Reuben passed his 'exam' to go to the nursery school attached to the prep school Nicholas was attending. The nursery was half a mile away from the prep school, and the only way to get Reuben there was for me to travel with Nicholas and Reuben on the school bus. Then I would walk Reuben down to the school. I liked the walk as I had liked walking with Nicholas, because it was time to be with Reuben with nothing to distract me. Often, we'd get to the nursery early and walk round the field. Such routines sound boring but they set a relationship.

The best time was when we went to Greece, as I've explained in an earlier chapter. One day, I had Nicholas in the morning and Aileen wrote; the next day, I wrote in the mornings. Even then, the need to make a living intruded and one or two days a week I'd go to Athens to file a story, but I loved walking with Nicholas on the beach day after day.

I went back to work. I didn't choose to do something different and Aileen didn't choose to, either. In our different ways, we were both ambitious and wouldn't sacrifice those ambitions in order to create a better a marriage and a fairer division both of child care and of earning money.

In Greece, being with Nicholas so much, I became interested in what made children laugh. I had vaguely wanted not to abandon psychology and thought of doing a Ph.D. Children's laughter was neglected since it can't be fabricated in the laboratory easily. It needed to be studied in the family. I got a grant to observe my own children's laughter and, for some of the next three years, I scribbled down most of the times they laughed. There was a video-camera in the house to catch some moments. I found that children learn ridiculous games from their parents and, from an early age, know they can use humour to deflect rebukes and, sometimes, to provoke. I've given a long account of this in *The Development of Play* (1987) and, of all the pieces of research I've done, it was the most fun.

I didn't stop making films. Partly, the grant money wasn't enough to live on comfortably and, partly, ironically, I got opportunities to make films that I had never had before. It was an imperfect compromise and, of course, at the time, much was wrong in my marriage. Taking more care of the children couldn't be isolated but it was always, at the very least, a simple, consoling pleasure.

Very little research has looked at what fathers gain from being more involved with their children. Generally, studies have only compared children whose fathers are completely absent and those who have them. 'Father-absent' children score lower on every achievement test

(Blanchard and Biller 1971), and are poor at motor skills, perceptual designs, and, especially, in reading comprehension (Lessing 1970). The whole style of personality alters. Carlsmith (1964) found that boys brought up without fathers had a distinct, far more feminine pattern of responses on aptitude scales. Girls were less affected because they didn't face the problems of a lack of a proper role model for their sex.

Few studies actually looked at what fathers did with their children. Biller (1982) in his work on 'father-absent' children used the following criterion for high father involvement. The father would spend two hours or more a day with the child. Ironically, that shows how low expectations were of what the father would do. Fathers were not expected to be either present or active.

FATHERING SKILLS

It is virtually impossible to define the skills that a good parent needs. There have always been fads and fashions in child care. We have veered from the very disciplined to the very liberal. It is hard, therefore, to be able to write a manual of good fathering. It seems clear to me that many of the things parents (male or female) need to do aren't particularly skilled and need to be demystified. The most basic one is to spend time with one's children and to talk to them. It's important to have sense about how to handle crises, which often means saying 'no' to certain requests or insisting that little Harry can't get away for the third night running with not doing his homework and rushing it on the school bus. But it is also important for fathers not to be bamboozled into thinking that child care needs specialist training. Everyone will learn to be a parent in different ways, but the rules are few and obvious. Take care of the safety of your children. Enjoy them. Show them love and interest. Never hurt them physically. Listen to them and make sure you talk to them. The list sounds banal. But it's important for men not to feel that somehow this is a mysterious feminine skill that is beyond them.

Sandra Bem (1974), in her studies of androgyny, found that men did rate child care as a feminine kind of task. Nevertheless, many men were surprisingly competent. She showed that on average men spent three hours a day with their children. Men who bottle-feed their children stick at it as long as women and give their infants as much formula, S and M. Later studies have shown that fathers respond quite as much as mothers to the cries of their infant children and that, given the chance, they play with them as long as mothers. Two differences emerge, however. Men tend to play rougher, more physical games and, after an infant is a year old, they play in a way that reinforces conventional sex roles. They play soldiers with their sons and dolls with their daughters. It has been suggested that men cling to these stereotypes because playing with children is seen as being risky for the male. To prove you are not engaging in some form of perverse behaviour, you act supermale. This is paradoxical, of course, but not hard to understand.

It is possible to argue that the kind of results Bem found were based on men's desire to give a good impression. Everyone wants to seem caring and if not liberated, at least not the kind of reactionary male who regards a baby's bottle as some kind of taboo. The laboratory evidence might suggest that men were nurturing whether they thought they were being watched or not, but was that real? It's a problem that many psychology experiments face.

The imperfect design of this study certainly made it possible that the men were being crafty and trying to put on a good show of caring. Few psychological experiments are so perfectly designed to rule out the possibility that subjects fake 'good', ie, what is socially desirable. Subjects tend to know what is being studied, especially if the basic situation is that men are with children. One of the most famous social psychology experiments was Stanley Milgram's study of obedience (1974). Milgram discovered that nice, decent, democratic Americans were willing to deliver what they believed were 'electric shocks' to other decent Americans when the latter failed to answer maths problems correctly. The subjects who gave the shocks could hear screams and pleas for mercy but, though some sweated, they persevered with punishing the mathematically inadequate even when the level of pain they were told to inflict passed red danger marks and a skull and crossbones. Milgram argued that this compliance showed how prone we all were to obey orders. For him, it helped explain the power of the Nazis. The social psychologist Rom Harre (1981) argued that Milgram simply didn't give his subjects credit. They knew they were at Yale, in a reputable university, where people didn't get maimed or killed. Many of them had an inkling that psychologists played a variety of weird games. So when they were asked to give shocks they weren't fooled. Nothing Milgram could manipulate in the lab could supersede the more important social setting of a respectable university. The Milgram-Harre argument illustrates a perpetual problem in psychology – that of making sure that subjects don't know too much about what is being studied. Imperfect as it might be, the evidence suggests that men aren't so frightened and clumsy in their dealings with children. Men have everything to gain in developing those skills but, to do it, we need the support of women. It has been argued, worryingly, by some writers like Katharine Whitehorn that women ought to be wary of helping men become good fathers. We are robbing them, Whitehorn argues, of one of the domains that women have preserved as their own. I don't think women or men will gain much from such defensiveness.

In my work as a film-maker, it's become anecdotally clear that some men are making a rather different commitment to fatherhood. I got clear evidence of this when I was commissioned to direct my first drama.

The first cameraman I wanted, Mike, was eager to work with me. Like me, he had made many documentaries. A drama would be wonderful, a step towards the fabled world of features. Two days after he agreed to do it, he rang me and sounded anxious. He was in the country. His wife had just given birth. To do the film would mean leaving her alone with the baby at a critical time. He was very sorry but he couldn't take on the drama. In two or three months, he would love to but, just at the moment, it wasn't possible. He had other priorities.

Outside King's Cross, a man with long grubby hair pushes a baby in a buggy. The man wears cowboy boots, a horror movie T-shirt, and tatty jeans. He looks rough and paradoxical. Tough boots, macho, lurid T-shirt. But he has soft hair and, even softer, he is pushing the baby. He waves across the road to a friend. The friend wanders over. There is no softness about this man, who completely ignores the baby. The father pays total attention to his friend so that the buggy becomes something alien, detached. Then, the friend wanders off and the father bends down, smiles at his kid, and gurgles at him before walking on down the road.

Carl, the second cameraman I approached, asked where the filming was going to take place.

'London.'

'Oh that's very attractive, I don't like to be away from my kids too much,' he said.

Cameramen are not saints or the vanguard of enlightened new men, but these anecdotes illustrate a trend that statistics and research support. It is true, of course, that the entertainment industry is

187

privileged. Cameramen can earn £200 a day, so they don't have to work every day. But the choices these two men made were telling: of a conscious decision not to put work first, on some days at least.

If the commitment of these cameramen illustrates a well-documented trend, one should not get idealistic about it. Lamb (1976) showed that even highly participant fathers do little caring for the children compared with women. Stewart Clarke (1978) found that very present fathers didn't engage in as much child care as mothers, though both of these studies don't rate just spending time with children as important.

A recent study shows how important it is for men not to retreat into thinking that looking after children is some female mystery full of activities men can't master. Hill (1987) found that about half the fathers (29 out of his sample of 62) were said to care for the child alone at least once a week. Most commonly fathers did it to let their wives have an evening out on their own. Hill gave couples diaries to fill, and learned that men tended to engage more in fun tasks, like playing, and the lesser burdens of housework like washing up. Less pleasant tasks, like changing shitty nappies, were left to the women. Hill snipes: 'There were a number of evasive techniques employed by fathers to justify not doing certain things.' Looking incompetent and expressing distaste were good ploys. Hill rated the domestic contribution of fathers. How much did they shop, wash up, wash clothes, clean the house, cook, change nappies, get children ready for bed? In 12 families out of 62, the father made little contribution. In 34 families, the father or the outside carers made an important contribution. In 16 families, the father won his domestic spurs with a high domestic score. Even participating fathers, however, rarely take initiative in making the arrangements for baby-sitting.

Hill suspected that men were prone to exaggerate their contribution. Hill noted dryly that fathers 'were said to care'. Whitbourne (1986) was similarly sceptical. There were a number of embarrassing pauses when she interviewed couples. A husband had just declared he regularly did much child care or housework: his wife looked deeply sceptical or said he was lying or dreaming.

Despite the need for sceptical caution, this suggests the start of positive changes. At least, many men are beginning to understand what we lose by not caring for our children. I have argued that we risk much by too much concentration on work. Feminists rightly point out that the unfair burden of looking after children, especially little children, causes much unhappiness. The benefits of change seem obvious. Here is an instance where one could achieve what feminists sometimes deride as 'Utopian heterosexuality' because there is much to be gained all round. It requires both personal and political action. Men need to be more willing to change their work lives to focus on children. Women need to accept men as equal parents, which is not always easy for them. Most crucially, we need a political agenda for change which gives women better job opportunities and men far more flexibility in their careers. This I look at in the next chapter.

Chapter Nine

A GENDER FOR CHANGE

I am writing this chapter after the children have gone to school. Aileen and I live in different houses now, half a mile apart. The children come to me on Sunday afternoon and stay till Tuesday morning. In order to be a practical and present father I've done what I once told myself was impossible; I've rescheduled my work. I organize things so as to have plenty of time on Monday to be back when they get in from school. Or nearly always. Ironically, it's no longer that necessary. Nicholas is 16 and Reuben is 13. They can both let themselves in, get on with their homework, even cook themselves a meal if they have to. They like me to be here but suffer little if I get in at six or seven. Often, like many teenagers, the last thing they want is to have to tell a parent what their day was like or what happened at school.

To some extent, I am able to arrange Sunday and Monday in this way because I feel more secure in my work. I wish I had been around more when the children were younger but I believed, as men are conditioned to believe, that I couldn't take the risk of neglecting work. That feeling wasn't all illusion. Getting work becomes easier with time, contacts, and confidence. At 25, everyone asks you to prove that you can write an article or make a film. By the age of 35, if you are still fighting those particular battles, something has not worked out right.

There are exceptions to this arrangement. If something absolutely has to be done on a Monday (and now that means that some event has to be filmed), Aileen will have the children. Despite living separately, we spend some time together. We've managed to forgive each other the pain we've caused each other, which is why I've dedicated this book to her. I hope our relationship will get better.

I know, however, that I am lucky. Far more than most people, I can set the timetable for my work. It wasn't easy for me to believe that I could and it was only after we separated when I had rigorously to make time to be with my children, that I tried as hard as I could to make it possible. I have often failed but at least I can see that the assumption that work generally has to come first can be obsessional and can be untrue.

In the last year, there has been much nostalgia and contemplation of 1968, the year when the revolution nearly happened or failed. It is all too clear that the glorious, if nebulous, revolution never came. When students were marching, the one item that was not on the agenda was sex roles. Oddly, it could be argued that one of the most important social changes of the last twenty years has been in precisely those areas that were ignored in the demos and street battles of 1968. Despite many setbacks and disappointments, feminists have succeeded in making clear the justice and necessity of equal rights and opportunities for women. Slowly, the attitudes of many men are changing. I am not suggesting some Panglossian scenario, but what is clear is that there have been large changes in the way women think of themselves and in the way we all view relationships between the sexes. In other parts of this book I've tried to suggest that men are not so wedded to the macho image. Macho itself has become something of a joke. Only those who are insecure have to put on the macho. Masculine heroes are no longer so old-style masculine, and, as I tried to suggest, one of the problems men face is that there is a confusion of role models to identify with. Even as apparently diehard a hero as Clint Eastwood, heir to John Wayne, has in some of his films tried to cope with feminist heroines.

I've tried to analyse psychological evidence which shows that many men are willing to change and that it is no longer accurate to claim that hard men are exclusively interested in things while sensitive women are interested in people. Rather, what we know (which is limited and flawed) shows that, for both sexes, relationships seem central. We judge the success and failure of much of our lives by the success and failure of relationships. I don't deny the evidence of the violence of men. Nevertheless, the now orthodox feminist argument that men don't care about women seems wrong. Some men don't know how to care, but to feather and tar the whole sex seems extreme.

There is some suggestion too that couples can identify the ways their relationship is not working out for them and agree to try out changes. Change is never easy. Smithers (1986), for example, has found that when women return to higher education, the men they live with often find that very hard to handle. But not all the evidence is depressing. Cancian found many couples who managed to negotiate changes and, in the best mush of personal growth, to grow together. It's possible to see how changes would benefit both partners. Negotiating who will earn the money and who will look after the children and the house can improve relationships, especially if each partner comes to see the problems the other has been having.

Not everyone has the luxury of making such choices. Usually it's only an option for the well-off, the well-educated, and the well-qualified. It's much easier if there is some hope of tinkering with arrangements at work. If I can get to the office fifteen minutes later, then I can drop the children off at school, leaving my partner time for herself. In Britain, apart from a few local authorities and voluntary organizations committed to job-sharing, employers do very little to help such arrangements. Employees are supposed to work conventional hours. No one has made such restructuring of work a priority.

Given no official initiative, there are limits to what individual couples can achieve. Feminism started out with a political agenda. It involved equal opportunities, equal rights, and equal pay. These have all become left-wing issues in the last twenty years, but, ironically, in Britain, the main left-wing organization, the Labour movement, has done little to promote them. Women trade unionists have often complained of how hard they have had to fight to achieve any measure of equality within the union movement. There were women cabinet ministers and, indeed, a woman prime minister long before there was a woman general secretary of a union. Brenda Dean, the first woman general secretary, is the head of a small union. It is surprising that feminists have succeeded to the extent they have given the fact that the Right opposes most of their demands – women shouldn't be seen as an oppressed class – while the Left concedes the justice of their case but takes little action – working class men are perceived by their leaders as having too much to lose. (We won't be mean and ask just how much working-class leaders have to lose.)

One of the failures of feminism has been its failure to engage sympathetic men as allies. By focusing almost exclusively on the rights that women need to gain, feminists have seemed to suggest either that men will gain nothing from this at all or that they will lose. The Marxist perspective of many feminist writers has reinforced this trend. If the oppressed are to win freedom, the oppressors must lose power. These tactics are understandable and, given what feminists had to struggle against, perhaps inevitable. The silence and defensiveness of men contributed to this view. Feminism could only succeed against men by making men give up things they wanted. Ergo, men were the enemy even if, in order not to seem too hostile, the official enemy was patriarchy.

Feminism has important achievements but such divisive 'battle of the sexes' tactics are, perhaps, no longer the most effective ones. I have tried to show that men too have a lot to gain by the kind of political and economic changes discussed – but, often, we don't realize it. Feminists ought to attempt to make men see the potential advantages. There will, of course, be large numbers of angry, sneering, or frightened men who will insist that they want the world kept the way it always was. There are, however, many other kinds of men too who, I suspect, have already realized that expressing feelings doesn't wreck one's masculinity and that it is wonderful to help look after one's children. Feminists could help by reaching out to them.

Such reaching out is important because some of the changes that are necessary are political changes – and most focus around the way we work.

Writing as a middle-class man who likes his work, it's easy to forget that for most men work is a drag. Job satisfaction is often a myth. Many men and women work to earn a living. They do not like work, and the main status it provides is the status of earning money and providing for themselves and their families. It's not a simple question of class. Miners, railwaymen, and seamen, all traditionally working-class, take pride in their work. In some white-collar jobs, men express much dissatisfaction. But there is a large body of men for whom work isn't a pleasure or a source of power. Give such men the chance to think about how they work differently, create more options for flexible employment, and there will be hope of altering the way in which men and women in couples arrange the way they live. It's true that some men may lose some economic power, but they are likely to gain in quality of life.

I am not suggesting that men stop working. The social psychologist Marie Jahoda (1981) has shown that, in our organization of society at least, going to work provides structure and a way of passing time. The unemployed suffer. But there is a big difference between organizing your life round work (which is what we do now, even though few men work more than 45 hours a week) and fitting necessary work into the rest of your life which has at least equal importance. In the

1960s, when we were about to be pitched into the leisure society, with robots doing all the dirty jobs, a few social scientists did pay attention to how technological changes could promote better lives. The economic crises of 1973 and after brought such fear of unemployment that not working became something to be terrified of. Now, it is surely time to reconsider such questions as the use of leisure time, a topic that hasn't attracted much serious work because it doesn't feel serious. Taking leisure seriously for men, means being less involved and less invested in work. It means taking less competitive pleasure out of it. It means examining and seeing what they stand to gain out of the following issues:

1 Equal training for women.
2 Equal pay so that it will be economically easier for women to spend time working.
3 More flexible career structures so that you don't get stuck and bypassed for promotion if you take time off to look after children and/or house. Men need to confront their fears about that and to be willing to think far more radically about retraining.
4 Proper funding for proper child-minding arrangements. The continued failure of governments of all complexions to provide adequate facilities is scandalous.
5 Some analysis of the age structure by which we organize work. At present, the time when men are supposed to concentrate most on their careers – from the age of 25 to 45, say – is the period when family stresses are likely to be highest. What kind of jobs might give more opportunity from 40 onwards? Industrial psychologists argue that we waste executives after 40 and deny them all kinds of chances. It is worth considering what happened if men and women had a chance to share jobs or do part time jobs while their children were small knowing that, after 40, they had good job opportunities. More employment prospects for the over forties might make sharing child care easier.

There is a need of serious discussion and initiatives on job-sharing. This often appeared a radical fancy, but men do stand to gain much by way of the quality of their life especially through having more time for themselves.

No European country has yet taken seriously on board the question of the emotional quality of life. The psychological evidence makes it clear that even in a materialistic country like the United States income is not perceived as the main cause of happiness. Mr Micawber got it wrong. Consumerism does not guarantee bliss, and many people are more than dimly aware of it. The trouble is how to turn this perception that a new car, a new dishwasher, and a new carpet do not result in more happiness. So far, the only political movement to have raised such issues is the Green movement. Its focus is ecological. Similar questions can be asked from a humanist perspective. The 'good life' may involve fewer goods and more life.

Feminists have, of course, developed some links with the Green movement but, in general, they have not tried to show men that curing their own oppression can help men too. I'm not suggesting that feminism should exist to make life better for men. Rather, many of its goals are political and can only be achieved by getting some men on their side. Feminists have not bothered so far to do this. Their failure is perhaps especially ironic because, as women become more equal, they seem to be acquiring the diseases of stress (too much smoking, heart attacks, more strokes) that men have suffered from. Equality has not made women more free but enslaved them in different ways, in the ways men are enslaved. Patriarchal attitudes aren't much good for most men either.

Given the kinds of trends I've suggested, we need political debate on such issues. However, there is little sign of any British political party encouraging it. The Conservative Party is too wedded to greed. The Labour Party in its present orientation wants to shed any kind of profound radical image. The Social Democrats, who ought to be in the forefront of such thinking, have given no lead. If the Greens offer thinking here, they haven't publicized it well. This lack of debate is odd because some economists like Schumacher did raise such issues in the seventies. Moreover, resolving such issues isn't wholly unrealistic when you consider that more people are working for themselves, more people are working from home and the magic of some communication advances means I can fax the world from my living room while making sure baby sleeps. Electronic terminals do make it possible to think of working from places that it would once have been impossible to imagine. We need to troop to the factory or the office far less than any previous generation. We are potentially freer, but few are really thinking through the options.

We need to widen political debate in order to consider such issues. Men need to confront the possibility of losing some power so as to gain more joy and, oddly, more control of their lives. People aren't natural martyrs or masochists. Men won't give up what they have till they see that they might get something, something different but good, in return. I believe we have a lot to gain from considering such changes but we have to discuss and debate how they might happen. The psychological evidence suggests that many men are willing to be different. But such possibilities need to be put on the political agenda. It will take work. It will take improbable alliances. But I think it's possible.

It is time men reacted positively to changes that women have created for themselves. Many of us are trying – imperfectly. It's time that men and women, women and men, put such issues on the political agenda to enable us all to live better.

BIBLIOGRAPHY

Argyle, M. (1975) *Bodily Communication*, London: Methuen.
Argyle, M. (1985) *The Psychology of Happiness*, London: Methuen.
Argyris, M. (1957) *Personality and Organisation*, New York: Harper.
Aries, P. (1962) *Century of Childhood*, London: Cape.
Aristotle (1972) *The Poetics*, Harmondsworth: Penguin.
Astrachan, A. (1985) *How Men Feel*, New York: Anchor Books.
Barlow, D. (1983) 'Anxiety increases sexual arousal', *J. of Abnormal Psych.* 92: 49–54.
Beauvoir, S. de (1949) *The Second Sex*, Harmondsworth: Penguin.
Bem, S. (1974) 'The measurement of psychological androgyny', *J. of Consulting and Clinical Psych.* 42: 155–62.
Biller, H. (1982) 'Fatherhood: implications for child and adult development', in B. Wolman (ed.) *Handbook of Developmental Psychology*, Englewood Cliffs, NJ: Prentice Hall.
Blanchard, J. and Biller, H. (1971) 'Father availability and academic performance', *Developmental Psychology* 7: 301–5.
Bowlby, J. (1981) *Attachment and Loss*, Harmondsworth: Penguin.
Bromberg, P. and Hartmann, F. (1984) 'Childhood, death, anxieties', *Contemporary Psychoanalysis* 40: 439–48.
Brown, G. and Harris, T. (1975) *The Social Causes of Depression*, London: Tavistock.
Buck, R. (1984) *The Communication of Emotions*, New York: Guildford Press.
Cabinet Office Papers (1985) *Violence Against Women*, London: Cabinet Office.
Campaign for Homosexual Equality (1979) *A Teacher's Handbook*, London: Campaign for Homosexual Equality.
Campbell, A. Converse, P.E. and Rogers, W.L. (1976) *The Quality of American Life*, New York: Russell Sage Foundation.
Cancian, F. (1987) *Love in America*, Cambridge: Cambridge University Press.
Carey, G. (1958) 'Sex differences in problem solving performance as a function of attitudes', *J. Abnormal and Social Psych.* 4, 56: 256–60.
Carlsmith, L. (1964) 'Effects of early father absence on scholastic aptitude', *Harvard Ed Review* 34: 3–21.

Centers, R. (1972) 'The completion hypothesis and the compensatory dynamic of intersexual attraction and love', *Journal of Psychology* 82: 111–26.

Chodorow, N. (1978) *The Reproduction of Mothering*, Berkeley: University of California Press.

Cline, S. and Spender, D. (1987) *Reflecting Men*, London: Deutsch.

Cohen, D. (1987) *The Development of Play*, Beckenham: Croom Helm.

Comfort, A. (1968) *The Joy of Sex*, London: Quartet.

Cooper, C. and Smith, M. (1985) *Job Stress and Blue Collar Work*, Chichester: Wiley.

Coward, R. (1984) *Female Desire*, London: Paladin.

Coward, R. (1987) 'New men', *New Internationalist* August, no. 190.

Crandall, V.C. (1969) 'Sex differences in expectation of reinforcement', in C.P. Smith (ed.) *Achievement Related Motivation in Children*, New York: Russell Sage Foundation.

Csikzentmihalyi, M. (1982) 'Self awareness and aversive experience in everyday life', *J. of Personality* 50: 15–29.

Darwin, C. (1872) *The Expression of the Emotions in Animals and Men*, London: John Murray.

Dearnley, E.J. (1981) 'Self Monitoring' – paper presented to the British Psychological Society Conference.

de Quincey, T. (1822) *Confessions of an English Opium Eater*, London: Tressey and Huss.

Derryberry, D. and Rothbart, M.K. (1984) 'Emotions, attitude and temperament' in C. Izard, J. Kagan and R. Zajonc (eds) (1984) *Emotions, Cognition and Behaviour*, Cambridge: Cambridge University Press.

Dominian, J. (1968) *Marriage*, Wiley: Chichester.

Duck, S. (1987) *Human Relationships*, London: Sage.

Ekman, P. (1980) 'Asymmetry in facial expression', *Science* 209: 833–4.

Ekman, P. (1981) 'The symmetry of emotional and deliberate facial action', *Psychophysiology* 18: 101–6.

Elster, J. (1986) *The Multiple Self*, Cambridge: Cambridge University Press.

Emerson, G. (1985) *Some American Men*, New York: Simon and Schuster.

Equal Opportunities Commission (1983) *Paternity Leave*, Manchester: Equal Opportunities Commission.

Ethelridge, G. (1964) *The Man of Mode*, London: Methuen.

Eysenck, H.J. (1969) *The Biological Basis of Personality*, Oxford: Pergamon.

Eysenck, H.J. and Wilson, G. (1982) *The Psychology of Sex*, Temple Smith: London.

Firestone, S. (1970) *The Dialectic of Sex*, New York: William Morrow.

Flanagan, W. (1978) 'A research approach to improving our quality of life', *American Psychologist* 33: 138–47.

Frank, E., Anderson, C., and Rubinstein, D. (1978) 'Frequency of sexual dysfunction in normal couples', *New England Journal of Medicine* 299: 111–15.

Frankl, V. (1968) *In Search of Meaning*, Harmondsworth: Penguin.

Freud, S. (1913) *Totem and Taboo*, London: Hogarth Press.

Freud, S. (1930) *Moses and Monotheism*, London: Hogarth Press.

Gavron, H. (1966) *The Captive Wife*, London: Routledge.

Gay, P. (1986) *The Tender Passion*, Oxford: Oxford University Press.

Goffman, E. (1969) *The Presentation of Self in Everyday Life*, Harmondsworth: Penguin.

Goldrich, J. (1967) 'A study in time orientation', *J. of Pers. and Social Psych.* 67: 216–21.

Gove, W.R. and Hughes, M. (1980) 'Re-examining the ecological fallacy: a study in which aggregate data are critical in investigating the pathological effects of living alone', *Social Forces* 58: 1157–77.

Graves, R. (1974) *Greek Myths*, Harmondsworth: Penguin.

Greer, G. (1970) *The Female Eunuch*, London: Paladin.

Halper, J. (1989) *Quiet Desperation: The Truth about Successful Men*, San Francisco: Jossey Bass.

Hamblin, A. (1983) 'Is a feminist heterosexuality possible?', in J. Ryan and S. Cartledge (eds) *Sex and Love*, London: The Women's Press.

Hardy, T. (1960) 'In the Time of the Breaking of Nations', in *Selected Poems*, London: Macmillan.

Harre, R. (1981) 'Obedience and authority', *Psychology News* no. 21: 10.

Hill, M. (1987) *Sharing Child Care in Early Parenthood*, London: Routledge and Kegan Paul.

Huizinga, J. (1949) *The Waning of the Middle Ages*, New York: St Martins Press.

Ingham, M. (1984) *Men*, London: Century.

Izard, C. (1977) *Human Emotions*, New York: Plenum.

Izard, C. (1984) 'Emotion, cognition, relationships and human development', in C. Izard, J. Kagan and R. Zajonc (eds) *Emotions, Cognition and Behaviour*, Cambridge: Cambridge University Press.

Jahoda, M. (1981) *Employment and Unemployment*, Cambridge: Cambridge University Press.

James, W. (1918) *Principles of Psychology*, New York: Macmillan.

Jardine, A. and Smith, P. (eds) (1987) *Men in Feminism*, London: Methuen.

Jong, E. (1979) *Fear of Flying*, London: New English Library.

Jung, C.G. (1925) *Archetypes*, London: Routledge and Kegan Paul.

Kaplan, H.S. (1974) *The New Sex Therapy*, New York: Brunner/Mazel.

Kasl, W. (1984) 'Stress and health', *Annual Review of Public Health* 5: 319–41.

Kerridge, R. (1987) 'Predatory homosexuals', *The Spectator* 8 August: 18–19.

Kinsey, A.C., Pomeroy, D.C., and Martin, C.E. (1948) *Sexual Behaviour in the Human Male*, Philadelphia: Saunders.

Kobuta, H. (1984) 'Tests in Japanese industry', *APA Monitor* Washington, December: 12.

Krech, D., Crutchfield, R., and Ballachey, D. (1962) *Individual in Society*, New York: McGraw Hill.

Ladurie, Le Roi (1978) *Mountaillou*, London: Scolar.

Laing, R.D. (1968) *The Politics of Experience*, Harmondsworth: Penguin.

Lamb, M.E. (1976) 'The role of the father', in M.E. Lamb (ed.) *Child Development*, New York: Wiley.

Landreth, C. (1941) 'Factors associated with infant crying'; *Ch. Dev.* 12: 81–97.

Lasch, C. (1980) *The Culture of Narcissism*, London: Norton.

Lawrence, D.H. (1971) *Fantasia of the Unconscious*, Harmondsworth: Penguin.

Lessing, E.E., Zagorin, S.W., and Nelson, D.D. (1970) 'WISC subtest and IQ correlates of father absence', *J. of Genetic Psychology* 67: 181–95.

Levinson, D.J. (1978) *The Seasons of a Man's Life*, New York: Ballantine.

Lewis, C. (1985) *On Becoming a Father*, Milton Keynes: Open University Press.

Locke, J. (1692) *Some Arguments Concerning Education*, Oxford: Oxford University Press.

Lorenz, K. (1972) *On Aggression*, London: Methuen.

Lummis, T. (1982) 'The historical dimension of fatherhood', in L. McKee and M. O'Brien (eds) *The Father Figure*, London: Tavistock.

Lunneberg, P.W. and Rosenwood, L.W. (1972) *Need Affiliation and Achievement*, Washington: Bureau of Testing.

Luria, Z., Friedman, S., and Rose, M. (1986) *Human Sexuality*, Chichester: Wiley.

Lurie, A. (1987) *Foreign Affairs*, London: Methuen.

Maccoby, E.E. and Jacklin, C.N. (1974) *The Psychology of Sex Differences*, Oxford: Oxford University Press.

McClelland, D. (1969) *The Roots of Consciousness*, New York: Bantam.

McLean, A. Jr (1981) *Emotional Imagery: Stimulus Information Imagery Ability and Patterns of Physiological Response*, unpublished Ph.D. dissertation, Madison: University of Wisconsin.

Marcuse, H. (1968) *Eros and Civilisation*, London: Abacus.

Maslow, A. (1968) *The Farther Reaches of Human Nature*, Harmondsworth: Penguin.

Masters, W.H. and Johnson, V.E. (1970) *Human Sexual Inadequacy*, Boston: Little Brown.

Mayne, J. (1987) 'Walking the tightrope of feminism and male desire' in Jardine, A. and Smith, P. (eds) *Men in Feminism*, London: Methuen.

Milgram, S. (1974) *Obedience to Authority: An Experimental View*, New York: Harper and Row.

Mill, J.S. (1924) *Autobiography*, New York: Columbia University Press.

Millett, K. (1970) *Sexual Politics*, New York: Doubleday.

Montaigne, Michel de (1972) *Essay on Fathers*, Harmondsworth: Penguin.

Moreno, J.L. (1946) *Psychodrama*, New York: Beacon.

Morris, D. (1965) *The Naked Ape*, London: Cape.

Mort, F. (1988) *Dangerous Sexualities*, London: Routledge.

Moscovici, S. (1976) *Social Influence and Social Changes*, Cambridge: Cambridge University Press.

Murray, H.A. (1938) *Explorations in Personality*, Cambridge, Mass: Harvard University Press.

Nicholson, J. (1984) *Men and Women*, Harmondsworth: Penguin.
Nietzsche, F.W. (1890) *Thus Spake Zarathustra* translated by H. Kauffman, New York: Viking Press.
Norwood, R. (1988) *Women Who Love Too Much*, New York: Bantam.
Oakley, A. (1980) *The Sociology of Housework*, Bath: Martin Robertson.
O'Brien, S. (1986) *The Negative Scream*, London: Routledge.
Ornstein, R. (1987) *Multimind*, London: Macmillan.
Orton, J. (1984) *Diaries*, J.Lahr (ed.), Harmondsworth: Penguin.
Ovid (1978) *Erotic Poems*, Harmondsworth: Penguin.
Penrod, S. (1983) *Social Psychology*, Englewood Cliffs, NJ: Prentice Hall.
Perls, G., Hefferline, T., and Goodman, P. (1972) *Gestalt Therapy*, London: Souvenir.
Pitcher, E.G. and Schultz, L.H. (1983) *Boys and Girls at Play*, South Hadley, Mass: Bergin and Garvey.
Plato (1963) *The Republic*, Harmondsworth: Penguin.
Pollock, L. (1984) *Forgotten Children*, Cambridge: Cambridge University Press.
Pyne, K. (1982) *Where Is He Now?*, London: Century.
Rank. O. (1922) *The Myth of the Birth of the Hero*, (in German *Der Mythus vom Geburt des Helden)* Vienna: Leipzig and Wien.
Read, H. (1953) 'To a Conscript of 1940', in *Collected Poems*, London: Faber and Faber.
Reedy. M. (1977) *Age and Sex Differences in Personal Needs and the Nature of Love*, Ph.D. Dissertation: University of California.
Reich, W. (1942) *The Function of the Orgasm*, New York: Noonday Press.
Rhyne, D. (1981) 'Bases of marital satisfaction among men and women', *Journal of Marriage and the Family*, 43: 948–60.
Rich, A. (1974) 'From an old house in America', in *Dreams of a Common Language*, New York: WW Norton.
Robinson, P. (1981) 'What liberated males do', *Psychology Today*, 15: 81–4.
Ross, W.D. (1954) *The Ethics of Aristotle*, Oxford: Oxford University Press.
Scherer, K., Wallbott, N., and Summerfield, A. (1986) *European Emotions*, Cambridge: Cambridge University Press.
Schofield, M. (1964) *Sexual Behaviour in Young People*, Harmondsworth: Penguin.
Schwartz, M.F. and Masters, W.H. (1984) 'The Masters and Johnson treatment programme for dissatisfied homosexual men', *Am. J. of Psychiatry* 141 (2): 173–81.
Scruton, R. (1986) *Sexual Desire*, London: Weidenfeld and Nicholson.
Seaman, B. (1972) *Free and Female*, Greenwich, Conn: Fawcett.
Segal, L. (1983) 'Sensual uncertainty or why the clitoris is not enough', in J. Ryan and S. Cartledge (eds) *Sex and Love*, London: Women's Press.
Shaw, G.B. (1934) 'Arms and the man', in *The Complete Plays of G.B. Shaw*, London: Odhams.
Shaw, G.B. (1934) 'The man of destiny', in *The Complete Plays of G.B. Shaw*, London: Odhams.

Simple, P. column, *Daily Telegraph* 11 November 1975.

Smith, P. (1987) 'Men in feminism and feminist theory', in A. Jardine and P. Smith (eds) *Men in Feminism*, London: Methuen.

Smithers, A. (1986) *The Growth of Mixed A Levels*, Manchester: Carmichael.

Spence, J.T. and Heimreich, R. (1978) 'The Personal Attributes Questionnaire', *JSAS Catalogue of Selected Documents in Psychology* 4, 43 Ms 617.

Spock, B. (1970) *Baby and Child Care*, London: New English Library.

Steinem, S. (1988) *Men Are Pigs and Deserve to Die*, Tucson, Arizona: Thunderbird Press.

Stellman, J. and Snow, B. (1984) 'The health and well being of video display terminal operators'.

Stengel, O. (1961) *Suicide and Attempted Suicide*, Harmondsworth: Penguin.

Stewart, Clarke K.A. (1978) 'And daddy makes three', *Child Development* 466–78.

Taylor, M.C. and Hall, J.A. (1982) 'Psychological androgyny: series, methods and conclusions', *Psychological Bulletin* 92: 347–67.

Thurber, J. and White, E.B. (1950) 'Six day bicycle riding as a sex substitute', in *Is Sex Necessary?* J. Thurber and E.B. White, Harmondsworth: Penguin.

Trew, K. and Kilpatrick, R. (1984) *The Daily Life of the Unemployed*, Dept of Psychology, Queens University Belfast.

US Bureau of Statistics (1985) *Criminal Victimization*, Washington, DC: Government Printing Bureau.

US Department of Justice (1970) *Obscenity and Pornography*, Washington, DC: Government Printing Bureau.

Watson, J.B. (1928) *The Psychological Care of the Infant and Child*, New York: WW Norton.

Wertz, R.W. and Wertz, D.C. (1977) *Lying In: A History of Childbirth in America*, New York: The Free Press.

Whitbourne, S.K. (1986) *The Me I Know*, Heidelberg: Springer.

White, T.H. (1963) *The Age of Scandal*, Harmondsworth: Penguin.

Williams, T. (1965) *A Streetcar Named Desire*, Harmondsworth: Penguin.

Wilson, E.O. (1975) *Sociobiology*, Cambridge, Mass: Harvard University Press.

Wolfe, T. (1970) *The Right Stuff*, New York: Bantam.

Zilbergeld, B. and Evans, M. (1980) 'The inadequacy of Masters and Johnson', *Psychology Today* 14: 28–43.

INDEX